Game of My Life
NEW YORK RANGERS

John Halligan
John Kreiser

SportsPublishingLLC.com

ISBN-10: 1-58261-956-5
ISBN-13: 978-1-58261-956-9

Publishers: Peter L. Bannon and Joseph J. Bannon Sr.
Senior managing editor: Susan M. Moyer
Developmental editor: Doug Hoepker
Art director: K. Jeffrey Higgerson
Dust jacket design: Heidi Norsen
Interior layout: Kathryn R. Holleman
Photo editor: Erin Linden-Levy

Sports Publishing L.L.C.
804 North Neil Street
Champaign, IL 61820
Phone: 1-877-424-2665
Fax: 217-363-2073
SportsPublishingLLC.com

Printed in the United States of America

   Library of Congress Cataloging-in-Publication Data

Halligan, John, 1941-
    Game of my life : New York Rangers / John Halligan and John Kreiser.
        p. cm.
    ISBN-13: 978-1-58261-956-9 (hard cover : alk. paper)
    ISBN-10: 1-58261-956-5 (hard cover : alk. paper)
    1. New York Rangers (Hockey team) 2. Hockey players--United States--
Anecdotes. I. Kreiser, John. II. Title. III. Title: New York Rangers.
GV848.N43H23 2006
796.962'64097471--dc22
                                            2006030847

CONTENTS

Acknowledgments   vii

I: IN THE BEGINNING   1

Chapter 1
FRANK BOUCHER   3

Chapter 2
CLINT SMITH   13

II: DOWNS AND UPS   21

Chapter 3
DON RALEIGH   23

Chapter 4
ANDY BATHGATE   31

Chapter 5
GUMP WORSLEY   41

Chapter 6
HARRY HOWELL   51

III: YEARS OF THE CAT   59

Chapter 7
ROD GILBERT   61

Chapter 8
VIC HADFIELD   73

Chapter 9
EMILE FRANCIS   81

Chapter 10
BRAD PARK   93

Chapter 11
PETE STEMKOWSKI 103

Chapter 12
STEVE VICKERS 113

IV: REBUILT, BUT STILL NO CUP 121

Chapter 13
DON MALONEY 123

Chapter 14
JOHN DAVIDSON 131

Chapter 15
JOHN VANBIESBROUCK 141

Chapter 16
MIKE GARTNER 151

V: TO THE CUP ... AND BEYOND 159

Chapter 17
ADAM GRAVES 161

Chapter 18
MARK MESSIER 169

Chapter 19
STEPHANE MATTEAU 185

Chapter 20
MIKE RICHTER 193

Chapter 21
BRIAN LEETCH 201

Chapter 22
NEIL SMITH 209

Chapter 23
WAYNE GRETZKY 219

Chapter 24
JAROMIR JAGR 235

ACKNOWLEDGMENTS

This book would not have come together without the assistance of a number of people to whom we owe a debt of thanks.

First and foremost, thanks to the former (and in the case of Jaromir Jagr, current) Rangers who were kind enough to give us their time and share their memories. From Clint Smith, 92 years young near Vancouver, to Mark Messier in the Bahamas and everyone in between, we are terribly grateful. We hope our readers enjoy reading your reminiscences as much as we enjoyed talking with you about them.

Special thanks to Rich Nairn, the Phoenix Coyotes' vice president of communications, for helping us with the chapter on Wayne Gretzky, and to Mary-Kay Messier, Mark's sister, whose efforts to arrange for us to talk to her brother were invaluable. Being able to include first-person remembrances from these two hockey immortals made this book just a little more special.

We also owe a debt of gratitude to John Rosasco and Jason Vogel of the New York Rangers, and especially to Adam Evert, who handles alumni relations for the Rangers and was of tremendous assistance in helping us track down some key alumni. Thanks also to Tyler Currie of the NHL Players Association and Wendy McCreary of the NHL Alumni Association for their assistance and good wishes.

No book of this type comes together without the availability of good research materials. We were fortunate to find useful material on a number of web sites, including NHL.com, the NHL's official site; NHLPA.com, the players' association site; sihrhockey.org, the web site of the Society for International Hockey Research (especially to Ernie Fitzsimmons for his help with several photographs); and hhof.com, the web site of the Hockey Hall of Fame, whose Legends of Hockey series was especially valuable. We were also aided by stories filed over the years by numerous writers for *The New York Times*, the *New York Daily News*, and the *New York Post*, as well as many of the *Sun* papers in Canada, which were especially helpful in researching a couple of the more recent events.

We also have to credit *When the Rangers Were Young*, written by Frank Boucher with Trent Frayne (Dodd, Mead & Company, 1973), which provided us with much of the background for the chapter on the Rangers' first great center and the team's NHL debut, supplementing personal interviews we conducted in the 1960s and early 1970s.

We also had the assistance of three fine editors at Sports Publishing LLC. Doug Hoepker, Mark Newton, and Elisa Laird all made major contributions to this book, as did Mike Pearson, who initiated this project, Erin Linden-Levy, our photo editor, and Letha Caudill, our marketing manager. Thanks to all of you for your help.

Last, but certainly not least, thanks to Janet Halligan and Helen Kreiser for listening to our successes and disappointments and putting up with us throughout this project. We couldn't have done it without you.

—John Halligan and John Kreiser
August 2006

I

IN THE
BEGINNING...

The Rangers were not New York's first hockey team. That honor went to the New York Americans. After the Hamilton Tigers went on strike in 1925, Big Bill Dwyer, New York's most famous bootlegger, shelled out $75,000 to bring the team, and the National Hockey League, to the Big Apple.

Dwyer rented out the newly constructed Madison Square Garden, dressed his team in star-spangled red, white, and blue uniforms, and began selling tickets. He sold more than 17,000 of them to the Americans' first game, a 3–1 loss to the Montreal Canadiens on December 15, 1925. Though the Americans finished fifth, they did well at the box office—so well that Garden management decided to get into the hockey business itself (despite having said that it wouldn't do so).

Tex Rickard, the head of the Garden, didn't know much about hockey, so he brought in someone who did—Conn Smythe. But Smythe got into a dispute with management and didn't make it to opening night. Instead, Lester Patrick, a member of hockey's most famous family, took over as general manager and coach.

The Patrick-built and coached Rangers were an immediate hit. The line of **Frank Boucher** and the Cook brothers (Bill and Bun) quickly became the league's best, and hard-hitting Ching Johnson anchored a tough defense. Boucher recounts his memories (via personal remembrances and his autobiography) of the Rangers' first game, a 1–0 victory that began a division-championship season.

One year later, the Rangers were NHL champs. With Patrick shedding his tie and jacket for goalie pads and gloves in a famous playoff game, the Rangers beat the Montreal Maroons in a best-of-five game to win their first Stanley Cup.

Throughout the 1930s, the Rangers were among the NHL's elite teams. They captured a second Stanley Cup in 1933, and after some brilliant rebuilding on the fly by Patrick (now a GM only after moving Boucher into the coaching job in 1939), won again in the spring of 1940. One of the young players on that 1940 team was center **Clint Smith**, who reminisces about being young and a Cup winner.

CHAPTER 1

FRANK BOUCHER

The Skinny

When the Rangers got their man, their main man, it was fitting that he was a former member of the Royal Canadian Mounted Police, since a Mountie, as the saying goes, "always gets his man." The year was 1926, and the man was Frank Boucher, one of two superstars (the other was Bill Cook) on the first Rangers team.

Boucher's arrival actually predated the arrival of Lester Patrick, who later became his coach and, ultimately, his boss. Conn Smythe, the Rangers' first general manager, started building the franchise by signing the Cook brothers, Bill and Bun. Bill was a right wing, and Bun played on the left side. All Smythe needed was a center. He was determined to get the Cooks anyone they wanted—no questions asked. The list included some of the game's biggest stars, such as Nels Stewart and Frank Nighbor. But the Cooks had their own ideas. They chose Frank Boucher. It was a choice made in hockey heaven.

No one among the original Rangers, not even Patrick (Smythe's successor), stayed with the franchise for as long as Boucher. He took the franchise's opening face-off in 1926 and played until 1938 (he also had a brief cameo for the war-ravaged team of 1943-44, went behind the bench as coach from 1939 to 1948, and served as general manager from 1946 to 1955—30 years in all).

The longer schedules and faster game played today don't do justice to Boucher's offensive numbers. But Boucher was one of the greatest players of his era, a cunning playmaker who developed into one of the most popular Rangers of all time. It's not much of a stretch to say Boucher was the Wayne Gretzky of his day. Both were brilliant, lefty-shooting centers who played "like they had the puck on a string," to paraphrase legendary broadcaster Foster Hewitt's description of Boucher and his linemates on the Rangers' famous "A Line." The trio owed its name to the A train, the subway line that was being built beneath the third Madison Square Garden (the one between 49th and 50th streets and Eighth and Ninth avenues, about a mile north of the current Garden) when the Rangers were born in 1926.

Though he was a native of the Canadian capital city of Ottawa, Boucher developed a great fondness for the Big Apple and all of its pleasures. On and off the ice, he became the most recognizable hockey face in town.

Boucher was one of the cleanest players of all time. He drew only one major during his career. Ironically enough, that penalty came in the Rangers' very first game, a 1–0 victory over the Montreal Maroons on November 16, 1926. Boucher won the NHL's Lady Byng Trophy for "clean, effective play" so many times—seven in all—that the league finally gave it to him permanently and had a new trophy struck.

Boucher must have needed a large trophy room to accommodate all the honors he won. In addition all to the Lady Byngs, there were three Stanley Cups, two as a player (1928 and 1933) and one as a coach in 1940. He also made the First All-Star Team three times and the Second Team once as a player, and earned another place on each team as a coach.

One of Boucher's innovations is still with New York hockey fans today. He and publicist Herb Goren founded the Rangers Fan Club in 1950. The club's leadership immediately established a "most popular Ranger" award, and named it the Frank Boucher Trophy. The Rangers Fan Club continues to flourish today, more than a half-century after its founding.

The Setting

The Rangers weren't the first hockey team to call Madison Square Garden home. That honor went to the New York Americans, who joined the NHL in the fall of 1925 and did so well that Garden management decided

Notes on Frank Boucher

Name:	Frank Boucher
Born:	October 7, 1901 (Ottawa, Ontairo)
Died:	December 12, 1977 (Kemptville, Ontario)
Position:	Center
Height:	5-foot-9
Playing Weight:	170 pounds
How Acquired:	Traded to the Rangers from the Vancouver Maroons for $15,000— September 28, 1926
Years with Rangers:	1926-27 to 1937-38; 1943-44
Stats as Ranger:	533 games, 152 goals, 261 assists, 413 points, 114 PIM
Uniform Numbers:	7, 17
Accomplishments:	Lady Byng Trophy 1927-28, 1928-29, 1929-30, 1930-31, 1932-33, 1933-34, 1934-35
	First-Team All-Star 1932-33, 1933-34, 1934-35
	Second-Team All-Star 1930-31
	Hockey Hall of Fame 1958
	Lester Patrick Trophy 1993

to get its own franchise to capitalize on the Big Apple's newfound interest in hockey.

Legend has it that the nickname "Rangers" began with "Tex" Rickard, who was running the Garden at the time. Rickard was really a boxing man but had become fascinated with hockey and was convinced the game, even with two teams in town, would draw plenty of fans to the Garden, "the world's premiere sporting arena," which had opened its doors just a year earlier. Local sportswriters dubbed the new club "Tex's Rangers," and though Tex is long gone, the latter part of the name lingers eight decades later.

If the Rangers have an actual "birthday," it would be May 15, 1926, the date the National Hockey League awarded a franchise to the Garden. The nation as a whole and New York in particular were at the height of the Roaring Twenties—the Great Depression was still three years away. It was the "Golden Age Of Sports" in America, meaning that the Rangers would have to compete for newspaper headlines (there was little radio, and television and the Internet weren't even a gleam in an inventor's eye) with the likes of Babe Ruth, boxing champ Jack Dempsey, football star Red Grange, golfer Bobby Jones, and tennis great Bill Tilden.

A lot of New Yorkers cared more about their sports heroes than they did about politics or foreign affairs. It was an era when secretaries made about $15 a week and sirloin steak was 41 cents a pound. There were 13 daily newspapers in New York, and they trumpeted the exploits of heroes like trans-Atlantic flier Charles Lindbergh, English Channel-swimmer Gertrude Ederle, author Ernest Hemingway, and film star Ronald Colman.

As Boucher remembered decades later, both in interviews and his 1973 book, *When The Rangers Were Young*, "It was the era of the sheik and the flapper, and the world was different. There were 20,000 speakeasies in New York as Prohibition marked its seventh year. Three days before we opened our season, there were 72,000 people in Yankee Stadium when Notre Dame, coached by Knute Rockne, beat Army, 7–0. The next day, a mere 20,000 watched Red Grange score three touchdowns for the New York Yankees as they beat the Boston Bulldogs, 24–0."

Rickard and his associate at the Garden, Col. John S. Hammond, were determined to ice much more than a mere expansion team (not that anyone would have known what that term meant in 1926). And that's just what they did. Recalled Smythe, "I knew every hockey player in the world right then. Putting that whole team together, many of whom had never played pro hockey before, cost the Rangers about $32,000."

But Smythe didn't get to stick around to see his handiwork pay off. He was fired after a series of disagreements with Hammond and Rickard. With opening night drawing closer, Hammond and Rickard turned to the dapper and magisterial Patrick, a hockey legend who was 42 at the time.

The Rangers wanted their opening night to be memorable. In particular, they wanted it to at least equal (and preferably outdo), the pomp and circumstance of the Americans. The "Amerks," who were tenants at the

Frank Boucher. *Courtesy of the John Halligan Collection*

Garden, had officially brought hockey to New York on December 15, 1925, when they faced off against the Montreal Canadiens and lost by a score of 3–1.

Though the Americans were losers on the ice that night, they were winners in terms of prestige. The game was treated like a gala international social affair. Among those on hand were the Canadian Governor General's Royal Foot Guards from Ottawa and the United States Marching Band from West Point.

Almost a year later, it was the Rangers' turn to herald their arrival. The *New York Daily News* described preparations for the big game: "The Garden has been transformed into a veritable winter palace, and a pretentious program has been arranged between periods for the entertainment of hockey patrons, including Katie Schmidt's ice ballet. West Point's cadet orchestra also has been secured."

The Game of My Life
OPENING NIGHT—NOVEMBER 16, 1926
RANGERS VS. MONTREAL MAROONS
AT MADISON SQUARE GARDEN

"We arrived in New York on the overnight train from Toronto the morning of November 12, 1926. That was four days before our opening game. People who live there now would have marveled at the New York we knew. There were about six million people. Nearly a million of them traveled on the subway every day. The fare was five cents.

"The Garden was a teeming oven that night. It must have been about 70 degrees. When I stood at the blue line lofting warm-up shots at Hal Winkler, our goaltender, I was edgy and nervous.

"The crowd of more than 13,000 was still coming in. In the boxes down close to the ice, the women were wearing furs and evening dress; their men were natty in tuxedos. Up in the balcony above the mezzanine, the smoke was already building into a haze. We were about to play our first game.

"It was pretty theatrical. There were some celebrities there, but I don't remember exactly who. In time, we drew a lot of big names to the Garden. Babe Ruth used to come into the arena in his flashy beige camel hair coat and matching cashmere cap. So did Lou Gehrig, the Babe's running mate on the Yankees, a big, quiet rusty-haired fellow with a huge cheek dimple and wide smile. They often came to the dressing room to visit us.

"Humphrey Bogart and the Duke and Duchess of Windsor and Lucille Ball and Desi Arnaz were hockey fans. So were George Raft, Jack LaRue, and Cab Calloway.

"The game was even on radio. Madison Square Garden Corporation bought its own frequency and started a station called WMSG. Jack Filman from Hamilton, Ontario, was the broadcaster. He did the same thing for the Americans. Jack was quite a character and he stayed on the scene for a long time, probably until the late '30s."

"I took the first face-off, against Montreal's Nels Stewart, and won it cleanly, drawing the puck back to Bill Cook. We were off and skating. The real face-off came after a ceremonial face-off conducted by movie star Lois Moran, who was slim, blonde, and very attractive. With that tiny ceremony, the Rangers had arrived in New York."

"It was a great game ["fast and savagely played" was the description of Seabury Lawrence, who covered the opener for the *New York Times*. I actually fought Montreal's Bill Phillips—the first and only time I ever had a fight on the ice. I am grateful for that.

"Bill Cook, the team's first captain, scored the only goal of the game, assisted by Bun, at 18:37 of the second period. The Rangers won by a score of 1–0."

Afterword

Boucher wasted little time establishing himself as one of the best centers in the NHL. The line of Boucher between the Cook brothers quickly became one of the league's most feared trios. With the A Line leading the way, the Rangers finished first in the American Division in their first season.

"That first season, we followed a pattern we set in our opening-game victory over the Maroons," Boucher recounted some years later. "We headed Boston by 11 points to win the American Division championship. Bill Cook won the scoring championship, and was also the NHL's top goal-scorer with 33 goals in a 44-game schedule." The A Line was so good that Patrick often left them on their own at practices at one end of the ice while he coached the rest of the club at the other end.

But the Rangers lost to Boston in the opening round of the playoffs, leaving them with some unfinished business. There were no loose ends in their second season, when they took home the Stanley Cup—with Boucher scoring the Cup-winning goal in the fifth and deciding game against the Maroons. But Boucher may have made a bigger contribution earlier in the series: Depending on whom you believe, Boucher was the one who persuaded the 44-year-old Patrick to put on the pads and gloves and take over in goal when goaltender Lorne Chabot was injured in Game 2.

Boucher set team scoring records that took decades (and much longer schedules) to break. In an era when players were vassals whose movement was totally controlled by management, few players were as identified with their teams as was Boucher with the Rangers. That's why it was a foregone conclusion that Boucher would turn to coaching at the end of his playing career. It happened right on schedule at the end of the 1937-38 season, when Boucher managed only a single assist; this from a player whose line had put up more than 1,100 points in their decade together—big numbers in an era when schedules were less than 50 games and teams rarely combined for as many as six goals in a game.

"It was clear, painfully clear, that my time had come," Boucher said in *When the Rangers Were Young*. "The others knew it, too. Bun [Cook] was already gone, sold to the Bruins, and Bill [Cook], Ching [Johnson] and Murray [Murdoch] all made it plain that they, too, had had enough."

Boucher's playing career may have been ending, but his time with the Rangers was far from done. Patrick named Boucher as coach of the New York Rovers, the Rangers' top farm club in the Eastern Amateur Hockey League. That gave him a chance to get his feet wet as a coach before moving up to the big club in 1939-40, with Patrick keeping his job as general manager. The rookie coach led the team to its third Stanley Cup. "That team," Boucher would often say, "was the greatest hockey team I had ever seen."

Unfortunately for Boucher and the Rangers, World War II destroyed any hopes of an emerging dynasty. Boucher led the Rangers to the playoffs in 1940-41 and to the Prince of Wales Trophy for finishing first in the regular season in 1941-42. But the third-place Bruins upset the Rangers in six games in the semifinals, and the team was never the same.

Much of the team was off to the war by the fall of 1942, and the Rangers plummeted to the basement of the six-team league (the Americans folded the previous spring). Things got even worse in 1943-44, and the Rangers needed some spark. Boucher thought he could provide it. He put the skates on again at the ripe old age of 42. Despite fairly decent numbers (four goals and 10 assists for 14 points in 15 games), Boucher knew it just wasn't going to work, so he quit for good as a player.

Boucher would stay behind the bench for 10 seasons, however, including a brief stint in 1953-54. But after his fast start, Boucher never recaptured the touch he had before the war. Boucher would also become the Rangers' second general manager, succeeding Patrick in 1946 and serving until midway through the 1954-55 season. In 1958, he was elected to the Hockey Hall of Fame.

Sadly, all of Boucher's trophies and memorabilia were lost when a fire destroyed his home on February 23, 1965. The blaze wiped out "Byng Farm," a 160-acre apple orchard that Frank ran with his son Earl in Mountain, Ontario, outside of Ottawa.

"That was one of the saddest days of my life," Boucher often lamented. "But they didn't burn my memories. No sir."

Boucher left Rangers fans with one final memory on February 11, 1968, when the Rangers bid farewell to the third Madison Square Garden. Boucher and the Cook brothers made one last appearance together in the building where all three became Hall of Famers, headlining an unprecedented collection of 62 hockey greats. Boucher set up Bill Cook for one last goal, to the cheers of the sellout crowd on the Garden's last day.

Boucher died on December 12, 1977, at age 76. Thirty of those 76 years were devoted to the Rangers. No one had served the Rangers longer. Few have served them better.

CHAPTER 2

CLINT SMITH

The Skinny

His nickname was "Snuffy," after the character in the comic strip *Barney Google*, but there was nothing funny about the way Clint Smith played hockey. The native of Assiniboia, Saskatchewan, was an offensive force in an era when every goal was precious and was instrumental in the Rangers' third Stanley Cup victory.

Had he been playing today, Smith would have been a high draft pick, perhaps No. 1 overall. But in the early 1930s, he had to settle for being one of the youngest players ever to turn pro.

"I think I brought myself to New York," Smith says in recounting how he wound up in the Big Apple. "That's the reason [Rangers general manager] Lester Patrick and I never got along. I was about 18, and I think I was the third-youngest player to ever turn pro in those days.

"The president of the Rangers was Colonel [John] Hammond, and I made my deal with Col. Hammond on the telephone. But when came to sign my contract with Lester, he had me down for one just year. I said, 'No, Lester, I made a deal with Col. Hammond for a two-year contract for this amount of money,' and I insisted on it. I was a 17-, 18-year-old kid talking back to Lester Patrick. That wasn't supposed to be. He always held that against me.

"We were training in Lake Placid that year, and he said to me, 'Col. Hammond is in Lake Placid. He'll probably be over here tomorrow, and I'll see him then.' The next day, he called me in after practice, and Col. Hammond was there, and Lester said, 'This young fellow said that you said you'd give him a two-year contract.' And Col. Hammond said, 'Yes, Lester, I told him that.' So Lester had to eat a little bit of crow, and he didn't like it.

"I didn't make the [Rangers] that year and I was sent to Springfield, the Rangers' farm team in the Can-American League. At Christmas time, that league broke up, so I was loaned back to Saskatoon in the Western Hockey League. The next year I was loaned out to Vancouver in the Pacific Coast League because Lester's brother, Guy Patrick, owned the Vancouver Lions. I played for Vancouver for three years, and I had big years with the Lions."

That's an understatement. Smith had 25 goals and 39 points in 34 games in 1933-34, and boosted his point totals in each of the next two seasons.

"The third year I played with Vancouver, I had an argument with Guy Patrick. I know I was making the top dollar of the players out there, but I had played for three years, and I was leading the league in scoring every year. So the third year, I had it added to my contract that I had to go to another league the next year. He signed that; he said, 'We can take care of that.' The next year, I was still with the Rangers, but I went to Philadelphia. At the same time, [linemates] Bobby Kirk and Charlie Mason didn't make the Rangers—they had a little stint, but they didn't stick. So they're in Philadelphia. I was with [Bryan] Hextall. Of course, Lester was calling all of the shots in Philadelphia. He put our line together—Hextall and Bobby Kirk and I, and we broke records in that league."

Smith finished with 25 goals and 54 points in 49 games and then scored his first NHL goal during a two-game call-up with the Rangers.

"The next year, we went up as a line to the Rangers, Kirk and Hextall and me. We played about five or six games, and we were doing all right. But you didn't lose three or four games in a row with Lester, and he broke our line up. He put Hextall with Phil Watson, and I forget with whom Bobby Kirk played. But it didn't hurt me—I went between Lynn Patrick and Cecil Dillon. Cecil was left-hand shot who played right wing. We all went together like ham and eggs. We had a heck of a line there."

By 1938-39, Smith was among the NHL's top players. He won the Lady Byng Trophy while finishing fourth in the league with 41 points while taking only one minor penalty.

Notes on Clint Smith

Name:	Clint Smith
Born:	December 12, 1913 (Assiniboia, Saskatchewan)
Position:	Center
Height:	5-foot-8
Playing Weight:	165 pounds
How Acquired:	Signed as a free agent by the Rangers—October 13, 1932
Years with Rangers:	1936-37 through 1942-43
Stats as Ranger:	281 games, 80 goals, 115 assists, 195 points, 12 PIM
Accomplishments:	Lady Byng Trophy 1938-39

The Setting

The Rangers had entered the NHL in 1926 and won a Cup the next season, beating the Montreal Maroons in the final. They won a second Cup five years later and were looking for Cup No. 3 after finishing second in 1940.

The Blueshirts rallied in the semifinals and beat Boston, the defending Stanley Cup champions, in six games. Next up were the Toronto Maple Leafs, who had split a pair of finals with the Rangers, winning in 1932 and losing a rematch in 1933.

But the Rangers had a problem: Though they should have enjoyed the home ice advantage, they faced the prospect of having to play as many as five games away from Madison Square Garden. In those days, the Ringling Brothers Circus came to the Garden in the spring and took over the building, forcing the Rangers to make other arrangements.

The Rangers won the first two games, 2–1 in overtime and 6–2, to take a two-game lead to Toronto. The lead didn't last long, as the Leafs won 2–1 and 3–0 to even the series.

But the Rangers rebounded to win Game 5. Muzz Patrick, one of Lester Patrick's two sons on the team, scored 11:43 into the second overtime to give the Rangers a 2–1 victory and a 3–2 lead in the series.

Smith and his teammates came to Maple Leaf Gardens on April 13, 1940, hoping to close out the series. Sixty-six years later, he still remembers that night—both the game and the celebration that followed.

The Game of My Life
1940 STANLEY CUP FINALS, GAME 6
RANGERS AT TORONTO MAPLE LEAFS—APRIL 13, 1940

"We got locked out of the Garden because of the circus coming in. The circus came into the Garden every spring. They used quite a bit of money from the circus to build the Garden, so the circus had a priority there in the spring. They had that agreement for years. So we only got to play two games in the finals at home. Then we had to play the rest of the series in Toronto. That was a pretty tough job, even then. There weren't many Rangers fans in that rink.

"We won the first two games in New York, but we lost the next two in Toronto. We won the fifth game in Toronto in overtime. In the sixth game, we were down 2–0 in the third period, but we rallied to force overtime.

"I don't remember the winning goal by Bryan Hextall. You know, I'm 92 now. But I remember that you could have heard a pin drop when we scored. It got awfully quiet. It really didn't matter who scored it. All I know is that we won. That was the big thing. I did get a lot of ice time in that series. We loved to beat Toronto in Toronto. We had quite a few Eastern boys on the club. Ott Heller, Dave Kerr, they were Easterners.

"I can't explain the feeling of winning the Stanley Cup. It's the ultimate. It's something you always strive for—just to get into the Stanley Cup Finals. And then when you win—it's something you always remember.

"The funny part of it was, after the game, team president John Reed Kilpatrick came in, and that was only about the second time I'd ever seen him in our dressing room. He was always at the games, but he never came into the dressing room.

"He said, 'I'd like your attention for a minute.'

"When he spoke, the hilarity stopped right there.

Clint Smith. *Courtesy of Ernie Fitzsimmons*

"He said, 'I have a room at the Royal York Hotel. I want everybody here to be there. I know a lot of you have friends here,' because we had a lot of players from Toronto, and when we went to Toronto, they always had relatives who came to the games. They used to come down to the hotel to see the boys, things like that. He said, 'I want everybody there, and if you have friends or family who were at the game, they're invited the same as you.'

"We got to the hotel and there was a little bit of hilarity starting. We were having a few drinks—mind you, we didn't drink that much in those days, mostly beer. I was strictly a beer drinker. We were just sitting around, and John Reed Kilpatrick came to Muzz Patrick and me; we were standing around, and he came to both of us, and he said, 'Boys, if I were younger, I think I'd be taking some of that booze up to my room for the train ride home tomorrow.'

"You see, the next day was Sunday, and there was no liquor on the train on Sundays. I'll tell you, he didn't tell us twice. We had some booze back in the room so fast …then we came back to the party.

"The next day on the train, there were quite a few sports reporters on the train who had come down with us, and after we had breakfast, about an hour later, we were starting to get a little thirsty, and we went back and brought a bottle back. We had one room there, and they asked, 'Where did you get the whiskey?'

"We said, 'We just happened to have some that we took back with us.'

"We thought we'd get away with that, and we'd have about three bottles apiece when we got back to New York. We never got a drink—they went through our bags. The party started all over again on the train. Muzz and I never got a bottle back to New York. But it was a lot of fun."

Afterword

Smith and the Rangers had two more fine seasons, including 1941-42, when the Rangers finished first overall but were unable to win the Stanley Cup. But by then, World War II was in full swing. No team was hit harder than the Rangers, who saw many of their top stars enter the military. Smith wound up being sold to the Chicago Black Hawks (that's the way they spelled it then) after the 1942-43 season.

"Lester and I, we were never the best of friends," Smith recalls. "We were good friends once we got the contract signed; then everything was fine. But we always had a problem with contracts. Lester and I had a pretty good argument, and he ended up selling me to Chicago."

The move turned out to be a good one for Smith's stats.

"I had some pretty big years with Chicago," he says. "I was playing between [Hall of Famers] Max Bentley and Bill Mosienko, and we set records. [Smith set the NHL record for assists in 1943-44 with 49 and finished with 72 points.] It ended up that it was a good trade for me. I didn't want to leave New York, but I was glad to get away from Lester. He was a great man, but he was a mean man in a lot of ways."

Smith wrapped up his playing NHL career with the Black Hawks in 1946-47, finishing with 185 goals and 397 points in 483 games—with only 24 penalty minutes. He also shares the NHL record for most goals in a period with four, set on March 4, 1945, against Montreal.

After 11 seasons in the NHL, Smith went to the USHL's Tulsa Oilers in 1947 and won the Herman W. Paterson Cup as the league's MVP in 1947-48. He stayed active in hockey as a player-coach for the St. Paul Saints of the USHL until he hung up the blades to coach full time with the Cincinnati Mohawks of the American Hockey League in 1952.

"I coached for several years," he says. "I started with the Rangers' farm club in St. Paul. Then they went into Cincinnati; they went into that team with Montreal and coached for a year [while also playing two games]. I enjoyed coaching. We won a cup with the St. Paul club. But you have to quit sometime, I guess."

He returned to Vancouver in 1953.

"After I coached, I went into the service station business with Imperial Oil near Vancouver, where I've lived since about 1941," he says. "I was in the service station business for 20 years. I had always worked around service stations during the summer. I never wasted a full summer like a lot of the other guys; they'd play golf all of the time, but I could never do that. I liked the service station, so it was natural that I'd go into that business. It treated me well."

But he didn't put his skates away. Smith played old-timers' hockey for a number of years. He also was a founding member of the British Columbia

Hockey Benevolent Association, serving as president and holding several other offices in the organization.

One highlight of Smith's post-playing career came in 1991, when he was inducted into the Hockey Hall of Fame.

"I was thrilled to be inducted. It's quite a privilege," he says. "It kind of gives you memories. I used to enjoy going back there, because I'd see five or six of the fellows I used to play against. But," he adds with a laugh, "not too many of the guys I played against are left—that's the problem of living too long."

Smith's loyalties were divided three years later when the Rangers went to the Stanley Cup Finals—against the Vancouver Canucks.

"I saw the games out here," he says. "It was a good series. It was hard to pick one team, because I had played for the old Vancouver Lions—that was my stepping-stone to the National Hockey League. I was torn between the two. I've lived in Vancouver for a long time.

"I still get to the games out here. They treat me well—I sit in the press box, and I enjoy seeing the Rangers come out here. That's the one disappointment this year; because of the schedule, they don't come to Vancouver this year."

Smith received a special treat in the summer of 2005 when he got something that players didn't get to enjoy in his era: a day with the Stanley Cup. With the 2004-05 season wiped out by the lockout, there was no Stanley Cup champion, so the practice of giving players from the championship team a day with the Cup was extended to a number of players from the past.

"Howie Meeker brought the Cup out to Vancouver Island, and while it was out here, they phoned and asked me if I would like it for a day—and, of course, I said I'd be glad to take it for a day," he says. "We enjoyed it. I went to the Winter Club in West Vancouver, and, of course, they just jumped at [the chance to get the Cup for a day]. We had a pretty good display. It was nice. But I had to laugh—the Cup was so small, you could carry it around. You couldn't carry the Cup that we won around. I think we had 13 rings on that Cup—I think they have five now."

II

DOWNS
AND UPS

With a load of young talent and an excellent farm system, the Rangers appeared set for more years of success. They finished first overall in 1941-42, though they were upset in the playoffs. Then World War II intervened.

No NHL team was ravaged by the war as badly as the Rangers. Patrick dissolved the farm system in anticipation that the NHL would go on hiatus; instead, like the other pro sports, hockey was allowed to continue to provide entertainment. With most of his top talent off to war, Patrick wanted to suspend operations, only to be told that the league couldn't afford to operate with fewer than six teams.

The Rangers struggled until making the playoffs in 1948, their first trip to the postseason since 1942. Two years later, the brilliant goaltending of Charlie Rayner and some clutch scoring by center **Don Raleigh** got the Rangers within one victory of the Stanley Cup. Raleigh recounts how his two overtime goals in the finals got the Rangers within one victory of a championship, and how a puck that bounced the wrong way kept them from being Stanley Cup winners. It was one of the most heartbreaking moments in franchise history.

The Rangers struggled into the mid-1950s before they finally rebuilt their farm system, generating future Hall of Famers like **Gump Worsley**, **Andy Bathgate**, and **Harry Howell**. The Rangers made the playoffs three years in a row in the late '50s, then struggled again until 1961-62, when they outlasted Detroit to make the playoffs. Bathgate recalls perhaps the most famous goal of his career, a penalty-shot tally against Detroit that lifted the

Rangers into the 1962 playoffs, while Worsley remembers his greatest—and most disappointing—game, a double-overtime loss to Toronto in Game 5 of the 1962 playoffs. Howell, who played more games than anyone in franchise history, shares memories of Harry Howell Night, the first ever given to a Ranger, and the highlight of his Norris Trophy–winning season in 1966-67.

CHAPTER 3

DON RALEIGH

The Skinny

Barring a change in the NHL's entry draft, Don Raleigh holds one record no Ranger will ever break: the youngest full-time player ever to wear the Blueshirt.

Tall and thin (hence his nickname, "Bones"), Raleigh was on a pair of bantam championship teams in Manitoba and played on a midget title team in 1941-42 before moving into junior hockey with the Manitoba Monarchs. With World War II having decimated their roster, the Rangers signed Raleigh to a pro contract. Although he spent most of the season with the Brooklyn Crescents, Raleigh actually played 15 games with the Rangers in 1943-44, scoring his first two NHL goals and adding two assists (one of his teammates was Rangers immortal and coach Frank Boucher, who came out of retirement at age 42 to become one of the oldest players in team history). Raleigh's first taste of NHL life ended when he broke his jaw against the Toronto Maple Leafs.

The Setting

Raleigh went back to Canada, joined (and played hockey with) the Canadian Army, and attended the University of Manitoba. But by the fall of 1947, at the age of 21, the Rangers thought he was ready for the Big Apple and brought him to New York full time.

Like many of his teammates, Raleigh wasn't a physical player, but he was a slick passer and shooter. The slender center became the first Ranger to score four goals in a game in the 7–4 loss to Chicago on February 25, 1948. He also played 42 NHL games that season before taking his first minor penalty.

Raleigh finished with 15 goals and 18 assists for 33 points (and only two penalty minutes) as a rookie and added another pair of goals in the Rangers' first-round playoff loss to Montreal.

Injuries limited Raleigh to 41 games and 10 goals in 1948-49, but he played all 70 games and was a solid contributor in 1949-50, scoring 12 goals and adding 25 assists for 37 points. He helped the Rangers to a fourth-place finish and their second playoff berth in three seasons.

Much to the surprise of the hockey world, the Rangers stunned the second-place (and heavily favored) Montreal Canadiens in five games. Led by the goaltending of Hart Trophy winner Chuck Rayner, the Rangers took the first three games; barely missed a sweep when the Canadiens won the fourth game 3–2 in overtime; and wrapped up the series at the Forum with a 3-0 victory.

That sent the Rangers to the Finals against the first-place Detroit Red Wings. It was their first trip to the Finals since their last Cup victory in 1940. But as it had 10 years earlier, the circus made life harder for the Blueshirts. In 1940, they were able to play two home games before the series moved to Toronto; in 1950, the Rangers' two "home" games were played in Toronto.

Detroit was without Gordie Howe, who suffered a severe head injury in the Wings' first playoff game, but they opened the Finals at the Olympia with a 4–1 victory—not unexpected for in a series between a first-place finisher (88 points) and a fourth-place team that ended up three games below .500.

But with the fans at Maple Leaf Gardens cheering them on (even then, the Wings weren't favorites in Toronto), the Rangers rode Rayner's goaltending to a 3–1 victory. But Detroit blanked the Blueshirts 4-0 in the third game and headed home to play the rest of the series needing only two victories in a building in which they had gone 19-9-7 during the regular season.

The Rangers, however, had other ideas.

Notes on Don Raleigh

Name:	Don Raleigh
Born:	June 27, 1926 (Kenora, Ontario)
Position:	Center
Height:	5-foot-11
Playing Weight:	145 pounds
How Acquired:	Signed as a free agent
Years with Rangers:	1943-44 to 1955-56
Stats as Ranger:	535 games, 101 goals, 219 assists, 320 points, 96 PIM
Nickname:	Bones
Uniform Numbers:	9, 7
Accomplishments:	Captain, November 4, 1953, through 1954-55 season
	West Side Association Award (Rangers MVP) 1950-51
	Frank Boucher Trophy 1951-52

The Game of My Life

STANLEY CUP FINALS, GAMES 4 AND 5
RANGERS VS. DETROIT RED WINGS—APRIL 18 AND 20, 1950

"It was tough not having any home games because of the circus. At first, they told us we were going to play the whole series in Detroit, then they were going to give us a couple of 'home games' in Toronto or Montreal. They finally gave us two games in Toronto. The people cheered for us, and we won the second game but lost the third.

"But we weren't discouraged, even though we knew it would be tough to win three games in Detroit. One thing we knew we had going for us was Charlie Rayner. He was the MVP that year and he gave us a chance to win every game. He really had a great season and a great series.

"I've always said the best shot in hockey is the one-timer—shooting the puck right off the pass. I don't remember who threw the pass to me, but I remember one-timing the puck past goaltender Harry Lumley to give us the win in Game 4. I do remember that the building got awfully quiet really fast—I think they expected us to roll over.

"Two nights later, we had a real goaltending duel. Charlie was great. We almost had them in regulation, but they scored in the final couple of minutes to send the game into overtime tied at 1–1. The building was really noisy. But I scored really quickly in the overtime—I think it was only a minute or two into the period. It was just like the other one, on a one-timer. That was always my best shot.

"There's nothing more special than scoring an overtime goal in the Stanley Cup Finals. To score two of them in a row is almost beyond words. It's something that I'll never forget. I was the first player to do it and the only one for a long time—I think John LeClair was the only other player to do it in 1993."

Afterword

Alas for Raleigh and his teammates, there was one more hurdle to climb, and they couldn't quite get there.

The Rangers grabbed a two-goal lead in Game 6. But the Red Wings' vaunted power play helped them rally for a series-tying 5–4 victory.

"Back then," Raleigh remembers, "when you took a minor penalty, you sat for the whole two minutes. The opposition could score as many power-play goals as it could. It wasn't like now, where they let you go after the team scores a goal."

Still, the Rangers had another chance in Game 7 and again they jumped out to an early lead. Tony Leswick set up a goal by defenseman Allan Stanley and then scored one himself to put the Blueshirts ahead 2–0 after one period.

But a penalty to Stanley early in the second period gave the Wings an opportunity, and again they took advantage. Pete Babando and Sid Abel scored power-play goals 21 seconds apart to tie the game.

The Wings pressed for the go-ahead goal, but New York's Nick Mickoski broke in alone on Lumley. Mickoski was stopped, but Buddy O'Connor knocked in the rebound at 11:42 to give the Rangers a 3–2 lead.

Again, though, the Rangers couldn't keep the lead. At 15:57, Jim McFadden scored the tying goal, evening the game at 3–3.

Don Raleigh. *Courtesy of Ernie Fitzsimmons*

Neither team was able to score during the third period, sending the game into overtime. Both goaltenders were perfect through the first overtime, although the Wings tested Rayner much more severely.

In the second overtime, the Rangers had their chance to win—and Raleigh had his opportunity to be an overtime hero for the third time.

"Twice in overtime, Bones was in alone," Rayner remembered years later, "but the puck rolled over his stick both times. One break there, and there never would have been a 54-year drought. It would only have been 44 years. Honestly, I think about it every day."

The vision of missed opportunity hasn't left Raleigh, either.

"I had a couple of chances, especially in the second overtime. I think one of them went over my stick, and I believe I hit the post or the crossbar on the other. To have the Stanley Cup that close and not get it was terrible."

The Wings finally got their chance and didn't miss. Prior to a face-off in the Rangers' end, Detroit center George Gee moved winger Pete Babando to a different spot and told him he'd get him the puck. Gee was as good as his word; he won the draw to Babando, a journeyman forward, who quickly whipped a backhander past Rayner for a stunning 4–3 victory.

"It was heartbreaking," Raleigh says. "To be that close and not get it really hurt. The funny thing was, Babando later played with me on the Rangers [in 1952-53]."

Raleigh finished the playoffs with four goals and five assists for nine points in 12 games. What he couldn't have known is that it would be his last trip to the playoffs.

For the next five seasons, Raleigh was one of the Rangers' most reliable players. He had a spectacular campaign in 1951-52, setting career highs with 19 goals, 42 assists (a team record), and 61 points, and then served as captain from November 4, 1953, through the 1954-55 season.

Along the way, Raleigh established another Rangers first: he became the first Blueshirt to move to Staten Island, then regarded as the country by most New Yorkers. Raleigh, who said he had problems sleeping in the "city," allowed that he slept much better on Staten Island.

Another problem for Raleigh was his weight—but his was keeping it on, not taking it off. He was once seen at training camp in Lake Placid eating two ice cream cones at once in order to put on a few pounds.

"I always had to work to keep my weight up," he says.

The arrival of fiery Phil Watson as coach in 1955-56 signaled the beginning of the end for Raleigh.

"I was never very heavy—about 145 or 150 pounds," Raleigh says. "I knew how to collapse my body so that when guys hit me, I didn't get hurt. I only had a couple of serious injuries. But Watson wanted us to be physical and run around and hit people and get hit. That wasn't for me, so after 1955-56, I left and went into coaching for a couple of years."

Raleigh served as player-coach with the Brandon Regals of the Western Hockey League in his home province of Manitoba in 1956-57, scoring 60 points and leading the team to 44 wins. But after coaching Saskatoon/St. Paul the following season, Raleigh left hockey for good.

"I was 32, which is young now," he says. "But I'd had enough. I had married a Winnipeg girl, and I got into the insurance business. My time as a hockey player came in handy—people knew my name, and I did pretty well."

Raleigh served as the president of J. D. Raleigh & Co., an insurance and consulting firm in Winnipeg. When the WHA Jets arrived in 1972, he also did some work as a TV analyst.

He also got to see his No. 7 jersey retired to the rafters of Madison Square Garden, though not with his name.

"We had a prestigious group of guys who wore No. 7—Frank Boucher, Phil Watson, me, and I believe Red Sullivan had it after I did," he says. "But Rod Gilbert was a great player, and he earned the right to have it retired."

It's been five decades since Raleigh's last NHL game, but he still follows the NHL avidly, and even wrote to NHL vice president Colin Campbell after the 2005 lockout was settled to suggest improvements in the way the game is played. He also keeps a special eye on his old team.

CHAPTER 4

ANDY BATHGATE

The Skinny

By the early 1950s, the Rangers had long since lost the aura of an elite team. World War II sent the franchise into a tailspin, wiping out a solid roster and a farm system that had been the envy of hockey. There was a brief uptick in 1948 and a stunning run to Game 7 of the 1950 Stanley Cup Finals, but by the early 1950s, the Rangers were back near the bottom of the NHL.

Help was on the way though. Defensemen Harry Howell and Bill Gadsby, plus solid goaltending in the persons of Lorne "Gump" Worsley and Johnny Bower gave the Madison Square Garden faithful plenty of hope. But the Rangers needed offense too, and they got it from an outstanding right wing who was as happy setting up his linemates as he was ripping one of his own shots past enemy goaltenders. His name was Andy Bathgate, and he would become the face of the Rangers for a decade.

Bathgate was born in Winnipeg and played his minor hockey in suburban West Kilodan, Manitoba. He signed with the Guelph (Ontario) juniors in 1951 but quickly suffered a left knee injury that required surgery in 1952 to have a steel plate fixed beneath the kneecap. Although the knee plagued him throughout his career, he missed only five games in 11½ seasons with the Rangers.

Bathgate's smooth skating and deft puckhandling were Hall of Fame caliber, but it was his shot that made goalies cringe. The great Jacques Plante of the Montreal Canadiens became the first modern goaltender to use a facemask after one of Bathgate's shots, a backhander, cut him during a game at Madison Square Garden on November 1, 1960. Bathgate was one of the first to master the slap shot, and in an era where face masks were still the exception rather than the rule, the site of Bathgate racing down right wing and winding up for a slapper was enough to make even the best goalies want to make sure their insurance was paid up.

Bathgate was the Rangers' captain and the team's first superstar since the era of Frank Boucher and Bill Cook. His leadership and scoring ability, not to mention his toughness, keyed the Rangers' return to the Stanley Cup playoffs in 1956 for the first time in six years. He did the same in 1957 and 1958, though they lost in the first round all three times.

Bathgate's best season was 1958-59, when he became the first Ranger to score 40 goals in a season and added 48 assists for 88 points. He won the Hart Trophy as NHL MVP, even though the Rangers stumbled down the stretch and missed the last playoff spot on the final night of the season.

That season, Bathgate was the first Ranger to appear on the cover of *Sports Illustrated*, a feat he accomplished on January 12, 1959. The headline, accompanied by a portrait photograph of the handsome right wing was a simple one: Andy Bathgate Hockey Hero. For fans of the New York Rangers, Bathgate was all that and more.

Even though the Rangers returned to their struggling ways in 1959-60 and 1960-61, Bathgate continued to excel. In 1961-62, he was particularly brilliant, tying Chicago's Bobby Hull for the Art Ross Trophy as the NHL scoring leader. Hull got the hardware, though, because he had more goals, 50. More important for New York fans, though, Bathgate was fueling the Rangers' drive for a playoff berth.

The Setting

The Rangers and Detroit Red Wings battled tooth and nail for the NHL's fourth and final playoff spot in 1962. With player-coach Doug Harvey providing a lift on the blue line, the Rangers were enjoying their best season since 1957-58. But Detroit had plenty of firepower up front with Gordie Howe and Alex Delvecchio. All-Star Red Kelly led the defense, and the peerless Terry Sawchuk was in goal.

Notes on Andy Bathgate

Name:	Andy Bathgate
Born:	August 28, 1932 (Winnipeg, Manitoba)
Position:	Right wing
Height:	6 feet
Playing Weight:	175 pounds
How Acquired:	Product of the Rangers organization
Years with Rangers:	1954-55 to 1963-64
Stats as Ranger:	719 games, 272 goals, 457 assists, 729 points, 444 PIM
Uniform Numbers:	12, 10, 16, 9
Accomplishments:	Hart Trophy (NHL MVP) 1958-59
	First-Team All-Star 1958-59, 1961-62
	Second-Team All-Star 1957-58, 1962-63
	Rangers MVP 1956-57, 1957-58, 1958-59, 1961-62
	Players' Player Award 1962-63
	Frank Boucher Trophy 1956-57, 1957-58, 1958-59, 1961-62

Bathgate led the Rangers' attack, and he was bolstered by linemates Dean Prentice and Earl Ingarfield. Harry Howell and newly acquired Doug Harvey anchored the defense in front of goalie Gump Worsley. Harvey was also the team's coach. Statistically, the 1961-62 team was unspectacular. There were flashes of brilliance at times, but mostly, the team stumbled along at a pace below .500.

The Rangers were an aging team, to be sure. Their general manager, Murray "Muzz" Patrick, son of the great Lester Patrick and a member of the 1940 championship team, was desperate for a playoff contender. He may also have sensed the nearing of the end of his managerial career, although he had a long-term contract that would allow him to remain with the Madison Square Garden Corporation regardless of how the Rangers fared.

Rangers fans have always been a special breed. In 1961-62, the Rangers would regularly draw raucous sellout crowds of 15, 925 to the third Madison Square Garden. However, not much could prepare those avid fans for what they would see, courtesy of Andrew James Bathgate, on Wednesday, March 14, 1962.

Coming into the game against Detroit that night, the Rangers were in the throes of a slump, having won only once in their previous seven outings. The playoffs were in danger of slipping away. The teams were dead even in points, 57 apiece, but Detroit had a slight edge—the Wings had six games remaining to the Rangers' five.

The game had a feel of "winner take all" to it. Both teams—and certainly the fans—seemed to sense it.

[The game started slowly, caution being the watchword on both sides. Bathgate struck first, with an early goal at 3:02 of the first period, his 26th of the season. He would have no idea that his 27th would probably be the most important one of his career.

Claude LaForge would tie the score for the Red Wings at 17:40 of the first. The great Gordie Howe would score the 500th goal of his magnificent career at 17:10 of the second period, lifting a backhander past Lorne (Gump) Worsley after putting the puck through Harvey's legs and scoring shorthanded. Howe thus became the second NHL player to reach 500, and the Garden crowd gave him a long, standing ovation.]

"You know, I don't even remember that," Bathgate says today. "There were so many guys who seemed to get milestone goals against the Rangers. I just don't remember it." [However, the Rangers quickly pulled even at 2-2 on a goal by Ingarfield. What happened next is something Bathgate remembers with great clarity more than four decades later.]

"Actually, Dean Prentice should have taken the penalty shot," Bathgate says today. "I had given him a pass and he got tripped (Detroit goalie Hank Bassen actually threw his stick at Prentice) when he went in, and Dean hit the boards pretty hard. He was just kneeling there, trying to get his wind back – I guess he had the wind knocked out of him, more than anything. The referee [Eddie Powers] came up, called for a penalty shot and pointed at me. I looked and I didn't say anything. The Detroit guy came up and said,

Andy Bathgate. *Courtesy of the John Halligan Collection*

'He wasn't tripped. Dean was tripped,' But the referee had pointed and me and said, "You take it.

"Hank Bassen was the goalie for Detroit. I hadn't made up my mind what I was going to do, but when I got in over the blue line, he started moving out at me. I thought he was going to come out and back in, but he came out and tried to give me a poke check. I stepped around him, and it was very easy to put it into the empty net, because he was maybe 10 or 12 feet out of the net after he tried to make the poke check, and he fell down. I think I was going to go to my right, and he went for it, fortunately.

"I was very surprised that the goalie moved out that quickly on me. I played with [Bassen] later in my career, in Detroit, and he would make up his mind what he was going to do. Once you're committed, you're dead, and luckily, I could get around him.

"I remember the goal very vividly, and I think a lot of people in New York, from my old bunch, they remember it too. It's a once-in-a-lifetime thing really, especially the way the atmosphere was in the Garden that night. If I missed, I would have been a complete bum, but I scored, so I was a hero for years. No doubt that was one of the highlights of my career in New York. That put us in the playoffs and the Red Wings out."

The Game of My Life

DETROIT RED WINGS AT RANGERS
MADISON SQUARE GARDEN—MARCH 14, 1962

"Actually, Dean Prentice should have taken the penalty shot. I had given him a pass and he got tripped when he went in. The defenseman pulled him down, and Dean hit the boards pretty hard. He was just kneeling there, trying to get his wind back—I guess he had the wind knocked out of him, more than anything. The referee [Eddie Powers] came up, called for a penalty shot, and pointed at me. I looked and I didn't say anything. The Detroit guy came up and said, 'He wasn't tripped. Dean was tripped,' But the referee had pointed and me and said, 'You take it.'

"Hank Bassen was the goalie for Detroit. I hadn't made up my mind what I was going to do, but when I got in over the blue line, he started moving out at me. I thought he was going to come out and back in, but he came out and tried to give me a poke check. I stepped around him, and it was very easy to put it into the empty net, because he was maybe 10 or 12 feet out of the net after he tried to make the poke check and fell down. I think I was going to go to my right, and he went for it, fortunately.

"I was very surprised that the goalie moved out that quickly on me. I played with [Bassen] later in my career, in Detroit, and he would make up his mind what he was going to do. Once you're committed, you're dead, and luckily, I could get around him.

"I remember the goal very vividly, and I think a lot of people in New York from my old bunch, they remember it too. It's a once-in-a-lifetime thing really, especially the way the atmosphere was in the Garden that night. If I missed, I would have been a complete bum, but I scored, so I was a hero for years. No doubt that was one of the highlights of my career in New York. That put us in the playoffs and [left] the Red Wings out."

Afterword

What happened after the goal will never be forgotten by those who were there. In the words of Kenneth Rudeen, the erudite writer who covered the game for *Sports Illustrated*, "The Garden's grimy old steelwork rang with a million-decibel shout of jubilation, for in this one rare penalty shot, New York Rangers fans not only saw a victory assured but a whole season redeemed."

Emotionally, Bathgate's shot and the 3–2 victory over the Wings certainly gave the Rangers the jolt of energy they needed, but they still had four games left. They won twice and tied once in those four games to edge the Wings for the final playoff spot, 64 points to 60.

Despite the euphoria surrounding the "Bathgate Penalty Shot Game," as it came to be known, and the mad rush of fans to acquire Stanley Cup playoff tickets, it was to be a short playoff run for the 1961-62 squad. They were unable to get past the Toronto Maple Leafs in the first round. The teams split the first two games, but the Leafs won the next two, primarily on the strength of emerging superstar Frank Mahovlich. The Leafs would go on to win the Cup that year, their first of three in a row.

Bathgate continued to score in 1962-63—not as dramatically as he did on the penalty shot, but equally as compelling. Rather than one memorable goal, Bathgate set an NHL record by scoring a goal in 10 straight games— showing that at age 30, he certainly hadn't lost his scoring touch. The streak began with an otherwise remarkable goal that helped propel the Rangers to a 4–2 victory over the Canadiens on December 15, 1962, at the Forum in Montreal, something that certainly didn't happen all that often in that era.

The streak continued for the next nine games (11 goals in all), and reached 10 in a row when he scored in a 2–2 tie on January 5, 1963, against the Canadiens, again in Montreal. The streak ended the next night at the Garden, January 6, as Plante blanked the Blueshirts, 6–0. During Bathgate's streak, the Rangers went 4-3-3, and hope for the playoffs dimly flickered for a while. But the team could win only 10 of its last 32 games and missed the playoffs by a bundle, 22 points to be exact, to the Red Wings.

With the Rangers struggling again the following season, GM Patrick decided to shake up his team, and he did it with a blockbuster trade, the biggest in team history at the time. The deal, a seven-player stunner with the Maple Leafs, included the great Bathgate. To some fans, it was unthinkable, but it was true. The date was February 22, 1964.

Don McKenney, a veteran forward, was shipped to Toronto with Bathgate. In return, the Rangers got five players: veteran forwards Dick Duff and Bob Nevin, plus young defensemen Rod Seiling and Arnie Brown and forward Billy Collins. The trade worked for both teams. In the long run, the Rangers won the trade—Nevin was a solid regular for several years and became captain, while Seiling and Brown formed the basis of a solid defense that fueled the Rangers' return to respectability. But in the short run, Bathgate and the Leafs won—with the former Ranger star in the lineup, the Leafs won their third straight Stanley Cup less than two months after the stunning trade.

Was Bathgate disappointed in the trade after more than a decade in New York? "No, not really," he recalls, "because I knew I wasn't going to be on a Stanley Cup winner [in New York]. When you're there 12 years, you see the caliber of players who went through there, and they were traded. We weren't picking up any good young players at the time. They were waiting and waiting. You could see it.

"I was always treated very well in New York. I would never say a bad word about the treatment I got from the fans. But you're playing and hoping to see some bright young star come along, like Rod a couple of years behind me. Toronto and Montreal and Detroit were getting their hands on them before we could get them."

The failure, he says, was with management, which at that time didn't make the commitment needed to compete with powerhouses like Montreal and Toronto.

"When I first when to New York, we had one goalie—we used a big board on the other goal. You make the most of it—you do the best you can do at that time. To see the way the players are treated these days—we can't even imagine it. The training facilities and everything they have, it's unreal. That's life and how it changes, from one extreme to another. You have to be hungry when you play hockey, and have to be sort of mean.

"If you're satisfied, if you have that 'If you don't want me, I'll go somewhere else' attitude, I don't think that's a good attitude. You want to produce for that team and stay there if you can. If you give the effort, the people really appreciate it. That's all I could do in New York. People say 'You didn't win anything in New York.' But you can only do what you can with the players that you have there. The players can't do anything else about it. You try to use everyone as best you can."

Bathgate was eventually acquired by the Red Wings, and then by the Pittsburgh Penguins in the 1967 expansion draft. He played his last NHL game with the Penguins in 1970-71. But hockey was still Bathgate's passion. He was player-coach with Ambri-Piotta in Switzerland for a season, and such was his renown that fans actually chartered trains to see him play.

There is no doubt that Bathgate was the greatest Ranger from World War II until the "Rise of the Rangers" era in the late 1960s. Of his 973 NHL points, 729 came in 719 games as a Ranger. He made four All-Star teams in an era that also included fellow right wingers by the names of Gordie Howe, Maurice "Rocket" Richard, and Bernie "Boom Boom" Geoffrion.

Bathgate was inducted into the Hockey Hall of Fame in 1978. Initially, the Hall displayed Bathgate's final jersey with the Penguins. Andy quickly had that replaced with a Rangers sweater.

At 74 years of age, Bathgate is still quite active. He runs a golf facility in Mississauga, Ontario, outside Toronto, and is on the ice two or three times a week, helping to coach his son's youth hockey team. "My son does the coaching, and I just encourage the kids to shoot the puck and pass the puck," he says—just what Andy Bathgate always did best. And to this day, in his own words, "I am still a Ranger fan at heart."

CHAPTER 5

GUMP WORSLEY

The Skinny

For the better part of a decade, Gump Worsley had one of the most thankless jobs in hockey—starting goaltender of the Rangers, then one of the NHL's have-nots. Few goalies in hockey history had to stand up to the workload Worsley faced as the last line of defense for a team that wasn't very good for most of his time in the Big Apple.

Though Worsley's given name was Lorne, he picked up the nickname that would accompany him throughout his career at an early age. George Ferguson, a boyhood pal, thought Worsley resembled Andy Gump, a popular comic strip character at the time. The nickname stuck for a lifetime. "Certainly, no one ever called me Lorne," Worsley remembered years later. "Well, maybe my parents, but that was a long, long time ago."

Worsley wasn't exactly an overnight sensation. Before he established himself as an NHL regular with the Rangers, he played in five different leagues, piling up honors and trophies along the way. He made the Eastern Hockey League's First All-Star Team with the New York Rovers in 1949-50, then was named the top rookie and best goalie in the USHL with the St. Paul Saints in 1950-51. He was a Second-Team All-Star with the Saskatoon Quakers of the PCHL in 1951-52, leading the league in shutouts (five) and playoff wins.

Worsley was 24 when he finally made the NHL, and even that required a break.

"I was in Saskatoon," he says, "and Chuck Rayner [the Rangers' starting goaltender] got hurt in Detroit right before the start of the season. I was called up, got the starting job, and won the Calder Trophy."

He won the Calder despite a 13-29-8 won-lost record, a testament to his heroic play on a team that finished last with a 17-37-16 record. Amazingly, he found himself back in the minors that fall, winning the Western League MVP award with the Vancouver Canucks by leading the league in victories (39) and goals-against average (2.40). But while he was starring in the minors, Johnny Bower played the full season in goal with the Rangers.

"I won the Calder Trophy, and the next year I wound up back in the minors. Johnny Bower got the job, and I played in Vancouver," he says. "The funny thing was that [Rangers forward] Camille Henry won the Calder the next year [1953-54], and he wound up back in the minors, too. I think they were afraid we were going to ask for raises."

By 1954-55, Worsley was back in New York to stay (This time, Bower was sent to the minors; he later resurfaced with Toronto, where he also went on to a Hall of Fame career). A year later, Worsley backstopped the Rangers to the first of three straight playoff appearances, the team's best performance since the organization was torn apart by World War II. He also matched the team record set by Bower two years earlier by playing every minute of all 70 games—no Ranger goaltender since has matched Worsley's total of 4,200 minutes played in a season.

By then, Worsley was well into a long-running battle with his coach, Phil Watson. The two didn't see eye to eye on a lot of things. Watson, a French-Canadian who was a member of the 1940 championship team, was invariably described with adjectives like *fiery* and spoke his own version of English (think of Esa Tikkanen with a French-Canadian background and you'll get the idea). Watson had his own ideas about how things should be done, and he and Worsley soon had little use for each other.

Once asked if he disliked Watson, Worsley retorted, "*Hate* would be a better word." Asked about Watson's coaching skills, he replied, "As a coach, he was a good waiter."

Watson didn't have much affection for Worsley either. He once lambasted the goaltender for being out of shape and "having a beer belly." Worsley's response: "That shows you what he knows. I only drink VO."

Notes on Gump Worsley

Name:	Lorne "Gump" Worsley
Born:	May 14, 1929 (Montreal, Quebec)
Position:	Goalie
Height:	5-foot-7
Playing Weight:	180 pounds
How Acquired:	Product of Rangers Organization
Years with Rangers:	1952-53, 1954-55 to 1962-63
Stats as Ranger:	582 games, 204 wins, 271 losses, 101 ties, 3.10 goals-against average
Accomplishments:	Calder Trophy 1952-53
	All-Star Game 1962, 1963
	Rangers MVP 1960-61, 1962-63
	Frank Boucher Trophy 1955-56, 1960-61, 1962-63
	Hall of Fame 1980

(That wasn't always true—Gump drank beer and referred to it as "the champagne of the common man.")

Nearly five decades later, Worsley still has memories of playing under Watson.

"We had some pretty good players in the late 1950s. But Phil Watson, he was a beauty," Worsley says. "If we won, it was him. If we lost, it was one of us. That's the way he was. It's not going to make guys real happy, that's for sure."

At 5-foot-7 and a generously light listing of 180 pounds, Worsley was among the most popular Rangers. He won the Frank Boucher Trophy as the most popular Ranger on and off the ice three times. In an era where masks for goaltenders were more of a rarity than a necessity ("My face is my mask," he joked), fans could see every emotion from Gump, from joy at the not-often-enough victory to frustration at the all-too-often-allowed goal. He called a night in the nets "going into the barrel," and when asked which team he had the most trouble with, quipped "the Rangers."

Watson heaped a lot of blame on Worsley for the team's late-season collapse in 1958-59, when the Rangers fell apart down the stretch and missed a playoff berth. But the team's struggles in 1959-60 cost Watson his job, ending one of the great player-coach feuds in NHL history. Alf Pike replaced Watson, but Worsley was still seeing rubber by the bushel—a 40-save performance was far more the rule than the exception. "I used to feel like a duck in a shooting gallery," he said at the time.

Worsley's style wasn't always pretty. Like Dominik Hasek in today's modern era, he would do anything he could to succeed. "Gump would do anything to keep the puck out—anything," remembered defenseman Harry Howell, a longtime teammate and the Rangers' all-time leader in games played (1,160). "He'd flop around a lot. The coaches didn't always like it, but he got the job done."

The Setting

By 1961-62, the Rangers hadn't made the playoffs for three seasons. But with future Hall of Fame defenseman Doug Harvey having come from the Canadiens to serve as player-coach and give the blue line a boost, the Rangers and Detroit battled down the stretch for the final playoff berth. Thanks to a 3–2 victory over the Wings on March 14 at Madison Square Garden—a game in which Andy Bathgate scored the deciding goal on a third-period penalty shot—the Rangers pulled ahead down the stretch and secured the final playoff berth, earning their first trip to the postseason since 1958.

Another reason the Rangers made the playoffs was Worsley, who finished with his best numbers since 1957-58, compiling a 2.97 goals-against average, a 22-27-9 won-lost record, and two shutouts. Though the numbers don't show it (the NHL didn't keep shots faced and save percentage figures back then), 1961-62 was probably the best season of his time on Broadway.

The Rangers were big underdogs in the playoffs against the Toronto Maple Leafs and surprised no one by dropping the first two games of their semifinal series at Maple Leafs Garden in Toronto. Things looked bleak for the Rangers as they returned home for Games 3 and 4, but the arrival of rookie Rod Gilbert gave the Rangers a spark, and they evened the series with 5–4 and 4–2 victories.

Gump Worsley. *Courtesy of Ernie Fitzsimmons*

That sent the series back to Maple Leaf Gardens for Game 5, with the outcome very much up for grabs.

The Game of My Life

1962 STANLEY CUP SEMIFINALS, GAME 5
RANGERS AT TORONTO—APRIL 5, 1962

"We had beaten the Leafs two games at the Garden. We had some pretty good talent—Doug Harvey and Harry Howell on defense, and guys like Andy Bathgate up front. They traded Andy a year or two later—I could never figure out why. He was the best player they had.

"I don't know how many shots they had, but it was a lot. I always seemed to see a lot of rubber—it was an occupational hazard, and everybody really only used one goaltender at that time.

"We finished regulation time tied at 2–2 [Earl Ingarfield had forced the overtime by scoring a goal with 7:29 in regulation time, and the teams went through a full 20-minute overtime period without scoring]. Early in the second overtime period, Frank Mahovlich took a shot, and I took it on the shoulder. I thought I had it covered, but [referee] Eddie Powers wouldn't blow the whistle. I was on my back, and I think the puck was under my shoulder. I moved a little bit, and Red Kelly found the puck and took a whack at the puck, and it went into the net.

"I had figured I was down long enough that the play must have been stopped, that the referee must have blown his whistle. Since nothing was happening, I lifted my head, and that's where the puck was—under my head. Kelly found it and tucked it in. ["I couldn't see the puck after Worsley went down," Kelly said after the game. "But I just kept looking for it, and suddenly, he lifted his head and there it was—so I tucked it in."]

"It was a really frustrating loss," Worsley adds, the frustration of 40-plus years still in his voice. "Another hard thing was that we had to play Game 6 in Toronto, too. The circus was in the Garden, and we couldn't play there. That made it tough—we didn't get to go home. Madison Square Garden figured we wouldn't make the playoffs, so they put the circus in there. We had to get out."

Afterword

Worsley finished Game 5 with 56 saves, even earning an ovation from the fans at Maple Leaf Gardens, who were no doubt relieved that their team had avoided an upset loss. With Game 6 also scheduled for Toronto because of the circus, the Leafs rolled to a 7–1 victory that closed out the series.

The Rangers went backwards in 1962-63, missing the playoffs again. With Harvey not up to his form of the previous season, the defense corps made life tough for Worsley, who was subjected to 40-plus shots on a nightly basis. He led the league in games played (67) and minutes (3,980), finishing with a 22-34-10 record, a 3.27 goals-against average, and two shutouts. In one six-game span, he was called on to stop 269 shots—more than 44 per game.

But Worsley's life was about to get a lot easier. On June 4, 1963, the Rangers and Montreal Canadiens made one of the biggest trades in NHL history at the time. The centerpieces were goaltenders: the Rangers acquired Jacques Plante, who had backstopped the Canadiens to five consecutive Stanley Cups from 1956 to 1960. The Canadiens got Worsley. Gump got a chance to go home—and to win.

"I was told I wasn't being traded. In the morning, I was told I'd be with the Rangers for my career," he says of the day he was traded. "I was traded by noon. The Rangers forgot to tell me that they'd traded me. I found out when the Canadiens called me."

Worsley's homecoming wasn't a big success at first, statistically at least. He hurt his knee and wound up spending a lot of the 1963-64 season with the Quebec Aces of the AHL. He played the first part of the 1964-65 season with Quebec as well, but made it back to Montreal later in the season and won the No. 1 job for the playoffs, winning five of eight starts as the Canadiens won their first Stanley Cup in five years. Worsley shut out Chicago 4–0 in Game 7 of the Finals to get his name on the Cup for the first time.

In 1965-66, Worsley had the best season of his career. He won 29 of his 51 appearances, finished with a 2.36 goals-against average, won the Vezina Trophy as the Canadiens led the league in fewest goals allowed, and was a Second-Team All-Star. Worsley was even better in the playoffs, going 8-2 with a 1.99 goals-against average as the Canadiens repeated as champions by beating Detroit in the Finals.

Worsley says the difference between playing for the Rangers, where 40 shots a night was the rule rather than the exception, and Montreal was an incredible change.

"It was a nice feeling to go from a team where I was seeing so many shots to a team like Montreal," he says. "It sort of made up for everything."

Worsley missed much of 1966-67 with injuries but rebounded in 1967-68. He shared time during the regular season with newcomer Rogie Vachon, and the combo worked—the Canadiens won the Vezina Trophy again, and Worsley was named a First-Team All-Star after going 19-9-8 with six shutouts and a 1.99 goals-against average. Worsley was the star of the playoffs, going 11-0 in 12 games with a 1.88 goals-against average as the Canadiens won their third Cup in five years.

By now, Worsley was among the few remaining goaltenders who played without a mask. "I didn't wear a mask until the very end of my career," he says. "They were very hot. They didn't have the cage masks like they have today. They were form-fitting, right on your face. Too hot."

Vachon got the majority of the playing time in 1968-69, but Worsley was still sharp, going 19-5-4 with a 2.25 goals-against average and five shutouts in only 30 games. He was 5-2 in the playoffs as the Canadiens won another Cup.

But by 1969-70, Worsley was 40 and had developed a fear of flying in airplanes that got the better of him. He retired on November 28, 1969— only to be talked back onto the ice late in the season by Minnesota North Stars GM Wren Blair. The North Stars, in need of a goaltender and not having many plane trips remaining, lured Worsley back for what turned out to be four more seasons.

"I finished up in Minnesota. That was different. I got a lot of work," he says of his final NHL stop. "I went from a shooting gallery to a lot of calm with the Canadiens to another shooting gallery."

Though Worsley finished with a sub-.500 regular-season record (335-352-150), his 43 shutouts, 2.88 goals-against average, 43 shutouts, and 40-26 playoff record with four Stanley Cup rings were more than enough to convince Hall of Fame voters that he belonged. He was inducted in 1980 along with fellow goaltender Harry Lumley and Lynn Patrick, the son of Lester Patrick and a star on the 1940 championship team.

"It was great to get into the Hall of Fame after all those years in the shooting gallery," he says. "I went in with Harry Lumley and [Lynn] Patrick. What a thrill."

Worsley was on hand in 2000 when the Rangers celebrated their 75th anniversary. "I was down there on the 75th anniversary of the Rangers— there was a picture of me, Chuck Rayner, and Ed Giacomin—three Hall of Fame goaltenders," he says.

Worsley is retired these days, living outside Montreal. "I played in New York for 11 years and have some great memories," he says. More than 40 years after he left, Gump is still a favorite with a generation of Ranger fans that saw him try to do the impossible on a nightly basis.

CHAPTER 6

HARRY HOWELL

The Skinny

No one in Rangers history has worn the Blueshirt as many times as Harry Howell. Not many have worn it as well, either. For 17 seasons and 1,160 games, Howell was Mr. Reliable on the Rangers' blue line. It's a record that has stood for more than three decades, and one that the current crop of Rangers will be hard pressed to surpass.

Howell arrived in the Big Apple in 1952, fresh out of junior hockey—something that rarely happened in the Original Six era. Though he was 6-foot-1 and 190 pounds, a fairly big guy at that time, Howell wasn't a physical kind of defenseman. That earned him some boos from the fans who came out to the old Madison Square Garden. They wanted to see their defensemen banging opposing forwards into the boards, not just stripping them of the puck and starting the play back the other way.

But the fans eventually grew to appreciate Howell's subtle skills. So did management—he was named captain at the start of the 1955-56 season, but gave back the C after two seasons, saying he wasn't playing well enough.

"Hey, Sully [Red Sullivan], Andy Bathgate, and Camille Henry were all on those teams," he recalled. "They all had more experience than me. I just wanted to do my job."

That he did. Howell continued to provide the Rangers with solid play on the blue line—nothing flashy, but consistent and productive.

Howell especially remembers the late 1950s, when Phil Watson was coach. Watson was, to put it mildly, tempestuous during his reign from 1955 to 1959. The Rangers made the playoffs in 1956, 1957, and 1958, and were headed for another trip to the postseason in 1959.

"Phil was most definitely a character, one of a kind," Howell recalls. "One night [February 15, 1959], he made us practice *after* a game, which we lost at the Garden to Montreal. Can you imagine that? That practice was a killer, not only physically, but psychologically. We were dead after that, and Toronto knocked us out of the playoffs on the final night of the season.

"We had some pretty good teams in those years. Bathgate was in his prime, so was Gump Worsley. Camille Henry was a great sniper. We made the playoffs a couple of times but never got out of the first round."

Unlike most players, Howell seemed to get better with age, even as the team struggled in the early 1960s. He made the All-Star Game (the format back then matched the Stanley Cup champs against a team made up of the best players from the five other Original Six teams), in 1954-55, but not again until a three-season run in 1963-64, 1964-65, and 1965-66.

The Setting

By the fall of 1966, Howell was the 34-year-old dean of the Rangers defense, a group that included impressive young players like Rod Seiling, Jim Neilson, and Arnie Brown. But little did anyone know that the Rangers, who hadn't made the playoffs since 1962, or Howell, who had never been a big scorer, were about to take off.

With Howell playing the best hockey of his life, the Emile Francis-built Rangers got off to the kind of start they hadn't had in decades. Ed Giacomin's goaltending, the emergence of young forwards like Rod Gilbert and Jean Ratelle, and solid play from veterans like Bob Nevin, Phil Goyette, and newcomer "Boom Boom" Geoffrion sparked the Rangers into first place at Christmas time.

"We hadn't been a good team for a long time, but we started to get better after Emile [Francis] came," Howell says of the Rangers' improvement. "He was the one who built the team."

Howell was putting up points like he never had before and says Geoffrion was a major reason why.

Notes on Harry Howell

Name:	Harry Howell
Born:	December 28, 1932 (Hamilton, Ontario)
Position:	Defenseman
Height:	6-foot-1
Playing Weight:	190 pounds
How acquired:	Product of Rangers organization
Years with Rangers:	1952-53 to 1968-69
Stats as a Ranger:	1,160 games; 82 goals; 263 assists; 345 points; 1,147 PIM
Uniform Number:	3
Accomplishments:	Norris Trophy 1966-67
	First-Team All-Star 1966-67
	Rangers MVP 1963-64
	Players' Player Award 1964-65, 1966-67
	Frank Boucher Trophy 1964-65, 1965-66, 1966-67

"That year, I scored more goals than I ever had before," Howell says. "Part of the reason was that I was playing the point on the power play with Boomer [Geoffrion]. In the past, I had played with guys like Andy Bathgate and Rod Gilbert, who had big shots. I always fed them. But when I passed to Boomer, he'd send it back to me and say, 'You shoot it.' It was funny, because Boomer was one of the first guys to use the slap shot a lot."

Howell was also approaching a milestone—his 1,000th NHL game (a much tougher feat to achieve in the days of the six-team league and 70-game schedules). He became the first Ranger to play 1,000 games on January 21, 1967, during a 6–2 loss at Boston that was part of the Rangers' annual January road trip.

By then everything was in place for the first night in Rangers history set up to honor a specific player. Harry Howell Night was scheduled for January

25, 1967, with the Boston Bruins coming to town. It was game No. 1,002 in Howell's career, and a night he'll never forget.

The Rangers had never honored a player with his own night, and with the team enjoying the kind of success it hadn't seen in years, Harry Howell Night was sure to be a festive occasion.

The celebration actually started the day before, when then-mayor John Lindsay presented Howell with the medal of the City of New York.

"I was the first hockey player to get a medal from the city," Howell remembers. "It was pretty special."

Then it was time for the big night. The old Madison Square Garden was packed.

The Game of My Life

HARRY HOWELL NIGHT—JANUARY 25, 1967

"I had played in my 1,000th career game the previous Saturday in Boston—I was the first Ranger to do that. Harry Howell Night had been set for the first home game after that—it was January 25, with Boston coming to town. It was the first 'Night' that the Rangers had ever had for any of their players, so that made it special.

"It was quite a night. We had two planeloads of people coming down from Hamilton, but some of them didn't get there until after the game started because there was fog at the airport in Toronto.

"One of the things I remember was Toots Shor, who was a big restaurateur, spending time with my 90-year-old uncle. He spent a couple of hours with him—that was amazing, him spending all this time with a farmer from Hamilton.

"When we came out, they had all these tables at center ice with gifts (a year's supply of cheese, watches, and a gas barbecue). We got some trips to resorts—the people who owned Grossinger's gave us a holiday there. They gave my wife, Marilyn, a bouquet of roses—I still have a picture of it in my office here.

"I also got a Mercury Cougar. That was a big deal—the Cougar was a brand-new model in its first year, and getting a car like that was really something.

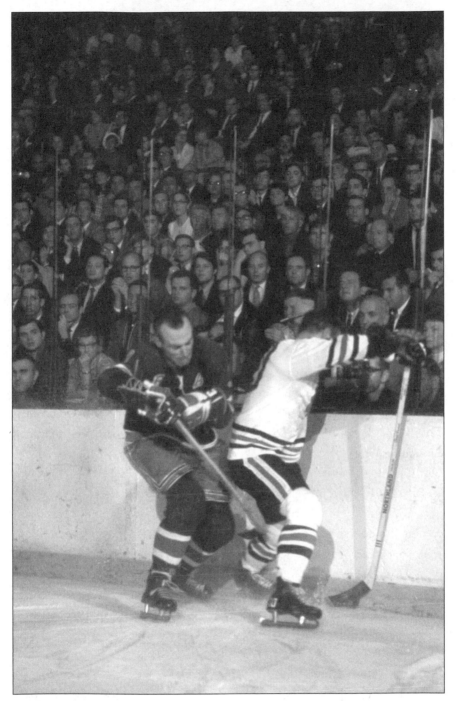

Harry Howell. *Courtesy of the John Halligan Collection*

"The fans were always great to me. On Harry Howell Night, after all the gifts were presented, I spoke for about eight to 10 minutes, and they cheered. That was a nice thing. The fans were always good to me. I was a big guy for the time I played—I was 6-foot-1 and I played at about 190 to 200 pounds. But I wasn't the type of guy to go run people. I could take them out of the play, but I wasn't going to skate 50 feet to hit someone. But they grew to appreciate me.

"I don't remember much about the game itself, except that we won— we beat Boston 2–1. That was an important thing, because I remember we were the visiting team in Montreal when they honored Rocket Richard and Doug Harvey—and we won those games. The fact that we won made the night extra special."

Afterword

The Rangers struggled down the stretch after Howell's big night, but they finished a solid fourth and made the playoffs for the first time in five years. Not even a four-game sweep at the hands of the Canadiens could dim the accomplishments of that season. Howell finished 1966-67 with 12 goals and 28 assists for 40 points—the biggest offensive totals of his career and enough to win the Norris Trophy as the NHL's top defenseman.

During the luncheon ceremony at which he picked up the Norris Trophy, Howell also proved to be an expert prognosticator.

"I'm glad I won it this year," he quipped, "because I think some other guy is going to win it for the next decade."

The "other guy" turned out to be Boston's star young defenseman Bobby Orr, who took home the Calder Trophy as Rookie of the Year that afternoon and then proceeded to win the Norris for the next eight seasons.

The Rangers continued to improve, finishing second in 1967-68 with 90 points and third in 1968-69 with 91. But by then, Howell's back was giving him trouble.

"I was always pretty healthy, I think I only missed maybe 16 games in my first 15 years," he says. "But in my last year [1968-69], I had back problems and missed more games than I had missed in my career to that point.

"I wound up having a spinal fusion—I was the oldest athlete to have one at the time. While I was in the hospital, Emile [Francis] came in and told me I wouldn't be playing in New York anymore. He offered me a job with the organization, but I told him I hadn't gone through all this [the surgery and rehab] to take a front-office job. Emile made a couple of deals and I wound up playing seven more seasons, four on the West Coast and three in the WHA.

Howell played 1½ seasons with the Oakland/California Seals and 2½ more with the Los Angeles Kings, plus a total of four seasons with three different teams in the old World Hockey Association—the New York–New Jersey Knights, the San Diego Mariners, and the Calgary Cowboys. In all, he played 1,581 games as a pro—1,411 of them in the NHL and 1,160 as a Ranger.

After his playing career was done, Howell spent time as general manager of the Cleveland Barons and then briefly coached the Minnesota North Stars after those two teams merged.

Following that, he went into scouting—and although he never won a Stanley Cup as a player, Howell eventually got his name etched on hockey's most cherished prize as a scout with the Edmonton Oilers in 1989-90. He was elected to the Hockey Hall of Fame in 1979.

"When it comes to the Stanley Cup, you never give up," Howell says. "I'm sure glad I didn't. Eventually, I got my ring. I wish it could have been with the Rangers, but a ring is still a ring."

After returning to the Rangers as a part-time scout in the 1990s, Howell finally retired and lives in Hamilton with his wife, Marilyn.

III

YEARS OF THE CAT

As a goaltender, **Emile Francis** never really had a full-time NHL job. But as an executive and coach, he turned out to be just what the Rangers needed.

"The Cat" took over as general manager in the fall of 1964 and quickly made himself coach as well. By the late 1960s, he had turned a doormat into a contender thanks to a combination of good player development and shrewd dealing.

It was an era of memorable games and stars. **Rod Gilbert** recounts two memorable nights: a two-goal playoff performance as a rookie call-up and a four-goal, 16-shot effort in his home town of Montreal—perhaps the most dominant individual effort in Ranger history. **Vic Hadfield**, Gilbert's linemate, remembers what it was like to become the first Ranger to score 50 goals, getting the final two on the last day of 1971-72 and capping the greatest offensive season in team history to that point.

The most amazing offensive performance in Rangers history came on April 5, 1970, when the Blueshirts scored nine goals in the season finale to miraculously earn a playoff berth that appeared all but lost. Francis talks about that game from the perspective of a coach trying to rally his troops, while **Brad Park**, a young defenseman on the way to a Hall of Fame career, remembers what it was like to be on the ice that day.

Center **Pete Stemkowski**, one of Francis' best acquisitions, earned a place in Rangers history in 1971. Stemkowski shares his memories of becoming the only Ranger in the past 70 years to score a triple-overtime tally.

The 1972-73 season brought the arrival of **Steve Vickers**, a left wing who wasted little time making a big impression. Vickers recounts a magical four-day stretch in November 1972 when he became the first player to score hat tricks in consecutive games.

CHAPTER 7

ROD GILBERT

The Skinny

No one in the Rangers' 80-plus NHL seasons has been more identified with the team and with hockey in the New York metropolitan area than Rod Gilbert. Few have done as much for the team on the ice and off.

Gilbert was the fourth of five children, and like so many Canadian youngsters, he started skating young. By the time he was seven, he was playing seven or eight hours of hockey a day.

At age 10, Gilbert met another young hockey player, a slender center named Jean Ratelle, who was attending Roussin Academy, a boarding school next to the Gilberts' home. The two began playing together and were linemates for the better part of 25 years, from peewee hockey through most of Gilbert's NHL career.

"Jean was a classic player," Gilbert says of his old friend and linemate. "We played together since we were 10 years old. I knew his moves, and vice versa."

Like most French-Canadian youngsters, Gilbert was a Montreal Canadiens fan; his idol was Bernie "Boom Boom" Geoffrion. Gilbert might have wound up with his hometown team, except for a man named Yvon Prudhomme. Gilbert's hockey skills drew the attention of Prudhomme, who had been hired by the Rangers to start a Junior B league in Montreal. Not only did Gilbert sign the contract offered by Prudhomme, he convinced him to offer a contract to Ratelle, reuniting the two boyhood friends.

Part of Gilbert's deal was a promise that he would get a chance to try out with the Guelph Biltmores, the Rangers' Junior A team. Not only did he get the tryout, he made the team and finished fourth on the club in scoring in 1957-58 as a 16-year-old, even though he played only 32 games.

In 1958-59, Gilbert blossomed into a star—and a scout. He convinced the Biltmores' coach, Eddie Bush, to bring Ratelle to the team and let the two play on the same line. The reunited pair proved to be an explosive combination: Gilbert had 27 goals and 34 assists for 61 points, while Ratelle collected 51 points as a rookie. The two were teammates for three seasons in Guelph. In 1959-60, Gilbert had 91 points while Ratelle piled up 86 as the Biltmores won the Memorial Cup.

Gilbert almost won the scoring title—Chico Maki edged him on the last day of the season. He did win the title in 1960-61. With the team now known as the Guelph Royals, Gilbert led the OHA in scoring with 103 points, including a league-high 54 goals. He made the OHA's First All-Star team; Ratelle, who had a league-best 61 assists and finished with 101 points, was a Second-Team All-Star. Gilbert also got his first taste of NHL action. On November 27, 1960, he made the most of a one-game call-up by assisting on Dean Prentice's third-period goal that gave New York a 3–3 tie with Chicago.

All looked promising, but then disaster struck on the last day of the season.

"I fell against the boards on a piece of debris," Gilbert says of the junior hockey accident that would affect his entire career. "I had broken my back, and I felt my career was in jeopardy then. They sent me 22 hours on a train to Minnesota, to the Mayo Clinic, because the chairman of the board of Madison Square Garden, Admiral [John] Bergen, was a firm believer in the Mayo Clinic, even while they had a very important doctor here, Dr. [Kazuo] Yanagisawa. He performed [my second] spinal fusion. He also did them on Harry Howell, Orland Kurtenbach, Jean Ratelle—he saved a lot of guys' careers.

"But since I was the best prospect, Admiral Bergen said, 'We want him to go to the best. This guy here [Dr. Yanagisawa] was offended; he actually consulted—he met with the doctor who did the operation, in Chicago, and was in total disagreement with him. They took some bone from the tibia and fused it in my back, but the operation took so long that the blood didn't

Notes on Rod Gilbert

Name:	Rod Gilbert
Born:	July 1, 1941 (Montreal, Quebec)
Position:	Right wing
Height:	5-foot-9
Playing Weight:	175 lbs
How Acquired:	Product of Ranger organization
Years with Rangers:	1960-61 to 1977-78
Stats as Ranger:	1,065 games, 406 goals, 615 assists, 1,021 points, 508 PIM
Uniform Numbers:	14, 7
Accomplishments:	First-Team All-Star 1971-72
	Second-Team All-Star 1967-68
	All-Star Game 1964-65, 1965-66,
	1967, 1969, 1970, 1972,
	1975, 1977
	Bill Masterton Trophy 1975-76
	Lester Patrick Trophy 1991

coagulate, and I got a staph infection in the hospital. I was there for two months, on morphine every three hours. Finally, when I got back, I met with Dr. Yanagisawa here, and he said, 'The operation hasn't been a great success. You play three or four years, and then I'll redo it.' I said, 'I'm not doing that. I just went through that.'

"I was inactive for eight months—couldn't drive a car, couldn't do anything. When I came back in December, they sent me to Kitchener [in the Eastern Professional Hockey League] with [coach] Red Sullivan. I played there for about 30 [actually 21] games. But all that time, the Ranger fans knew that I was one of their top prospects. They were told that this kid was going to come up and change the whole thing. I was good in juniors until I got hurt. Then, the games in Kitchener, I was good, but I didn't break any records."

Thanks to Andy Bathgate's memorable penalty-shot goal that gave the Rangers a key victory over Detroit, the Rangers finished fourth and made the playoffs in 1962 for the first time since 1958. Their opponent: the second-place Toronto Maple Leafs.

The Setting

The series opened in Toronto, with the Leafs winning 4–2. Toronto took the second game 2–1, sending the series back to Madison Square Garden with the Rangers desperately needing a victory.

They also needed another forward, due to injuries.

"Kenny Schinkel, who happened to be a right wing playing with [center] Johnny Wilson and [left wing] Dave Balon, broke his toe," Gilbert says. "I was an emergency call-up."

With Dean Prentice also sidelined with an injury, the 20-year-old took the ice at Madison Square Garden on April 1 and looked right at home. Before a sellout crowd at the Garden, he, Wilson, and Balon were the Rangers' best line against the Leafs. Gilbert earned an assist on Balon's third-period goal that proved to be the game-winner in New York's 5–4 victory.

With the Leafs leading the series 2–1, the Rangers had a chance to pull even on the night of April 3. Before another full house of 15,925 fans, New York's love affair with Rod Gilbert was about to begin.

The Game of My Life (Part I)
1962 STANLEY CUP SEMIFINALS, GAME 4
RANGERS VS. TORONTO MAPLE LEAFS—APRIL 3, 1962

"We had lost the first two games at Maple Leaf Gardens, and then we came back here, to the old Madison Square Garden [the third Garden, on Eighth Avenue between 49th and 50th streets] and won Game 3. In the next game, the first time I got on the ice, I scored a goal [41 seconds into the game]. I was very excited about that—just being in New York and finally playing here was amazing, and then my first time on the ice, I scored against Johnny Bower. Not only that, but toward the end of the first period [at 15:46], I got another one. It was 2–0 Rangers, and I had both goals.

Rod Gilbert. *Courtesy of the John Halligan Collection*

"I came into the locker room at the end of the period. Muzz Patrick was our [general manager] and I said, 'Can you hit me in the head so I can wake up? I think I'm dreaming about this.' He said, 'No, you're here. Don't worry. Go get another one.' I went back out there, and I did get an assist. We won the game, 4–2. The fans were pretty excited—we hadn't been in the playoffs for a while, I think.

"Sometimes I tell Johnny Bower, 'Thank you so much for letting me score my first goal against you.' He says, "Don't worry, kid. I let every kid score their first goal against me.' I said, 'Did you let me score the second one too, at the end of the first period?' and he said, 'No, no, not that one.' I always see him and thank him, and he just says, 'Shut up!' …He's a good guy.

"That was probably my most impressive game. There was nothing to compare with the atmosphere. Everything was new. The lights were shining. I was on Broadway! I also knew then that there was a chance that I was good enough to make it [in the NHL]. I didn't know that before. When you get this kind of success right away, it gives you some pep. I was playing with a brace to protect my back, so I didn't know. Everything was brand new and very exciting. My life made a lot more sense after I did that. My career took a big hop, and my confidence went up 100 percent."

Intermission

The Rangers went back to Toronto for Game 5 and played the Leafs to a standstill through 60 minutes. With goaltender Gump Worsley playing perhaps the finest game of his career, the game was tied 2–2 entering overtime.

Gilbert almost became the hero again.

"We went to overtime, and I hit the post in the first overtime. That would have made us a winner and put us ahead [in the series] 3–2. Instead, we wound up losing in double overtime when Red Kelly scored on Gump Worsley."

Worsley, who made 56 saves, stopped a shot by Frank Mahovlich but couldn't find the puck, which was under his right shoulder. Referee Eddie Powers never blew the whistle, and when Worsley moved his head, Kelly tucked the puck into the net at 4:23 of the second overtime.

The disappointment was compounded by the fact that because of the Garden's then-annual commitment to the circus, Game 6 would also be played in Toronto, with Game 7 back at the Garden—if the Rangers could win. They didn't, losing 7–1.

"The other problem was that we didn't come back here, because of the circus," Gilbert remembers. "We played the sixth game in Toronto and got whacked 7–1. We didn't come back here, and I didn't understand that. There's a big difference playing at home and at Maple Leaf Gardens. We were good enough to beat them. Had we come back here, we win the next game, and then who knows. We could play with them. We had a good team."

Gilbert made the Rangers as a 21-year-old rookie in 1962-63, scoring 11 goals and adding 20 assists. In 1963-64, he reached the 20-goal mark for the first of 12 times in his career. Garden fans loved his speed and booming slap shot as well as his willingness to go to the net despite a lack of size. He finished 1963-64 with 24 goals and 64 points, and improved to 25 goals with 61 points in 1964-65.

However, just as Dr. Yanagisawa had warned him, the surgery Gilbert underwent at the Mayo Clinic hadn't been totally successful. The bone graft loosened and eventually disintegrated as a result of bodily contact. Before his third NHL season, it was discovered that the surgically repaired vertebrae were damaged and had to be operated on again.

In 1965-66, Gilbert tried to play while wearing a custom-fitted brace, but it hindered his breathing and affected his stamina. In January 1966, he underwent a second spinal operation that saved his career. This time, Dr. Yanagisawa took a piece of Gilbert's pelvis and wove it between the fourth, fifth, and third vertebrae.

With his back healthy again, Gilbert scored 28 goals in 1966-67 as the Rangers made the playoffs for the first time since 1961-62. Though the Rangers were swept by Montreal in the semifinals, Gilbert again showed he could produce in the postseason with two goals and five points in the four games.

The Setting to the Second Game

By 1967-68, Gilbert had been reunited with his old boyhood center, Ratelle, who had worked his way through the Rangers' farm system. Veterans like Bob Nevin, Don Marshall, and Phil Goyette gave the Rangers three good forward lines. Harry Howell headed a solid defense that included youngsters Rod Seiling, Arnie Brown, and Jim Neilson, while Ed Giacomin was an All-Star in goal.

With the season entering its final weeks, the Rangers were solidly locked into a playoff berth when they came to the Montreal Forum for a game on February 24, 1968. But the Canadiens were the class of the league. They entered the night with a 22-2-2 record in their previous 26 games and had won eight in a row since the Rangers blanked them 3–0 on February 4, ending Montreal's 12-game winning streak. They were also 19-0-1 in their previous 20 games at the Forum.

The fans who turned out to see the Rangers come to town that night saw one of the greatest performances ever on Forum ice—by a player who wasn't even sure he'd be able to suit up.

The Game of My Life (Part II)
RANGERS AT MONTREAL CANADIENS—FEBRUARY 24, 1968

"I was sick as a dog the morning of that game. On Friday night I had dinner with my parents and my brother and sister, and I woke up the next morning with a 103-degree fever. I didn't think I could play that night. I didn't go to the pregame skate; I stayed in bed. I was hot, and I called the doctor from the hotel. He gave me some antibiotics, and I went back to sleep.

"I still wasn't sure if I could play, But I went out there—I had bought 15 tickets for the game, so I *had* to play. I wound up getting really hot in the warm-up and forgetting about the whole thing [feeling sick]. I went out there and just played.

"Our line was really going in high gear. I got 16 shots on goal, and I only scored four goals. I should have had maybe eight. Rogie Vachon [the Canadiens' goaltender] made some incredible saves against me.

"I was banging that thing toward the net—and remember, we didn't shoot from far out. Our line worked it in pretty close. I had a lot of chances. I also had an assist on Ratelle's goal, so I finished the night with five points. We didn't win often in Montreal, so to win 6–1 and score four goals, that was a pretty big night. I had a lot of friends in Montreal—it was my home town, so it was extra special."

Afterword

Gilbert finished 1967-68 with career highs of 29 goals and 77 points, fifth in the NHL scoring race and one point behind Ratelle. It was the first time since 1941-42 that the Rangers had two players among the NHL's top five scorers. Gilbert added five goals in the playoffs, but the Rangers fell in six games to Chicago.

Gilbert continued to produce, scoring 77 points in 1969-70 and reaching the 30-goal mark for the first time in 1970-71. But those performances were just a warm-up for the 1971-72 season, when everything came together for Gilbert and the Rangers.

With the tandem of Gilbert and Ratelle accompanied by Vic Hadfield on left wing, the 1971-72 Rangers were almost unstoppable. The trio, known as the GAG (Goal-A-Game) line, put up points like no Ranger trio in history. Ratelle set a team record with 109 points before a broken ankle ended his season prematurely. Hadfield became the first Ranger to score 50 goals in a season, and Gilbert had career highs with 43 goals, 54 assists, and 97 points, earning a First-Team All-Star berth. Despite the injury to Ratelk, the GAG Line became the first line ever to have all three members score 40 or more goals.

By then, Gilbert was a fixture on the New York scene. Young, handsome, single, and talented, he loved the Big Apple and was loved in return.

"I met a lot of other artists—Broadway stars and producers and doctors, and we were like a big family. Athletes from other [New York] teams—we were close. The Mets, the Giants, these guys were my friends. We supported each other. We'd hang out—it was fun. It was a different era. The athletes were more approachable then. I wrote a couple of books, I was on *What's My Line* [a popular game show], the Johnny Carson show with Don Rickles, I think I was more visible then. I was the mystery guest on *What's My Line*, and the panel didn't recognize me with the masks off or on."

The Rangers beat Montreal and Chicago to make the 1972 Stanley Cup Finals, but without Ratelle, they came up short against Boston and Bobby Orr. It's still one of the great disappointments of Gilbert's career.

"My hopes were always as high as could be," he says of missing out on winning the Cup. "I didn't understand why we couldn't win. It seemed like during the season, we could beat anybody. The year we played against Boston in the finals, we lost Jean in March [with a broken ankle]. He already had 109 points, and he had about 16 games to go. If he hadn't broken his ankle, [Jaromir] Jagr would have had a lot more work to do [to break the team scoring record]."

Gilbert remained among the NHL's best right wings through the mid-1970s, putting up a career-high 59 assists in 1972-73, scoring 36 goals the next season, and matching his career high with 97 points in 1974-75. Still the Rangers couldn't win the Cup.

The personal milestones began to come. On March 24, 1974, he scored his 300th career goal, beating Dave Dryden of the Buffalo Sabres to become the first player in team history to reach that mark. In June 1976, Gilbert was presented with the Bill Masterton Memorial Trophy as a tribute to his dedication on and off the ice. On December 12, 1976, he played his 1,000th game and set up three goals in a 5–2 win over the Stanley Cup champion Canadiens at the Garden.

Gilbert finished 1976-77 with 28 goals and 75 points for a team that was in transition from the Emile Francis–led clubs of the 1960s and 1970s to a team led by Gilbert's former Montreal nemesis, John Ferguson. Along the way, he scored his 400th goal and 1,000th career point. But before the start of the 1977-78 season, the two tangled over a new contract. Following a 15-day holdout, Gilbert had just two goals and nine points in 19 games before he was let go.

"John Ferguson fired me," Gilbert says. "[Team president] Bill Jennings was sick, and Ferguson and I didn't see eye-to-eye on many things. I was in his way to having total dominance, so he got rid of me. I was very disappointed. I got mistreated here at the end of my career, and I was bitter. I never really recovered for a long time, until I came back in 1989, when almost everybody [from that era] was gone."

Gilbert's numbers—406 goals, 615 assists, and 1,021 points—tell only part of the story of his Ranger career.

"I was very close to New York—I lived in town and met everyone and went to all the charity events," he says of his playing days, when he was one of the few NHL players who didn't go home during the summer. "I was single for a long time, so I was with the fans at these different locations all the time, and I guess it built up. I was fortunate to play—I had a really rough start, with my surgeries and such, so when I did get to play, I was very active everywhere, on the ice and off. My personality fit in here more than anyone else's, because I was excited and curious about a lot of things."

The Rangers wasted little time making Gilbert the first player in team history to have his number retired. On March 7, 1977, his No. 7 was raised to the Garden rafters. Five years later, Gilbert was elected to the Hockey Hall of Fame, following a time in which he coached the Rangers' top farm team in New Haven and opened a restaurant.

"It's the biggest honor you can have in hockey," he says. "It's not something you think about while you're playing. All those years in New York, I never thought about the honor. It was unexpected, and I was very honored."

The breach between the Rangers and the most famous player in their history has long since healed. For more than a decade, Gilbert has been active in the Rangers' community relations program, doing things such as giving clinics and meeting with fans. Much of his life is also devoted to charitable work.

"That's what's most important to me," he says. "I've seen the Rangers lose and win. But people that I meet that are generous and charitable off the ice, they became my friends, and there's plenty of those in New York.

"We do the Skate with the Greats for Ronald McDonald House. Our charity at the Garden is Cheering for Children. I do that. I also help the Rangers alumni quite a bit. I'm on different boards: for cystic fibrosis, Boomer Esiason's foundation, I do all the [fund-raising] walks, and I help with Ice Hockey in Harlem. I also have my own charity for diabetes—we've had it for 12 years. We do it at two golf courses, and we've raised so much money for the American Diabetes Foundation—that's probably my closest one.

"I do a lot of stuff for the Rangers too—clinics for kids, visits with people at the games. I think it shows the young kids that people care. They see that the older players are well treated, so they know that they're going to be well treated. I think it's very important."

CHAPTER 8

VIC HADFIELD

The Skinny

Rangers fans weren't exactly jumping up and down when the Blueshirts landed Vic Hadfield, a big left wing, from the Chicago Black Hawks in the 1962 waiver draft. Sure, Hadfield was big (for the 1960s, anyway) and rugged—two commodities that hadn't been in ample supply on Broadway in quite a while. But he wasn't much of a scoring threat. In fact, after bouncing up and down between the Rangers and the minors for a year or two, his biggest accomplishment was leading the NHL in penalty minutes in 1963-64 with 151.

But the 1960s was the era of curved sticks. Bombers like Bobby Hull terrorized goaltenders by launching slap shots with "banana" blades—sticks with unlimited curves that made life miserable for goaltenders. Hadfield started using the slap shot and the curved stick, and the goals started to come. Hadfield hit the 20-goal mark for the first time in 1967-68, helping the Rangers make the playoffs for the second consecutive season. He rang up 20 or more goals in each of the next three seasons while providing the Rangers with a physical presence on the left side of a line that included center Jean Ratelle and right wing Rod Gilbert.

Hadfield also became one of the best practical jokers in team history. One of his favorite ruses would send the victim on a wild goose chase. As a veteran, Hadfield always had credibility in the locker room.

"That helped a lot," he remembers, "but the most important thing was the timing. You had to get the guys at the right time."

The "right time" was usually when he was leaving, freshly showered and shaved, after a practice or a game. It went something like this: "Oh, [Willie, Tom, John]," Hadfield would say, "I forgot, the Cat [Emile Francis, the club's longtime coach and general manager] was looking for you before." That would send the victim scurrying off to the team's business office in search of Francis. Emile would just chuckle and tell the victim that he'd been had.

Hadfield's repertoire wasn't limited to wild goose chases. He perfected all the usual array of clubhouse pranks: switching teammates' neckties, fake phone messages (usually from females), Vaseline smeared inside of shoes, and on and on.

Still, on the ice, there appeared to be nothing terribly special about Hadfield until the 1971 playoffs, when he tied a team record with eight goals, including three in one game against Toronto—the first playoff hat trick by a Ranger since Pentti Lund had one in 1950.

During the summer of 1971, the Rangers traded team captain Bob Nevin to Minnesota for speedy forward Bobby Rousseau. That left the captain's *C* without an owner—until general manager Francis gave it to Hadfield.

The Setting

The Rangers had reestablished themselves as one of the NHL's elite teams; they finished second to Boston in 1970-71 and won a playoff series for the first time since 1950 before losing a heartbreaking seven-game semifinal series to Chicago. The Hadfield-Ratelle-Gilbert line was among the better lines in the NHL, but no one could have foreseen the kind of season they would have in 1971-72.

Hadfield, Ratelle, and Gilbert opened the season hot and got hotter. They piled up goals and points like no Rangers unit in history. The local papers picked up team statistician Arthur Friedman's nickname for the unit—the "GAG (Goal a Game) Line"—though that was understating the level of their performance.

Notes on Vic Hadfield

Name:	Vic Hadfield
Born:	October 4, 1940 (Oakville, Ontario)
Position:	Left wing
Height:	6 feet
Playing Weight:	190 pounds
How Acquired:	Claimed by Rangers from Chicago in the 1961 waiver draft
Years with Rangers:	1961-62 to 1973-74
Stats as a Ranger:	839 games, 262 goals, 310 assists, 572 points, 1,036 PIM
Uniform Number:	11
Accomplishments:	Captain 1971–1974
	Second-Team All-Star 1971-72
	Players' Player Award 1971-72

With the GAG Line leading the way, the Rangers battled the Boston Bruins for first place in the East Division and in the overall NHL standings. Hadfield, Ratelle, and Gilbert all were among the league leaders in scoring and made the All-Star Game.

The Bruins eventually took control, and any hopes the Rangers had of catching them were dashed on March 4, when Ratelle's left ankle was broken by a shot from teammate Dale Rolfe in an otherwise routine win over the California Golden Seals.

"It was a terrible break when Jean broke his ankle. Jean was such a workhorse," Hadfield says. "We just couldn't replace him with anyone. It was devastating when that happened. We couldn't survive with a hole as big as Jean Ratelle in our lineup. We had played together for so long. Jean killed penalties, worked the power play, he was a workhorse for our team."

But the loss of Ratelle didn't cool off Hadfield's hot stick. All three linemates had broken Andy Bathgate's team record of 40 goals in a season, set in 1958-59. But Hadfield outdistanced both Ratelle (46 before he got hurt) and Gilbert (43), and he came into the season finale against the

Montreal Canadiens at Madison Square Garden with 48 goals, a team record.

But Hadfield wasn't done yet. The game didn't mean anything in the standings—the Rangers were assured of finishing second, one spot ahead of the Canadiens. But with a national TV audience watching and the playoffs looming, Hadfield wasn't about to sit.

The Game of My Life
RANGERS VS. MONTREAL CANADIENS—APRIL 2, 1972

"I came into the game with 48 goals. But the ligaments were torn in both of my thumbs. It was painful, but it was important that I play because we were playing the team we were going to play in the playoffs. I couldn't let them know there was something wrong with me. The doctors were able to tape the thumb—it's tough to explain, but they were able to tape my thumb to the next finger so it was stabilized. Then I was able to cup the stick, not grab it the way you usually would. It was tough—it made it difficult to shoot the puck, but I could play. [After the game, Hadfield's right thumb was so sore that he had to accept greetings from well-wishers with his left hand.]

"I don't even remember the 49th goal, and I don't know who I was playing with—Rod and probably either Phil Goyette or Bobby Rousseau. I remember the second one being a play where I changed the direction of a pass from behind the Montreal goal. It came against goaltender Denis DeJordy. It was funny to score against him: I had played Junior B with Denis, and we roomed together in my first year as a pro in Buffalo in 1960. It was fun getting that goal off someone I knew.

"It was exciting to get the 50th. My son was there, and for him to be down there in the dressing room after the game—he was very excited. But to be honest, and not trying to sound corny, back then, individual awards didn't mean that much, because it's a team sport. We all stuck together.

"But having said all that, it was very nice to get No. 50. It was heartbreaking when we didn't win the Cup. That's just the way it was then. I know it's not like that today."

Vic Hadfield, No. 11. *Courtesy of the John Halligan Collection*

Afterword

Hadfield continued to fill the net during the 1972 playoffs. Despite the absence of Ratelle, the big left wing scored seven goals and added nine assists for 16 points, setting a team playoff record for points. The Rangers beat the Canadiens and the Black Hawks to advance to the finals for the first time since 1950, but lost to the Bobby Orr–led Bruins in six games.

"We were on a mission right from training camp: we were going to win the Stanley Cup," Hadfield said. "We had to do it as a team. Individual awards didn't mean anything. We were going to win it as a team or lose it as a team. Not winning the Cup was a big blow."

The Bruins were battered by the upstart World Hockey Association the next season, while Francis kept the Rangers together. A lot was expected, but the magic of the previous season was gone. Hadfield's goal output dropped from 50 to 28, and his point production from 106 to 62. Although the Rangers avenged the previous year's loss to Boston by routing the Bruins in five games in the first round, the Black Hawks followed suit by dumping the Rangers in the semifinals.

Hadfield's scoring dropped to 27 goals and 55 points in 1973-74, and after the Rangers were again ousted in the second round, this time in a bitterly fought seven-game series against the Philadelphia Flyers, Francis began to break up the team. Hadfield, who had just one goal in the 1974 playoffs and was going to be 34 in the fall, was among the first to go. He was traded to Pittsburgh for defenseman Nick Beverley.

Hadfield's scoring touch wasn't entirely gone: He had a pair of 30-goal seasons with the Penguins, but a knee injury that had become increasingly painful forced him to retire after he played just nine games in the 1976-77 season.

Though Hadfield's hockey career was over, his link with sports was not.

"I've always been in the golf business. I owned a golf course, which I sold in 1985. Since then, I've been into the golf driving range, teaching. I have a golf academy now in Oakville, Ontario. It's about 50 acres. We have it all here—miniature golf, sand traps, natural putting greens, tees. We're only a half hour from Toronto."

Golf also ties in with another of Hadfield's interests. He holds a one-day golf tournament each year to support the Daniella Maria Arturi Foundation, named after the daughter of a close friend who died at the age of three.

"In eight years, we've raised $1.4 million," he says. "We're very proud of that. It goes to Diamond Blackfan Anemia (DBA). It's a rare form of leukemia. A lot of the guys, like Eddie Giacomin and Brad Park, come and play to help us out."

Hadfield may be rooted in Oakville, but he's still a Ranger. His 50 goals remained a team record for more than 20 years, until Adam Graves scored 52 in 1993-94. And when the Rangers ended their 54-year drought that spring by winning the Stanley Cup, "I felt like I was part of the team," he says. "That was the Rangers—I'll always be a Ranger. My hometown, Oakville, all the minor hockey league teams are called the Oakville Rangers; all of them have the same colors. It's a big effort here. That's what that meant. I'm very proud of the fact that it was carried over here because I was a Ranger."

Hadfield even got to see his No. 11 raised to the Garden rafters on January 12, 2006, when the Rangers retired it in honor of Mark Messier. Hadfield was thrilled for his successor as captain.

"It was very nice to see No. 11 go up in the rafters," he says. "They certainly did it well, and I'm very glad for Mark. I've known him since 1980, and he's a wonderful individual. I couldn't be happier for him. A lot of people say, 'That should have been your number.' But it wasn't. Mark was able to win the Stanley Cup, and I wasn't able to do that. I don't have a problem with that."

CHAPTER 9

EMILE FRANCIS

The Skinny

The rebirth of the New York Rangers in the mid-1960s, following a remarkably dismal decade of failure, was orchestrated almost entirely by a remarkable general manager named Emile "The Cat" Francis. Francis, a quick-gloved goaltender during his playing days, bounced around hockey's high minor leagues for nearly 15 seasons as a player. He even had a few cups of coffee in the NHL with the Chicago Black Hawks and the Rangers themselves for 22 games.

Francis played his last pro game with Seattle of the Western League in 1958-59 and soon joined the Rangers-sponsored junior team in Guelph, Ontario, as coach. He stayed there only one season before coming to New York and worked his way through the Rangers' chain of command. Francis was named general manager in the fall of 1964, On December 5, 1965, he fired Red Sullivan and took over as coach as well.

As full-time general manager and three-time coach, Francis oversaw one of the greatest eras in Rangers history. By 1967, he had completely remade a team (his tenets were "youth, depth, and size") that had made the Stanley Cup playoffs only once in the previous eight seasons. In addition, the Rangers were preparing to move to the fourth Madison Square Garden (the current Garden) and were not selling out their games, particularly weekday games. That soon changed.

Francis had an eye for talent. He traded five players to Providence of the AHL for a minor-league goaltender named Ed Giacomin. He also shepherded a stream of young talent through the Rangers system, blending the kids with veterans like Harry Howell and Bob Nevin. In 1966-67, the new-look Rangers made the playoffs for the first time in five years. They celebrated their move into the new Garden in 1967-68 by finishing second, and made the playoffs again in 1968-69.

The Setting

After three straight playoff appearances but no series victories, the rebuilt Rangers looked ready to catch fire in 1969-70. They lost only four of their first 26 games and had a January-February streak that saw them lose only twice in 12 outings. The playoffs seemed assured for a fourth straight season, and inklings of a Stanley Cup began to resonate in some fans' heads—no mean feat for a team that hadn't won it all since 1939-40, three decades earlier.

The Rangers were in first place when they went to Detroit on February 28. They left with a 3–3 tie, but it was a costly point because they lost their best defenseman, Brad Park, who went down with a broken ankle. With Park out of the lineup, the team went cold—ice cold in fact, winning only once in 14 games. The playoffs were quickly slipping away. Instead of dreaming about winning the Stanley Cup, the Rangers were looking at the nightmarish possibility of missing the playoffs in a three-way race with the Red Wings and Montreal Canadiens for the final two berths in the East Division.

Amazingly, Park made it back for the last week of the season, but the Rangers' playoff hopes boiled down to the final weekend—home-and-home matches with the Red Wings on Saturday, April 4, at the Olympia in Detroit and Sunday afternoon, April 5, at the Garden. It was a do-or-die weekend, and everyone around the team, players and fans alike, knew it.

The Detroit half of the home-and-home series was a disaster. The Rangers were flat and lost badly, 6–2, at the Olympia as the Red Wings clinched their first playoff berth in four years. The loss hung hard on the Rangers. They had played sluggishly in what was their most important game of the season and headed for home in fifth place, two points behind the fourth-place Canadiens, who had lost at home to Chicago. That loss left a

Notes on Emile Francis

Name:	Emile Francis
Born:	September 13, 1926 (North Battleford, Saskatchewan)
Position:	Goaltender; General Manager–Coach
Height:	5-foot-6
Playing Weight:	145 pounds
How Acquired:	Traded to the Rangers with Alex Kaleta by the Chicago Black Hawks in exchange for Sugar Jim Henry— October 7, 1948
Years with Rangers:	1948-49 to 1951-52 (player) 1964-65 to January 6, 1976 (general manager) Three stints as coach, beginning December 5, 1965, through 1974-75
Stats as Ranger:	As a player: 22 games, 3.19 goals-against average, 7-9-5 record
As a coach:	654 games, 342 wins, 209 losses, 103 ties
Uniform Numbers:	1, 16
Accomplishments:	Lester Patrick Trophy 1982 Hockey Hall of Fame 1982

tiny sliver of hope that the Rangers could make the playoffs, but that opening was small, and only the feisty Francis seemed able to think it really could happen.

He stood wearily among a small knot of reporters in a tiny anteroom while his players slowly showered and dressed. As often would happen after hectic games, Francis was slightly hoarse, but he knew what he wanted to say.

"This game is slippery. It's played on ice. We're not out yet, and we won't stop fighting until the last soldier is dead," he said, using a military metaphor that he often invoked in tense situations. One by one, the players filed sullenly into the anteroom to retrieve their topcoats. None of them spoke. All that remained of their season was an afternoon rematch with the Red Wings on Sunday.

What the Rangers had to do to make the playoffs defied the imaginations of even the team's most optimistic supporters. The Rangers would have to beat the Red Wings the next day at the Garden; Montreal would have to lose Sunday night in Chicago against the Black Hawks; *and* the Rangers would have to score at least five goals more than the Canadiens—goals scored was the determining factor if two teams were exactly tied at the end of the season, and the Canadiens entered the final day of the season with a five-goal lead in that category.

It was an unlikely scenario to be sure, but Francis believed it could happen, and the team left the Olympia heading for the Windsor, Ontario, airport, across the Detroit River, where their chartered Air Canada jetliner awaited them. The bus was crowded with players, scouts, and newspapermen. It was about a 40-minute ride, and if one word was spoken, no one bothered to make note of it. The bus arrived at 11:30 p.m. The airport was deserted except for a dozen or so kids who flocked around the bus thinking the Red Wings were inside, not the Rangers, since the Wings were due at the airport at the same time for their own charter to New York.

Windsor is a small airport, and there were no departures or arrivals at that late hour other than the two charters. The dark bus took the players right out to the runway, and they went directly onto the plane. While most of the kids waited outside for the Wings to arrive, one slipped around back and cornered Francis for an autograph, telling him, "I still like the Rangers, Emile. You'll get them next time." The youngster had no idea how accurate he was.

Francis and two of his scouts, Lou Passador and Steve Brklacich, filed into the terminal to complete the ticketing arrangements while trainer Frank Paice and his assistant, Jim Young, helped to unload the baggage. A number of reporters were telephoning their papers with additions to their stories. Francis shouted at Passador and Brklacich, "Let's go ... Louie ... Steve ... don't look so glum. We're not out of this thing yet. We have to win our game and score five or more goals than the Canadiens do at night. Then we're in the playoffs."

Emile Francis. *Courtesy of the John Halligan Collection*

Landing in New York, the plane went to the International Arrivals Building at Kennedy Airport, which was bustling even at the late hour (2 a.m.). Outside the building, the Rangers again filed into a bus for the trip into Manhattan. Again, the bus was quiet, but through the windows, the Rangers could see the Red Wings, somewhat beery and perhaps smelling of champagne, coming into the terminal. Their charter had just landed, and there were smiles all around. It was 3:30 a.m. when the Rangers hit their hotel across from Madison Square Garden. Sleep, always difficult after a hectic game, was nearly impossible that night. Game time—the final game of a 76-game season—was only about 11 hours away.

Afternoon games following road games the night before were the toughest of all (in fact, the Collective Bargaining Agreement has since eliminated turnarounds this short). This one was even tougher. The morning came faster than usual, and it wasn't an overly joyous one. There was a power failure in the coffee shop at the Rangers' hotel, and breakfast was not available. Some players went elsewhere, others just skipped breakfast and pocketed the meal money—hardly an uncommon practice at the time.

At 11 a.m. some of the Rangers headed for church (it was Easter Sunday), while others simply wandered around the deserted fur district, killing time on a warm April day. The mood of silence continued as the Rangers drifted into the Garden for the final game. Things started to pick up a little as the players dressed. Eddie Giacomin and Ron Stewart were chattering, and it started to spread to the other players. "C'mon guys, we can do it. … Gotta get 'em early. … Put me down for two. … Would you believe 10 goals?" Snapped Francis, "Why not?"

CBS was showing the game on national TV. But the arena had large patches of empty seats at the scheduled 2 p.m. face-off. Many downhearted fans chose to stay home—including all of the Rangers' and the Garden's top management.

Those who came saw a game unlike any the Rangers had ever played. Bursting with energy, the Rangers raced after the puck following the opening face-off. They roared in on goalie Roger Crozier (substituting for normal starter Roy Edwards, who had done a little too much celebrating the night before). Many fans were still walking to their seats when Walt Tkaczuk came within a whisker of a goal 18 seconds into the game.

The Game of My Life

DETROIT RED WINGS VS. RANGERS
AT MADISON SQUARE GARDEN—APRIL 5, 1970

"I had a game plan, I really did," Francis recalls today, more than 35 years after the game. "I was going to keep changing lines and keep the shifts down to 30 seconds each, 45 seconds tops. It was the only way."

[Francis' plan to change his men as often as possible worked perfectly. Another line came over the boards before the Wings even mustered a single shot at Giacomin. Rod Gilbert, Jean Ratelle, and rookie Jack Egers thundered in on Crozier. Gilbert fired and scored. The time: 36 seconds. The sirens went off, and a window of opportunity opened.]

"Gilbert's goal ignited us for sure. Coming so quickly, even the guys who thought, 'Maybe we can't do it,' were now thinking, 'Hey, maybe we can.' I could almost feel it on the bench. As a team, something came over us.

"I told the guys right from the start, let's run 'em off the ice," recalls Francis, whose orders to his team to play "firewagon hockey" would work better than he could have dreamed. "And run 'em off the ice is what we did. I was pretty proud."

[Egers, a newly recalled left wing, scored the most important goal of his young career on a power play at 8:25. Dave Balon then posted his first of three at 12:21.] "It was incredible. I mean, we hadn't gotten three goals in a period in almost two months!" [Egers connected again, and even the most cynical fans were on their feet clapping and cheering. It was eerie and electric.]

"The goals by Egers were very important. They kept the momentum and the feeling going. I can tell you this much—that was probably the best game Jack Egers ever played in his career."

The second period began with the Rangers up 4–1, and Francis kept the fire stoked. Just 20 seconds into the period, Gilbert smoked a slapper past a reeling Crozier, and the fans went wild again. The Rangers already had their five goals, and if Tony Esposito could shut out the Canadiens at night, maybe, just maybe. ... Esposito already had a league-leading 15 shutouts that season. Was it possible? "Of course, it was possible," Francis says firmly. "I knew it, and it was my job to make sure the players knew it too."

[By this time, the Rangers were in complete domination. They peppered Crozier from every possible angle. At one point the acrobatic little goalie was in a complete frenzy, as the Rangers kept the puck in the Red Wings end for a full three minutes. Shot after shot thumped into Crozier's pads, ricocheted off the goal posts, slammed against the end boards and glass. It was hard to believe. Some fans, watching at home on TV, sensed history in the making and made their way to the Garden to be part of it. So did various sportswriters, radio interviewers, and television crews.]

"We all noticed it on the bench," Francis recalls. "At the beginning of the game, the building was maybe half-full; by the second period, there were about 12,000 fans; but by the start of the third, it was full … and loud. That helped us a lot."

[Stewart, all of 37 years of age, kept the fans roaring by scoring the Rangers' sixth and seventh goals for a commanding 7–2 lead. Crozier was clearly shaken after the second period. The Rangers had blasted 39 shots at him already, and their biggest salvo (26 more shots in the third) was yet to come. Balon scored his second at 1:21 of the final period and finished off a hat trick at 9:48. Bedlam broke out at the Garden, and the Rangers had nine goals. Francis desperately tried for more, lifting Giacomin for an extra skater four times in the final four minutes.]

"The Wings scored in the empty net twice," Francis recalls, "but that didn't matter, only total goals mattered. We had to win, of course, but goals were the key." The Rangers won 9–5.

Afterword

To this day, many of those Rangers don't even remember the thunderous ovation they received at game's end. The fans were in an uproar, many of them pounding the glass surrounding the rink. The dressing room was a wild scene. Said Balon, "If this is a dream, don't bother to wake me." Said Gordie Howe, "I don't think I've ever been in a game quite like that one." Neither had anyone else. Incredibly, the Rangers had fired a team-record 65 shots at Crozier that afternoon, something they had never achieved before, not in their previous 2,613 games.

Across the hall, Francis related his strategy to a rapidly growing swarm of notebooks, microphones, and cameras. "The adrenaline was flowing all game long," emphasized Francis. Years later, he added another salient note. "The fact that the game was on national television was a huge help to us. The Canadiens were in Chicago and no doubt watched what we did in the afternoon. That put the pressure right on them, no doubt about it."

The outcome also put pressure on Ranger fans. Throughout the Metropolitan area, dinners were gulped nervously or not eaten at all in anticipation of the game that night. Radio dials across the region were twisted and turned to bring in two distant stations (CBM, 950 AM in Montreal and WGN, 720 AM in Chicago). Most fans only found the Montreal station. Danny Gallivan's voice finally crackled over the air, "*This game is coming to you from the Chicago Stadium...* ." The "Madhouse on Madison" was living up to its name—a sellout crowd was on hand to see if the Black Hawks could finish first for only the second time in team history.

Gallivan: "*Mohns over to Pinder. ... Martin has it in front. ... He scores! ... Dennis Hull to Mikita to Koroll. ... Koroll scores! ... Vachon is out of the net. ... The Hawks lead 5–2. ... Pinder a shot. ... He scores! ... Dennis Hull has it. ... He scores!*"

With their season slipping away, the Canadiens emulated Francis and pulled their goaltender midway through the final period. With no goalie to stop them, the Black Hawks filled the empty net, rolling to a 10–2 victory and knocking the Canadiens out of the playoffs for the first time since 1948. The fans chanted, "We're number one. ... We're number one. ... We're number one. ... We're number one." They may as well have been cheering for the Rangers, who had done the impossible on one improbable April weekend.

Once the Montreal-Chicago game ended, radio and television stations blared the news: "The Rangers make the playoffs. ... The Rangers make the playoffs." It was the lead story for hours. Some stations even interrupted regular programming with the story. Said Francis that night, "It was like we won the Stanley Cup."

Figuratively, the "9–5 Game" as it came to be known, was the springboard into the era that is now called "The Rise of the Rangers," the touchstone of the Francis years that got the team ever so close, but not quite close enough, to a Stanley Cup championship.

The 1970 playoffs themselves were a disappointment, a letdown after such an emotional final regular-season game. The Rangers drew the rival

Boston Bruins for their opening-round opponent, hardly an enviable task. Boston was loaded. The Bruins had Bobby Orr and a top line of Phil Esposito between Wayne Cashman and Ken Hodge. Gerry Cheevers was the goalie.

Boston came out flying, pounding the Rangers 8–2 and 5–3 in the first two games at Boston Garden. The series moved to New York, and the Rangers responded to the crowd, some of whom were probably still celebrating the 9–5 game. The Blueshirts won a pair of fight-filled games, 4–3 and 4–2, and the series returned to Boston tied at two.

With Orr showing the way (he led all scorers in the series with seven goals), Boston grabbed control and won 3–2 in Game 5. Then the Bruins, led again by Orr, wrapped it up with a surprisingly easy 4–1 win in Game 6 at the Garden. "Except for the first two games, we played fine," Francis recalls, "but hey, Bobby Orr is Bobby Orr, and he just took over. It was kind of the same thing when we faced him in the Finals in 1972."

Francis knew his team was starting to peak. Late in the 1970-71 season, he acquired Hall of Fame defenseman Tim Horton from the Toronto Maple Leafs, kept almost all of his core players from the previous year, and set out for a Cup win. It was not to happen. The playoffs that year saw the Blueshirts oust the Toronto Maple Leafs in six games, but lose to the Chicago Black Hawks in seven, despite two dramatic overtime goals by Pete Stemkowski.

They got even closer the next season. For the first time since 1950, the Rangers made it to the Finals, disposing of Montreal and Chicago along the way. But once again they ran into Orr and the Bruins. The Bruins won in six, with the Rangers severely hampered by a subpar Jean Ratelle, their leading scorer, who suffered a broken ankle in early March. "With Jean, we might have done it," Francis says, "but without him, it was simply not meant to be."

The Rangers finally beat the Bruins in 1973, winning the opening round in five games. But the Black Hawks got revenge for being swept the year before, bouncing the Rangers in five games. A year later, the Rangers beat Montreal in the opening round (becoming the first team in NHL history to eliminate the defending Cup champs three years in a row), only to lose a bitter seven-game semifinal to Philadelphia, a series that saw the home team win all seven games.

"We had great chances also in 1973 and 1974, but Chicago beat us and so did Philadelphia," Francis says. "After that, I knew that particular team had run out of chances to win. But hey, we'll always have the Detroit game. That was our Stanley Cup, I guess."

Francis started to break up the core of his team after the 1974 playoff loss, dealing captain Vic Hadfield to Pittsburgh. After the Islanders stunned the Rangers in the preliminary round in 1975, he stepped down as coach for the final time in favor of Stewart (who was replaced by John Ferguson 39 games into the season) and turned his attention to his role as GM. With much of his team over 30, Francis knew it was time for a makeover. Ed Giacomin, Brad Park, and Ratelle were among those who were sent packing before the end of 1975.

But with the team still struggling in the first week of 1976, it was Francis who got the pink slip. He was let go after he refused to resign as GM. "If they want to remove me, remove me," he said after the move was made. "I never took the easy way out."

Ferguson added the GM's job to his position as coach, and Francis stayed on as a vice president. But that didn't last long. Later in 1976, he joined the St. Louis Blues as executive VP, general manager, and coach, building a team that set a franchise record with 107 points in 1980-81.

Francis was elected to the Hockey Hall of Fame in 1982. That same year, Francis, a longtime backer of youth and amateur hockey in the United States and the New York area in particular, also received the Lester Patrick Award for his contributions to hockey in the United States.

When the Blues went through an ownership shuffle, Francis left to join the Hartford Whalers in 1983 as president and general manager, building the team that won the Whalers' only divisional title in 1986-87.

Francis officially retired from the game after the 1992-93 season, retiring to Florida, where he remains today. But on June 14, 1994, The Cat was back in Madison Square Garden as an MSG Network analyst to see the franchise to which he gave so much achieve the one thing he was never able to achieve—a Stanley Cup triumph. Francis was in the tunnel below the press box as the final seconds counted down. "I didn't even watch the end," he says. "Instead, I turned and watched the fans. So many of them were crying. It was really something."

CHAPTER 10

BRAD PARK

The Skinny

A generation before Brian Leetch wore No. 2 on the way to a Hall of Fame career, Brad Park did the same thing. The only difference: Leetch won a Stanley Cup ring; Park never did, though not for lack of trying. In his 17 NHL seasons, Park's teams made the playoffs every time.

"One thing I'm proud of is that in 17 years, I never missed the playoffs. I was very proud of that," he says. "When I went to Detroit, they hadn't made the playoffs for seven years, they hadn't made it in back-to-back years in 22, and we made the playoffs both years."

Park was a standout in junior hockey with the hometown Toronto Marlboros. But in the early 1960s, the NHL reduced the number of players the six teams could control. That meant teams had to make decisions about which ones to keep, and happily for the Rangers, the Toronto Maple Leafs, who could have kept Park, didn't—reportedly, they thought he wouldn't be big enough to play in the NHL.

That left Park up for grabs, and the Rangers took him with the second pick in the 1966 Amateur Draft. "I tell people in Boston that it was ironic—when I got drafted, the Rangers had the second choice. The Bruins had the first pick and passed on me [they took another defenseman, Barry Gibbs]. If they had taken me then, I would have been in Boston from Day One. That would have been some combination."

Although the Rangers now owned his rights, Park stayed with the Marlboros, winning the Memorial Cup in 1967 with a team that included future pros such as Brian Glennie, Mike Pelyk, and Gerry Meehan, among others.

Park turned pro in 1968, and despite a strong training camp, was sent to the AHL's Buffalo Bisons, then the Rangers' top farm team. His coach there was Freddie Shero, who gave the 20-year-old all the work he could handle. But Park's minor-league career lasted all of 17 games, during which he racked up 14 points. With Rod Seiling and Harry Howell injured, Park stepped into the lineup in the fall of 1968 and never saw the minors again.

From the beginning, Park was a superb puck-mover with a big shot. It took him a while to get his first NHL goal—it came in a 9–0 rout of Boston on February 23, 1969. "I scored my first goal against the Bruins—the ninth goal in a 9–0 game," he remembers. "I was so excited about getting it that I fell down. You know it's going to happen, but you don't know when."

Bobby Orr had arrived in the NHL in 1966 and revolutionized the game by rushing the puck and joining the play, going into places where defensemen didn't normally go. Park wasn't the puck-rusher Orr was (no one has *ever* rushed the puck like Orr), but he quickly became an offensive force on the blue line—the likes of which Garden fans had never seen.

Neither did Park forget that his first job was to keep the puck out of his own net. Park was a solid, physical player in his own zone who was more than willing to mix it up if the need arose.

"I was probably more of an open-ice hitter and more physical than Bobby," Park says in comparing their styles of play. "Not long after I came to the Rangers, Orland Kurtenbach went down. We didn't have a lot of guys who would take on the policeman role, so for most of those years, I led the team in penalty minutes. Today, they wouldn't ask you to do something like that."

The Setting

Park turned into a star in 1969-70, his first full NHL season. He showed that he could do it all—skate, pass, shoot, and hit. With Park establishing himself as an elite player, the Rangers were rolling along in first

Notes on Brad Park

Name:	Brad Park
Born:	July 6, 1948 (Toronto, Ontario)
Position:	Defense
Height:	6 feet
Playing Weight:	200 pounds
How Acquired:	Rangers' first choice (second overall) in 1966 Amateur Draft
Years with Rangers:	1968-69 to 1975-76
Stats as Ranger:	465 games, 95 goals, 283 assists, 378 points, 738 PIM
Uniform Number:	2
Accomplishments:	First-Team All-Star 1969-70, 1971-72, 1973-74
	Second-Team All-Star 1970-71, 1972-73
	All-Star Game 1969-70, 1970-71, 1971-72, 1972-73, 1973-74, 1974-75
	Rangers MVP 1973-74
	Frank Boucher Trophy 1973-74
	Hockey Hall of Fame 1988

place until February 28, 1970, when he broke his ankle during a 3–3 tie in Detroit.

Without their top defenseman, the Rangers' magic began to fade. They went from fending off challengers for first place to a desperate quest just to make the playoffs. They went 0-6-1 in their next seven games (the tie was a 0–0 draw with the punchless Pittsburgh Penguins). They ended the slide with a 2–0 victory over the Pens, then went 0-2-2 before a solid 4–1 home victory over Montreal reinvigorated the team.

With Park back in the lineup, the Rangers won a key game, beating the last-place Maple Leafs 2–1 in Toronto. But the Rangers entered the final weekend of the season trailing the Canadiens by two points as they prepared for a home-and-home series with the Red Wings while Montreal faced a pair with Chicago.

The Wings rolled to an easyvictory at the Olympia on April 4, beating the Rangers 6–2 to wrap up a playoff spot. The only good thing for the Rangers was that the Blackhawks went into the Forum and smacked the Canadiens 4–1.

That left the Rangers with the smallest of chances. Not only would the Rangers have to beat the Red Wings on Sunday afternoon at Madison Square Garden, but they would have to score a lot of goals. Even if the Blackhawks were to cooperate by beating the Canadiens (the game meant a lot to Chicago, which needed a victory to finish first in the Eastern Conference), the Rangers had to fill the net. A New York win and a Montreal loss would leave the teams tied in the standings, but under the rules of that time, the next tiebreaker was goals scored—and Montreal entered the last day of the season with a five-goal advantage. The Rangers hadn't scored as many as five goals in a game in more than six weeks.

The Game of My Life

DETROIT RED WINGS AT RANGERS—APRIL 5, 1970

"That last game of the year in 1970 against Detroit was unbelievable. We had lost to Detroit the night before, and we had to win, and we had to score at least five goals to tie Montreal. That's probably one of the most vivid memories that I have.

"We started the first period—it was a Sunday afternoon game—and there were maybe 7,500 people in the stands. Rod Gilbert scored about 30 seconds into the game, and we kept going. At the end of the first period, we were leading something like 4–1. We came out for the start of the second period, and there were something like 12,000 people there. I think we were leading something like 7–2 after the second period, and we came out for the start of the third period, and the place was full.

"We ended up scoring nine goals. It was unbelievable. We even pulled Eddie Giacomin to play with the extra man to try to get more. We won 9–5 to tie with Montreal—and we were four goals ahead of them.

Brad Park. *Courtesy of the John Halligan Collection*

"That night, we were in Mr. Laffs, over on the East Side. We didn't know how Montreal and Chicago were doing—the game wasn't on radio or television. A friend of mine—his father was in Chicago, and he used a pay phone and called him. I was at Mr. Laffs, listening to the game on a pay phone. Montreal needed a tie or a win, and in the third period, they were down by a couple of goals and decided to pull their goalie. They wound up losing the game [10–2], and we got into the playoffs. I was so excited that I wound up buying a round at the bar—it was the most expensive round I ever bought.

"I had broken my ankle in Detroit, and I was back playing in four weeks, which was really unusual. I got back a week before the season ended. We ended up making the playoffs, and because of that game and with me bouncing back like that, I ended up making the First All-Star Team with Bobby Orr, and we were both only 21 years old."

Afterword

The Rangers went to Boston for their playoff opener on a high after their miraculous finale, only to be brought rapidly back to earth by the Big Bad Bruins, who won the first two games easily at home. The Rangers won a pair of fight-filled contests at the Garden to pull even, but the Bruins took the next two and went on to win the Cup.

"We hated each other," Park says of Bruins of the early 1970s, when the two teams met in the playoffs three times in four years. "In those times, we'd go to the All-Star Game, and there would be five Rangers sitting on one side and four to five Bruins on another side and four to five Montreal Canadiens on a third side, and we wouldn't even talk to each other. We had the All-Star Game in Minnesota, and it was 1–1 late in the third period, and I sent Pie McKenzie off on a breakaway and he scored. I wouldn't congratulate him, and he wouldn't say 'Thank you.'"

Park finished 1969-70 with 11 goals and 37 points in 68 games, helping him to finish second to Orr in the balloting for the Norris Trophy—the first of an NHL-record six times he would come in second. In four of those instances, he trailed only Orr in the balloting.

Park had only seven goals in 1970-71, but added 37 assists for 44 points and led a defense that helped goaltenders Ed Giacomin and Gilles Villemure win the Vezina Trophy (then given to the goalies on the team allowing the fewest goals) for the first time in more than three decades. But that was just a warm-up for his coming-out party.

No Ranger team has dominated teams offensively the way the 1971-72 team did. With the GAG Line of Jean Ratelle, Vic Hadfield, and Rod Gilbert leading the way, the Rangers shattered every team offensive record and kept pace with the Bruins, who had established themselves as the greatest scoring team in NHL history.

At age 23, Park was the quarterback of one of the NHL's top teams. He set team records with 24 goals, 49 assists, and 73 points while going plus-62. He was tough too—his 130 penalty minutes were second on the team to Hadfield's 142.

The Rangers opened the playoffs against Montreal and rallied from a 2–1 deficit to eliminate the defending Cup champs in six games. Next was Chicago, which had ousted the Rangers in a bitter seven-game semifinal series the previous spring. This time, it was all Rangers; the Blueshirts swept the Blackhawks in four games.

That set up another showdown with the Bruins, who had edged ahead of the Rangers and then pulled away after Ratelle went down with a broken ankle on March 4. The Bruins wiped out Toronto and beat Minnesota on the way back to the finals, seeking to win the Cup for the second time in three years.

Having spent much of the late 1950s and early 1960s fighting over the NHL's table scraps before recovering late in the '60s, the Rangers and Bruins had turned into bitter rivals. This wasn't like the Ranger-Islander or Ranger-Devil rivalries of later years, in which most of the animosity belonged to the fans. The two teams *and* their fans despised each other, and no one was more loathed in Boston than Park.

"I was hated in Boston," he remembers. "I had written a book [*Play the Man*, with Stan Fischler], and we had tailored it toward being an anti-Boston book. I spent a few years fighting everyone over that book. I used to get mail from there that was so bad I would turn it over to Emile Francis. The threats that I got, the threats that my wife got—when we went to Boston, I would get an FBI escort on and off the ice."

The finals opened on April 30, a warm Sunday afternoon at Boston Garden. The Bruins raced out to a 5–1 lead only to see the Rangers pull even. Overtime was looming before reserve forward Garnet "Ace" Bailey scored late in the third period to give Boston a 6–5 win. The Bruins won another squeaker in Game 2, edging the Rangers 2–1.

That sent the series back to Madison Square Garden on May 4 with the Rangers desperately needing a victory to get back into the series. With a raucous sellout crowd of 17,250 on hand for the first Stanley Cup Finals contest held in New York since Game 2 in 1940, Park made sure that the fans didn't go home unhappy.

"We had lost the first two games in Boston, and we *had* to win that third game," he says. "That was special. I scored two goals in the first period [a Stanley Cup Finals record for a defenseman], and that got us off to a fast start. We led 3–0 before they were able to score, and we won 5–2."

The Bruins won Game 4 at the Garden 3–2, but the Rangers spoiled their plans for winning the Cup in Boston by stunning the B's in Game 5. The 3–2 victory sent the series back to the Garden, but Orr led Boston to a 3–0 win in Game 6, giving the hated Bruins the Stanley Cup.

"It was disappointing," Park says of coming up short against Boston. "The two years that the Bruins won the Cup—they couldn't beat Montreal, but we had eliminated them both times, once at the end of the regular season [1970] and once in the playoffs [1972]. The Bruins couldn't beat Montreal, but we could." Park finished the Finals with six points in six games and wound up with 11 points in the Rangers' 16 playoff contests, then a team record for defensemen.

The Rangers finally beat the Bruins in the playoffs in 1972-73 but fell to Chicago in the semifinals. The loss capped a tough season for Park, who averaged a point a game but was limited to 52 games due to knee problems, though he still made the Second All-Star Team.

The knees were better in 1973-74, and Park had a career year with 25 goals and 57 assists for 82 points—good enough for another runner-up finish to Orr in the Norris Trophy voting. But the Rangers again came up short in the playoffs, losing a bitter seven-game semifinal series to Philadelphia, which went on to beat Boston for the Stanley Cup.

Park entered the 1974-75 season as captain following the trade that sent Vic Hadfield to Pittsburgh. However, when the Rangers were ousted in the preliminary round by the Islanders, winds of change began to blow at the Garden. GM Emile Francis brought in a young goaltender, John Davidson, from St. Louis during the off-season and dealt veteran Gilles Villemure. Ed Giacomin was put on waivers and claimed by Detroit in late October. But then came the deal no one could have foreseen: Park, Ratelle, and young defenseman Joe Zanussi to Boston for center Phil Esposito and defenseman Carol Vadnais.

Park was heartbroken. "I cried," he says of his first reaction to the trade. "I started my career there and loved those guys and loved New York, loved playing there. I had made it up to be the captain, and I was excited about that. When you get traded, you always feel like you're leaving with unfinished business. My first take on it was that I was very emotional. I called my wife, who already knew about it. I was welling up with tears. The next thing that happens is that after a couple of days you start to get mad. I think we went two or three years before the Rangers beat the Bruins. Ratty [Jean Ratelle] and I wouldn't let it happen.

"That was kind of a disbursement year. Emile [Francis], I believe, was told by the board of directors at Gulf and Western [which owned Madison Square Garden at the time] to get these guys out of there. [Francis himself] was gone pretty soon after that. I don't think he wanted to do those things, getting rid of Giacomin, Villemure, me, Ratty, Billy Fairbairn, and the three guys in the summer: Ted Irvine, Bert Wilson, and Jerry Butler [who were traded to St. Louis for Davidson in the summer of 1974]. I don't think he really wanted to break that team up."

Fans in both cities were shocked—Esposito was as hated by Rangers fans as Park was in Boston. But surprisingly, Park found out that the players he had hated as a Ranger were terrific teammates—and the fans who loathed him learned to love him.

"When I got to Boston, I found out they were great guys," he says three decades after the deal. "I got to play with Wayne Cashman, who was a wonderful, wonderful teammate."

He also got to play on the defensive pairing hockey fans had always dreamed off—if only briefly.

"We played 10 games together," Park says of his brief time playing with Orr. "On the power play, we had Jean Ratelle, Johnny Bucyk, and Wayne Cashman, with Bobby and me on the points. I think our power-play percentage was over 50 percent for those 10 games. Then Bobby's knees went out on him and he was out for the season—and the next summer he signed with Chicago."

With Orr gone, Park became the leader of the Boston defense, making the First All-Star Team in 1975-76 and the Second Team in 1977-78. He led Boston to the Finals in 1977 and 1978, only to run up against Montreal teams that were among the greatest clubs of all-time. Still, it was vindication for being dealt by the Rangers.

"I remember reading a quote from Jeff Jennings [son of team president Bill Jennings] saying that the reason I had been traded was because my knees were shot. I remember a couple of years later," he says with wry irony. "I was in the Finals against Montreal with the Bruins, and I told the New York reporters to ask him how my knees were now. I played another 10 years [after the trade]."

Park was plagued by knee problems for the next five seasons and finally left the Bruins after 1982-83. He signed with Detroit, helped the Wings to the playoffs twice before retiring and coached there for a couple of seasons before stepping away from the game. Five years after hanging up his skates, he was voted into the Hall of Fame.

"It was something I never thought about while I was playing," he says. "When it happened, I was excited. I was probably more excited for my father, who had such a huge, huge passion for the game. It was in Toronto, where I grew up. My father was bursting—I was more excited for him than for myself."

Park still lives in the Boston area, though he's spent time as a scout for the Rangers. He still follows the game. ("People ask me about it, so I have to keep up," he says.) And in 2005-06, he was able to watch his successor as the best Ranger ever to wear No. 2 up-close when Leetch signed with the Bruins.

As in New York, the two shared the same number.

"Brian is a wonderful player," Park says. "He's up here in Boston now, and I kidded him. I told him, 'Brian, you've got to stop following me around and taking my number.' When I got here, No. 2 had been retired for Eddie Shore. They said they were going to talk to Shore, and I said no, and I took No. 22. Brian came, and I said, 'You've got to stop following me. Not only are you following me, you took my number.'"

CHAPTER 11

PETE STEMKOWSKI

The Skinny

For a guy who later became a fixture on the New York hockey scene, Pete Stemkowski wasn't exactly thrilled to be traded to the Big Apple.

"I was a Midwestern guy," says Stemkowski, who was a vital cog in the Rangers' superb teams of the early 1970s. "I was born in Winnipeg, had won a Stanley Cup in Toronto, and was very happy in Detroit. It's a great sports town, and I'd had a pretty good year in Detroit the year before. We had a good mix of young guys like Garry Unger and Nick Libett and veterans like Gordie Howe and Frank Mahovlich. We had a good team. But Ned Harkness (who had coached the team in 1969-70) came in as general manager, and when we got off to a poor start in 1970-71, he decided to make some changes. That's when I was dealt to New York.

"Coming to New York was a culture shock. When we played at the old Madison Square Garden, we used to come in, land at the airport, come in and play the game, and then go jump on the plane and go back home. When I first got here, I didn't know what was going on or where anything was. I got lost a couple of times on the drive to Long Beach, coming back from the Garden. I'd see a sign that said 'Long Island Expressway' and end up way out in the boonies. I'd have to stop somewhere and ask for directions. That was a little tough to get used to.

"I had to make some adjustments here, and I had a serious head injury after I got here. But I settled here, got married here, had my children here.

Everything is fate in life—you get traded somewhere and you wind up living there. It's crazy how life is."

Stemkowski was a product of the Maple Leafs organization at a time when the veteran-laden Leafs were among the NHL's elite. He bounced back and forth between the Leafs and their Rochester farm team in the AHL for three seasons, spending more time in the NHL each time, until cracking the lineup to stay in 1966-67. He had 13 goals and 35 points in the regular season and then added five goals and 12 points (second on the team) in 12 games as the Leafs won their fourth Stanley Cup in six seasons (and the last one, to date, in franchise history), beating Montreal in six games in the Finals.

Both the Leafs and Stemkowski struggled in 1967-68, with Stemmer putting up just seven goals and 22 points in 60 games and the Leafs free-falling in an Eastern Division in which the Rangers and Boston Bruins were finally rejuvenated after years of battling each other for fifth place. With the season running out, the Leafs and Red Wings made a blockbuster deal, with Stemkowski going to Motown along with Frank Mahovlich, Garry Unger, and the rights to veteran defenseman Carl Brewer in exchange for center Norm Ullman and forwards Floyd Smith and Paul Henderson on March 3, 1968.

Stemkowski quickly made himself at home in Detroit, putting up back-to-back 20-goal seasons. The Wings missed the playoffs in 1968-69, but made it in 1969-70, beating the Rangers on the next-to-last night of the season to assure a third-place finish. (The Rangers routed the not-terribly-interested Wings 9–5 the next afternoon to sneak into the playoffs themselves.)

But the Wings were swept by Chicago in the 1970 playoffs, and general manager Ned Harkness decided it was time to shake things up. With the Rangers farm system churning out young defensemen like popcorn kernels, general manager Emile Francis decided young rear guard Larry Brown was expendable when Harkness told him Stemkowski was available.

The deal was made on Halloween in 1970, and after learning his way around New York's highways and byways, Stemkowski settled into the Rangers enclave on Long Island—an area that, before the Islanders arrived in 1972, was home to most of the team's players.

Notes on Pete Stemkowski

Name:	Pete Stemkowski
Born:	August 25, 1943 (Winnipeg, Manitoba)
Position:	Center
Height:	6-foot-1
Playing Weight:	205 lbs
How Acquired:	Traded to Rangers by Detroit for defenseman Larry Brown—October 31, 1970
Years with Rangers:	1970-71 to 1976-77
Stats as a Ranger:	496 games, 113 goals, 204 assists, 317 points, 379 PIM
Uniform Number:	21
Nicknames:	Stemmer; The Polish Prince

"We had it where Emile Francis got together with Nassau County and the city of Long Beach and built a rink here," Stemkowski said. "It's unfortunate that we were only here for two to three years [before the Islanders came] and then we all moved to Rye.

"We all lived here—there were a lot of summer homes, beach homes, and people used to come here for the summer and after Labor Day, they'd put a padlock on the door and go back into the city. We used to just move in—they were happy to have someone for seven to eight months, renting the houses. It worked out very well.

"We'd car pool into the city in the mornings and stay in the hotel across the street from the Garden. We'd have the morning skate, and then the wives or girlfriends would bring the car in. I remember one year I don't think I ever had a pregame meal in my own house. Emile would bring us into the hotel, we'd have the morning skate, we'd eat and play the game."

But not only did the Rangers get the perfect third-line center—a player who could check, win face-offs, and provide offense—they also got one of the funniest guys in the NHL.

Stemkowski had a passion for radio (it became a big part of his post-NHL career), and he would routinely go into his disk jockey mode on team buses and planes.

"It kept me loose, and it kept the rest of the guys loose," he often recalled. "That was definitely one of my favorite things."

Of Polish descent and proud of it, Stemkowski also loved to bring various varieties of kielbasa, the fragrant Polish sausage, for his teammates to consume on Saturday night charters back to New York from St, Louis, Chicago, Detroit, Pittsburgh, or Minnesota.

"Chicago was the best," he would tell just about anyone who would listen. "The Poles in Chicago have the *best* kielbasa. Pittsburgh was second best."

Once while traveling with the Rangers in the early 1970s, the team's bus took a wrong turn and ended up in a particularly rundown area of East St. Louis, Illinois. The bus was passing a burned-out school building that was barely standing.

"Looks like someone failed chemistry," Stemkowski cracked without missing a beat.

Stemkowski was also adept at verbally skewering opposing centers, a distinct advantage when he lined up for a face-off.

"Believe me, that stuff worked," Stemkowski recalled years later. "It's not hard to throw a guy off guard, especially on face-offs, by getting on his nerves. I won a lot more face-offs than I would have that way."

Stemkowski was a perfect fit as a third center behind high-scoring Jean Ratelle and two-way star Walt Tkaczuk. Francis put him on a line with left wing Ted Irvine and, after an early-February deal with the Wings, Bruce MacGregor on the right. The trio clicked, giving the Rangers as solid a group of three lines as any team in the NHL.

The Setting

The Rangers finished 1970-71 by setting a team record with 109 points and ended up second in the East, trailing only the Bruins. They also won the Vezina Trophy for the first time since 1939-40, which was also the last time they had won the Stanley Cup.

Pete Stemkowski is mobbed by his teammates after scoring his triple-overtime goal. *Courtesy of the John Halligan Collection*

The Rangers split the first four games of their opening-round series against Toronto, then captured Game 5 at home and won Game 6 in overtime at Toronto. The 2–1 victory gave the Rangers their first playoff series victory since 1950.

That sent the Rangers into the semifinals against the Chicago Black Hawks, the Western Conference champions.

The Rangers and Black Hawks battled to a 1–1 standoff in the series opener on April 18, but Stemkowski put the Rangers a game up just 1:37 into overtime, shoveling the puck over Tony Esposito for a 2–1 win. The Black Hawks evened the series with a 3–0 shutout, but the Rangers delighted a sellout crowd at Madison Square Garden with a solid 4–1 victory in Game 3.

It looked like the Black Hawks were on the ropes, but Bobby Hull & Co. had no intention of rolling over. They buried the Rangers in Game 4, knocking out Ed Giacomin and rolling to a 7–1 victory that quieted the Garden and sent the series back to the Windy City all even.

Game 5 was another thriller. For the second time in three games at Chicago Stadium, the teams finished the regulation 60 minutes all even, this time at 2–2. The teams battled evenly for the first 6½ minutes until Bobby Hull scored right off a face-off win by Pit Martin to give the Black Hawks a 3–2 victory and a 3–2 series lead.

The Rangers fans who filed into the Garden on April 29 (the latest date a game had ever been played at MSG) came with a combination of anticipation and apprehension: They knew the game might be the last one of the season, but also that a victory would move the Blueshirts within one win of their first trip to the Finals in 21 years,

The Game of My Life
1971 STANLEY CUP SEMIFINALS, GAME 6
RANGERS VS. CHICAGO BLACK HAWKS—APRIL 29, 1971

"I remember that we were down 2–0 midway through the game. But we kept coming, and we scored in the third period to force the overtime.

"You don't always remember every detail, but you remember the big highlights. I remember Stan Mikita hit both posts in overtime. But after a while, everyone on both teams was playing on fumes. I had never played a game that long.

"It was a game we could have lost very easily. I remember Bill White came in and took a shot that hit Eddie Giacomin in the throat—three feet lower and on the corner and it was in. Then Mikita took a shot that hit one post, skidded across, and hit the other post, and then Rod Seiling golfed it out of there. Those were two chances they had where they could easily have won the game.

"I think after the second overtime, someone must have said, 'I think they're running out of concessions. We better get this thing over with.'

"As for the goal—people who haven't seen it, I tell them it was an end-to-end rush. Basically, Timmy Horton shot the puck, and Teddy Irvine came sliding in there. I was the late guy coming in and jabbed it through Tony Esposito. (The *New York Times* noted the next day that Stemkowski didn't immediately realize that he had scored; the goal, at 1:29 of the third overtime, was the first ever scored by a Ranger after two overtimes.)

"It turned out to be the last point Tim Horton ever got as a Ranger. He went to Buffalo for a year and then died in a car crash. It's funny, because I see his daughter in Long Beach. I played with Tim in Toronto when his kids were very young, and I used to read them bedtime stories. Now I can sit in a bar and have a drink with them—shows you how old we're getting.

"I don't remember much about the noise after we scored. When you're playing, you hear the roar, you don't hear voices. The game was over, but it wasn't like we won the Stanley Cup and there was a huge celebration afterward. It was very businesslike. The emotion, the length of the game— we were so wired. I didn't get much sleep that night. I mean, we won, we went to Gallagher's 33 Steak House, we sat and ate, Dale Rolfe and I went to a little place in Long Beach and sat—just sat and talked about the game. We didn't get out of the Garden till about 1:30, and we didn't leave to go back to Long Beach until after 3:00. We got back to a place there about four, five o'clock and sat around there for an hour or so and we saw kids getting on a school bus. We didn't know what those kids would tell their parents if they saw us coming out of a place at that hour, so we ducked back inside until they left.

"I think I get more reaction now than when it happened. I was fortunate to have scored the goal because so many people remember it. I have more people come up and tell me, "I was listening to that game on my transistor radio. It was a school night and my parents wouldn't let me stay up, but I was able to keep the radio under the pillow." I have a lot of people tell me that.

"It was a great night, but it was all kind of tarnished by the fact that we went into Chicago and lost the next game. That was tough."

Afterword

The Rangers and Black Hawks stepped on the ice at Chicago Stadium on May 2, 1971, knowing that the winner would go to the Stanley Cup Finals and the loser would head for the golf course. The Hawks jumped on top early on a goal by Jim Pappin at 14:49, but Stemkowski tied the game with a goal at 18:31. The Rangers actually took the lead on a goal by Rod Gilbert at 11:43 of the middle period, but the Hawks tied the game on a power-play goal by Cliff Koroll less than two minutes later.

The teams exchanged chances until early in the third period, when Rangers defenseman Brad Park dumped the puck into the Hawks' zone a step before he reached the red line and was called for icing. With Martin on the bench nursing a bruised knee, former Ranger Lou Angotti stepped into the face-off circle and again won the draw cleanly to Hull, who stepped into a slap shot and beat Ed Giacomin. Chico Maki's empty-netter sealed the 4–2 win that sent the Rangers home for the summer.

Stemkowski says a change in the Rangers' routine on the day of Game 7 didn't help.

"We switched hotels going into Chicago," he remembers. "Back in those days, when you played a day game, you kind of grabbed your own meal. Usually if you had a night game, you had a pregame meal. At one o'clock or so, you'd sit down as a team. I specifically remember that we stayed at a different hotel than we usually did. The game was on a Sunday, and the coffee shop was closed. Guys were scrambling to find something to eat. We usually stayed at the Drake or the Executive House, but for some reason, we stayed at a different hotel. We woke up in the morning, and it was a kind of a 'get your own breakfast' thing. You've got to get proper nourishment, and I remember the coffee shop was closed.

"It may have had nothing to do with what happened on the ice, but I remember scrambling around trying to find something to eat. It was a hotel that we'd never stayed at before, so the day didn't get off to a good start—and then, of course, Chicago beat us."

Stemkowski and the Rangers did make it to the Finals the next season, only to lose to the Bruins in six games. He continued to provide the Rangers with solid two-way play for several more years, posting a career high of 70 points in 1973-74, when the Rangers again lost a heartbreaking Game 7 in the semifinals, this time to the Flyers in Philadelphia.

Stemmer had 24 goals in 1974-75, but after the Rangers were stunned by the New York Islanders in the opening round of the playoffs, Francis began to take the team apart. Stemkowski slumped to 12 goals in 1975-76 and scored just three times in 1976-77 as he became a part-time player. Stemkowski played 1977-78 with the Los Angeles Kings and then spent part of 1978-79 with the Kings' AHL team in Springfield before deciding to hang up his skates.

But Rangers fans hadn't seen the last of Stemmer. Having settled on Long Island, he began working in radio there. By the mid-1990s, he had expanded his horizons.

"I worked for the Sharks for nine years, doing their radio," says Stemkowski, who lost his job after the lockout. "I'm doing some radio now for the Rangers, and I have an interest in a travel agency on Long Island. Glen Sather has been really adamant about getting the alumni involved — having them make appearances, running clinics, meeting with clients. I'm grateful for that because it keeps a lot of us busy."

Though Stemmer will never make it to the Hockey Hall of Fame, he was honored in 2002 with induction into the National Polish-American Hall of Fame. He was only the second hockey-related inductee and the first NHL player to be honored.

But to Rangers fans, Stemkowski will always be the triple-overtime hero of 1971.

"I won a Stanley Cup in Toronto, but there aren't a lot of people in New York who are going to ask me a question about that," he says. "I get more people who remember that goal. I'm really flattered—I cherish that. It's nice that people remember that. They always seem to bring that up, and I'm happy about that."

CHAPTER 12

STEVE VICKERS

The Skinny

Steve Vickers grew up in Toronto, where he played the right side for much of his youth. That helped him develop a solid backhand shot—a skill that came to serve him well in his career.

He scored 43 goals in 36 games with Markham in Junior B hockey in 1967-68, then graduated to major junior (then known as Junior A) with the hometown Toronto Marlboros. By that time, Vickers was a prototype power forward—big, strong, and talented. He scored 28 goals and 66 points in 1969-70, his first season in juniors, and followed that with 43 goals and 107 points in 1970-71, earning First-Team All-OHA honors. Vickers added eight goals and 20 points in 13 playoff games.

That was more than enough to impress Rangers GM Emile Francis, who grabbed Vickers with the 10th pick in the 1971 Amateur Draft and sent the 20-year-old to Omaha of the Central Hockey League (then a top minor league) to begin his pro career.

Vickers' scoring touch made the trip from juniors to the pros. He made a name for himself by scoring 36 goals and 59 points. Many of his goals came from right in front of the net—he proved to be a master at getting position in the slot and getting off quick, accurate shots that found the mark.

The Rangers were one of the NHL's top teams, however, and were coming off a trip to the Stanley Cup Finals the previous spring. They were also loaded with young talent up front. In the fall of 1971, Francis had traded for Gene Carr, a speedy forward who could play center and left wing who was picked six spots before Vickers in 1971. Two other highly regarded kids, Tommy Williams and Curt Bennett, also were ahead of him on the depth chart. Vickers went in expecting to be sent back down to the minors before the regular season began.

"I wasn't really highly touted going into that season," Vickers said. "I think I was sixth or seventh on the depth chart for left wing for the Rangers then. I just bided my time. I figured first, let me make the team—that was my first goal—and then when I got into a game, I wanted to make the best of it. As camp wore on, I started getting more confidence."

Vickers scored a brilliant goal in a preseason game against the Islanders at the Nassau Coliseum and wound up earning a spot on the roster in training camp in the fall of 1972—quite an achievement for a 21-year-old.

The Setting

Vickers wasted little time showing he had what it took to be a goal-scorer in the NHL. He started the game playing on a line with Pete Stemkowski and Bruce MacGregor, but was moved up to play with Walt Tkaczuk and Bill Fairbairn when Carr missed a couple of point-blank shots and misplayed the puck a few times. The trio was a quick success: Vickers scored his first NHL goal on his first shot.

"I remember I wasn't getting a lot of ice time early on in the game, but they put me on in the third period a little more and I wound up scoring on my first shot on goal," Vickers recalls. "It was such a thrill. It was a pretty simple play: I came over the blue line, someone gave me the puck, and I shot it. Scoring on your first shot in your first game is something that will stay with you forever."

Considering Vickers' style of play, his first goal was a rarity—he beat Detroit's Denis DeJordy at the Olympia on a slap shot from about 50 feet. "It was probably the longest goal I ever scored," he says with a laugh. "I didn't score too many goals in my career on slap shots. I just came over the blue line, and I let one go on DeJordy. I think he must have been screened, because you usually don't beat a goalie from that far out—not with the slap shot I had."

Notes on Steve Vickers

Name:	Steve Vickers
Born:	April 21, 1951 (Toronto, Ontario)
Position:	Left wing
Height:	6 foot
Playing Weight:	185 lbs
How Acquired:	Selected in the first round, 10th overall, in the 1971 Amateur Draft
Years with Rangers:	1972-73 to 1981-82
Stats as Ranger:	698 games, 246 goals, 340 assists, 586 points, 330 PIM
Accomplishments:	Calder Memorial Trophy 1972-73 Second-Team All-Star, 1974-75

Vickers, nicknamed "Sarge" by Pete Stemkowski after he wore an old army shirt with chevrons to practice one day, was unlike anyone Ranger fans had seen. He didn't fly up and down the wing, and he didn't make slick passes or fancy plays. He became known for setting up in his "office," parking himself in and around the front of the net and generally making a nuisance of himself to opposing defensemen and goaltenders. He was big enough to hold his own against most defensemen, and his quick, accurate shot got the attention of opposing goaltenders. "It's a lot easier to score with the puck coming across the crease than it is from 30 feet," he says of his predilection for going to the net.

The rangy rookie started the season sharing time with Carr on the left side of the "Bulldog" Line with Tkaczuk and Fairbairn. Carr had played with Tkaczuk and Fairbairn for much of the 1971-72 season. But despite some flashes of brilliance, Carr had been a disappointment, and Francis was more than willing to try other options.

The two youngsters competed for the third spot on the Bulldog Line for most of the first month of the season. Vickers had four goals in the Rangers' first 14 games, while Carr managed only one. The Rangers, who had torn through the opposition in 1971-72, weren't scoring as easily or as often and were looking for one of their two young left wings to step up.

When the Los Angeles Kings came to the Garden on Sunday night, November 12, Vickers showed he was up to the challenge.

The Games of My Life

RANGERS VS. LOS ANGELES KINGS
AT MADISON SQUARE GARDEN—NOVEMBER 12, 1972
RANGERS VS. PHILADELPHIA FLYERS
AT MADISON SQUARE GARDEN—NOVEMBER 15, 1972

"I had scored in my first game, but I wasn't playing much. I was dressing but I wasn't getting the ice time. I was splitting time with Gene Carr, but I think they started to lose patience with him playing on the Bulldog Line. They put me on there, and immediately we clicked.

"The Bulldog Line was Walt Tkaczuk and Billy Fairbairn. They kind of turned me into a goal-scorer. I just kept going to the net, and more often than not, the puck would find my stick. I know we were always a high 'plus' line too. I only played with them for two years, and then they moved me onto the GAG Line after the Hadfield trade. But we were always a high plus line—I can remember going 10 games without our line being scored on. I think in my rookie year, I was one of the highest [plus-minus] in the league. I didn't kill penalties, so I didn't get a lot of ice time. I was lucky to get 30 goals in my first year.

"I got the first hat trick against Los Angeles on a Sunday night at the Garden, so obviously, they put me back on that line [the next game]. It was just one of those things. The first one, against LA, I went to the net three times, and the puck found its way there from Walter [Tkaczuk] or Billy [Fairbairn]. It was a great night. I don't remember if we had a big celebration after I got the first one, or even how I got it. It was late in the game.

"In the second one [against Philadelphia], I had two in the second period and one in the third. I didn't really think about it [back-to-back hat tricks] at the time, because I didn't know I was making history. I just kept trying to go to the net. Obviously, when you score a hat trick and you see all the hats on the ice, you know you've accomplished something.

"They didn't keep stats then like they do now. About a month later [after the second hat trick], they told me I was the first one who had ever

Steve Vickers. *Courtesy of the John Halligan Collection*

done it [scored hat tricks in back-to-back games]. They said they traced it back but they couldn't find anyone who had done it before. I think it's been done many times since. The biggest thing was that it established me as a regular. It proved to me that I could play in the league."

Afterword

Vickers' back-to-back hat tricks propelled him to one of the finest rookie seasons in NHL history. Although he was sidelined by a knee injury later in the season and wound up playing only 61 games, Vickers finished the season with 30 goals, 23 assists, 53 points, and a plus-35 rating—good enough to win the Calder Trophy as the NHL's top rookie, becoming the first Ranger to win the award since Camille Henry in 1953-54. Vickers also tacked on five goals in 10 playoff games. Three of them came in one memorable game. "I got one [hat trick] in the playoffs against Boston that year, the final game of the first round," he says "In a way, that was even more important to us as a team [than the back-to-back hat tricks]. We beat them in the fifth game at the Boston Garden one year after they beat us in the final—they had won the Cup at the Garden."

Though Vickers was a big guy by the standards of that era and plenty tough enough to earn space in front of the net, he wasn't a big fighter—sometimes to the chagrin of the Garden faithful.

"I fought a little bit early in my career, but not much after that," he says. "The fans probably wanted me to fight more, but you can't score goals from the penalty box. You had to earn your ground—if someone hit you, you had to hit them back, or else they would run you silly."

More than three decades later, Vickers has especially vivid memories of his first linemates.

"It was a treat playing with those guys," he says of Tkaczuk and Fairbairn, one of the NHL's premier checking and penalty-killing duos and among the elite two-way players of any era. "We played pretty basic hockey. They played good defensive hockey, but they could both score. People forget that Walter led the Rangers in scoring a couple of times, then he was called on by Emile Francis to play more of a defensive role and kill penalties. The GAG Line (Vic Hadfield, Jean Ratelle, and Rod Gilbert) got the glory and the goals, but a lot of people don't realize what a scorer Walt was or could be. He was needed more in the back end, and he was good on face-offs. I was very thankful that they put me on a line with him."

Vickers came back in 1973-74 and demonstrated his rookie season was no fluke. He improved his goal total to 34 and his point total to 58. When Vic Hadfield was traded after the Rangers lost to Philadelphia in the 1974 semifinals, Vickers moved up to the GAG Line with Ratelle and Gilbert and had the best offensive season of his career, scoring 41 goals and 48 assists for 89 points, good enough to earn a Second-Team All-Star berth and his first trip to the All-Star Game. As he did with the Bulldog Line, Vickers scored most of his goals by getting up close and personal with the opposing goaltender.

"You have to fight for your ground. You can't let the defenseman tie you up. Sometimes you have to sneak in there behind them or go to a hole. If you wrestle a defenseman all night, you're not going to score. You've got to get free. I scored a few goals that way, so I must have been doing something right."

Though the Rangers were upset by the Islanders in the preliminary round, Vickers continued to produce, scoring twice and adding four assists in the three games. But the stunning loss to their local rivals signaled the end of an era for the Rangers, and a major change for Vickers.

"After they traded Hadfield [in the summer of 1974], they put me up with the GAG Line, and I scored 40 goals with them," Vickers says of his season with Jean Ratelle and Rod Gilbert. "Then when they made the big trade with the Bruins [in December 1975], I never really hit it off. [Phil] Esposito, Gilbert, and I—we were quite awful as a line. We were three individuals with no chemistry as a trio. I kind of bounced around. I played with Walter for a while, then with Wayne Dillon. I think that trade really hurt me a lot. I was coming off a 40-goal season. I don't know why Emile Francis made that trade. We were an older team and had had a run at the Cup, and then the Islanders beat us in the opening round in 1975, a two-out-of-three series. I guess they thought they had to start dumping guys. They dumped Eddie [Giacomin] and Gilles [Villemure], and they started making trades. The team went reeling for a few years."

The Rangers struggled in 1975-76, missing the playoffs for the first time in a decade. But despite the shakeup, Vickers hit the 30-goal mark for the fourth consecutive season and added a career-best 53 assists for 83 points, earning another trip to the All-Star Game. He also had the greatest night of his career, a seven-point performance against Washington in a 10–4 victory over Washington at Madison Square Garden.

"Washington wasn't a real good team then," he says. "Of course, we weren't much better. I was playing with Wayne Dillon and Rod Gilbert. I think we beat them something like 10–4. I had three goals and four assists, and it was one of those evenings. It's still a team record. Wayne was on top of his game. I don't think John Ferguson [who had replaced Francis as coach and GM] was a big fan of Wayne. In today's game, he would have been a really good player. But back then, people were caught up in that whole Philadelphia Flyer syndrome—you had to be mean and tough. It was kind of sad, because I saw a lot of good players get cast aside because they weren't big enough or mean enough."

Vickers had the first off-season of his career in 1976-77. Despite some back problems, he managed to play 75 games but struggled to finish with 22 goals and 53 points as the Rangers missed the playoffs for the second season in a row.

Vickers and the Rangers both bounced back in 1977-78—Vickers with 19 goals and 63 points, and the Rangers with a playoff berth. Though injuries limited Vickers to 66 games and career lows of 13 goals and 37 points in 1978-79, he contributed both as a checker and a leader as the Rangers beat Los Angeles, St. Louis, and the Islanders on the way to their first Stanley Cup Final since 1972. Vickers contributed offensively too, scoring five goals in 18 games. "We rode [goaltender] John [Davidson] to the Finals that year," he says. "We had a terrific run, but we came up a little short against Montreal."

Vickers' health returned in 1979-80—and so did his scoring touch—he had 29 goals and 68 points while going plus-20. Amazingly, he scored his 29 goals on just 98 shots, setting a team mark for shooting accuracy. "That year I was playing with Ulf Nilsson and Anders Hedberg," Vickers says. "Ulf was a real good player—he was a little fragile and got hurt a few times. He got injured and couldn't repeat it the next year."

Vickers dropped to 19-39-58 in 1980-81, and his style of play was an increasingly poor match with new coach Herb Brooks. He split 1981-82 between the Rangers and their top farm team in Springfield, then called it quits that summer. He retired as the highest-scoring left wing in Rangers history with 586 points—and 25 years later, he still is.

"I tell people I retired for health reasons—the Rangers got sick of me," Vickers says with a rueful laugh. "It was a new coach, a new regime. Herb Brooks was one of the first guys to use that European style of play, the motion game. I had 10 coaches in 10 years—that was enough. I guess it was bound to catch up to me. I also had a young family and didn't want to test the waters. I didn't really pursue anything [with another team].

"I was getting my insurance license while I was playing hockey. I was in insurance for four years, then we moved back to Canada. I worked for Bell Yellow Pages for 16 years, then took a [retirement] package."

Vickers was also the first president of the Rangers Alumni Association, and though he lives near Toronto, he still gets to the Garden. He was on hand in spring 2006 for the team's first playoff games since 1997.

"I still follow the game," he says. "I'm still a true-blue Ranger fan—but there aren't too many of them up here."

IV

REBUILT, BUT STILL NO CUP

By the mid-1970s, Francis' powerhouse team had grown old and it was time to rebuild again. But Francis didn't get the chance to try a second time, he was let go in January 1976. Two seasons under John Ferguson yielded little, but ex-Flyer coaching legend Fred Shero's return to his former organization in 1979 produced quick and unexpected results.

Thanks to newcomers like rookie **Don Maloney**, a midseason call-up, and veterans such as goaltender **John Davidson**, the Rangers bounced back. Maloney, whose older brother Dave was team captain, talks about his NHL debut, a game in which he scored on his first shot in February 1979, marking the beginning of a Ranger career that continues to this day. Davidson, who became one of hockey's greatest broadcasters, recounts a night dear to all Garden fans, when the Rangers completed their upset series victory over the archrival (and heavily favored) Islanders in the 1979 semifinals.

The 1980s brought the arrival of a Garden favorite, goaltender **John Vanbiesbrouck**, who tells what it was like to make his NHL debut at the age of 18—the youngest goaltender to start a game for the Rangers.

By the early 1990s, the Rangers had begun to put together the beginnings of what would turn into the most famous team in New York hockey history. One of those early building blocks was **Mike Gartner**. The Hall of Fame right wing was the first player to get both his 500th and 600th goals as a Ranger, and he reminisces about both games.

CHAPTER 13

DON MALONEY

The Skinny

Don Maloney had an advantage that few other players enjoy—he had firsthand knowledge about life in the NHL from his brother. Dave Maloney had been the Rangers' first pick in the 1974 Amateur Draft. Younger brother Don was drafted by the Rangers with their first pick four years later. They were the first brother combination to be selected by the Rangers in the first round of the draft.

The fact that both boys were drafted by the Rangers was a relief to their mom. "I don't know what we would have done if the Rangers hadn't drafted Don," Regina Maloney said after her sons, two of her seven children (Dave was the oldest; Don was third) had established themselves as Rangers. "Having one son on one team and one on another might tear the family apart."

Both Maloneys came to New York from the Kitchener Rangers of the Ontario Hockey League. Dave was a defenseman who stepped right into the lineup on a team that was beginning to rebuild after the great Ranger clubs of the early 1970s began to get old. When he was named captain for the start of the 1978-79 season, he was 22—the youngest player in team history to wear the C.

By then, Don Maloney was on the horizon. The Rangers had traded away their first-round pick in the 1978 draft, but took him with their first selection in the second round.

The Setting

The glory years of the early 1970s were long gone as the last year of the decade approached. The Rangers entered 1978-79 after being bounced from the preliminary round of the playoffs by Buffalo the previous spring—their first playoff appearance since 1975. The addition of WHA stars Ulf Nilsson and Anders Hedberg gave the Rangers a second scoring option after aging superstar Phil Esposito, but the Rangers needed more as they tried to keep up with the powerful New York Islanders and Philadelphia Flyers in the Patrick Division.

Despite the boost from the two Swedes, the Rangers needed more help up front. Just after the All-Star Game, they called up the younger Maloney from the minors after he put up 18 goals and 26 assists at New Haven of the AHL. Maloney was set to make his NHL debut on Valentine's Day 1979.

The Game of My Life

BOSTON BRUINS VS. RANGERS
AT MADISON SQUARE GARDEN—FEBRUARY 14, 1979

"I was the first pick by the Rangers in the second round in 1978. I went to training camp that fall—and I was glad to go down to the minors. I guess I was intimidated. The Rangers had all these guys—Phil Esposito, Walter Tkaczuk, [Anders] Hedberg, [Ulf] Nilsson, and guys like that. They would come walking down the hallway, and I'd walk the other way. I don't know if I was intimidated or shy.

"Then I was called up right after a break in the schedule [instead of the usual All-Star break, the NHL took an 11-day break to play the Challenge Cup series against the Soviet Union. The three-game series was played at Madison Square Garden]. What happened was that they brought the whole New Haven team [then the Rangers' top minor-league affiliate] up to play a simulated game against the Rangers about three or four days before they were to resume play. I remember playing in that game, and I was awful. I had been told I was coming up prior to that game. I remember finishing that game and thinking, 'That's it. There's no chance.' I had been so bad. But they stayed with me, and I got called up.

"The night before—Don Murdoch was living with my brother Dave, and Dave had some appearance commitment. Donnie invited me over and

Notes on Don Maloney

Name:	Don Maloney
Born:	September 5, 1958 (Lindsay, Ontario)
Position:	Left wing
Height:	6-foot-1
Playing Weight:	190 pounds
How Acquired:	Rangers' first pick (second round, 20th overall) in 1978 Amateur Draft
Years with Rangers:	1978-79 to 1988-89
Stats as Ranger:	653 games, 195 goals, 307 assists, 502 points, 739 PIM
Uniform Number:	12
Accomplishments:	All-Star Game 1983, 1984 (MVP)
	Players' Player Award 1979-80, 1980-81, 1986-87
	"Crumb Bum" Award 1984
	Good Guy Award 1980-81

cooked dinner; I forget what he cooked. But he gave me some advice—probably the best advice I got. He told me, 'Just do what got you here. Don't try to be something you're not.'

"My mom and dad flew down [from Canada] for the game, and I got thrown on a line with Phil Esposito, of all people. I had grown up watching him. He was one of the greatest players who ever played, certainly one of the greatest scorers. I had played one preseason game with Espo, the first preseason game I ever played. To me, it didn't matter who I played with; I was just happy to get a chance. Donnie Murdoch was the other guy on the line. He had had his struggles, his off-ice issues. [Murdoch had been suspended for the first 40 games of 1978-79 for drug possession and had just returned to the lineup.] They kind of just threw the names against the wall and said, "Let's put the new kid together with those two guys." Obviously, we jelled.

"I remember going into the Garden for that first game and it was overwhelming—the noise, the fans leaning over the glass. Obviously, Dave was there; he was the captain of the team. It was great to have that support—someone I could talk to. You have to remember that we hadn't played together since, probably, squirt, when I was about eight years old. Not only was it my first NHL game, but it was also the first real game I'd ever played with my brother. He was only a couple of years older than me, but he was one of those guys who played with players older than him, so in hockey, he was four or five years older than I was—he was always ahead. He came to New York as an 18-year-old and left juniors a couple of years early. It was the one year that they had a junior draft that allowed young players to go [to the NHL]. So he was gone before I even hit major junior.

"It was really terribly exciting. We got out there on that first shift, and I got lucky and banged one in [5:14 into the first period].

"I think if you ask everyone [about their first NHL goal], it's one of those things you never forget. You picture the play in slow motion. I remember knocking someone off the puck in the corner, picking it up, and swinging out toward the net. I stepped out and threw the puck on goal. The goalie [Boston's Gilles Gilbert] actually made the save, but the puck came right back onto my stick, and I banged in the rebound. It was one of my typical goals—about three feet away from the net. Anything beyond that—no chance.

"I jumped about 10 feet in the air when I scored. And then the next shift, we actually scored again, Espo got the goal, and I got an assist on that one.

"I also remember that in the period, we held Boston to no shots—they didn't get a shot on goal. We were skating off the ice, and they announced that, and everyone was saying, "Why did they have to announce that? Now they're going to know about it, and they're going to be really teed off." It ended up being a really exciting night [the Rangers outshot Boston 15–0 in the first period and won the game, 5–1, their first win over the Bruins since March 23, 1975].

"I didn't get too much of a chance to celebrate the goal. It was Valentine's Day, and we were flying to Buffalo right after the game, but they had kind of a reception for everyone. It was a really special night when you're 20 years old and you're in New York and all the excitement that goes with

Don Maloney, No. 12. *Courtesy of the John Halligan Collection*

being in New York. Not only was it my first game and my first goal, but the team was having a terrific year. We had a good mixture of players. We had stars like Phil, John Davidson, Carol Vadnais. It was a very exciting time, certainly in my life, but also in New York hockey. The team had been a little down after the great years in the early 1970s, and now it had this really young group of exciting players. I just kind of slid in there and joined the party.

Afterword

Maloney, Esposito, and Murdoch developed almost instant chemistry, earning the name "The Mafia Line" (a Godfather [Esposito] and two "Dons."). Esposito gushed over his new left wing after the game, saying, "He's like [Wayne] Cashman to me. He gets the puck out of the corner. It's been a long time since I didn't have to help out in that respect."

With the new line giving the Rangers a boost (9-3-3 in the first 12 games after Maloney joined the team, they finished with a 40-29-11 record and 91 points, their best campaign since 1974-75. Maloney finished with nine goals and 27 assists for 36 points in only 28 games—and the scoring wasn't even his best attribute. "His scoring is a bonus," coach Fred Shero told reporters. "He's a bumper and a grinder. He reminds me of Bert Olmstead, the great left wing on the Montreal Canadiens' power play two decades ago."

Maloney says the three players were a perfect fit. "Our line just seemed to click right away. When you think about styles, our playing styles matched. Phil liked to park himself in front of the net, and he had a stick that was about 10 feet long. If you got the puck to him in the slot, there was a really good chance you'd be picking up an assist. That really fit into what my style was—picking up and finding pucks. Donnie Murdoch was one of those players who just had a knack for scoring. Some guys have a talent—they don't need much room to put the puck in the net. Not only was Donnie a good playmaker, he was one of those guys who knew where to go in the offensive zone, and it didn't take much for him to find that hole. It was a pretty good balance, and that line had a lot of success the rest of the year."

The Rangers blitzed Los Angeles in two games in the preliminary round, blew out Philadelphia in five games in the quarterfinals, and stunned the Islanders, the regular-season champions, in six games to advance to the finals against the three-time Stanley Cup–champion Montreal Canadiens. But after shocking the Canadiens 4–1 in the opener at the Montreal Forum, the Rangers were hampered by an injury to Davidson and dropped the next four games. Maloney led all playoff scorers with 13 assists and set a playoff record for rookie scoring (since broken) with 20 points.

"I was so naïve," Maloney says of playing in the Stanley Cup Finals less than three months after making his NHL debut. "I remember losing to Montreal that year, and I was physically and mentally exhausted. It was almost a relief that it was over. It was devastating that we didn't win, but we just said, 'OK, we'll win next year.' It's been 25 years, and I'm still waiting to get there. That was the closest I've been as a player or working for a hockey organization. It's pretty elusive to get there. If you were to ask everyone on that team who hadn't won before—if we could go back, maybe we should have sacrificed a little more."

Despite the disappointment of coming up short in the Finals, Maloney came back in the fall for his first full NHL season and picked right up where he left off—giving the Rangers consistent scoring and effort. He topped the

20-goal mark in each of his first five NHL seasons, twice scoring as many as 29. He was selected to play in the All-Star Game in 1982-83 and scored a goal for the Wales Conference at the Nassau Coliseum. One year later, he became the first Ranger to be named MVP of the All-Star Game, when he had a goal and three assists in the Wales Conference's 7–6 victory at the New Jersey Meadowlands.

The most heartbreaking day of Maloney's career was December 26, 1988, when he was dealt to the Hartford Whalers. He's still 11th on the all-time Rangers list in points (502) and 12th in goals (195). He also holds the team record for the fastest three goals, notching a hat trick in a span of 2:30 against Washington on February 21, 1981, and he scored a famous playoff goal in the final minute of regulation in the fifth and deciding game of the 1984 playoffs against the Islanders that sent the game into overtime.

He finished his playing days with the Islanders and began his postplaying career as an assistant to Islanders GM Bill Torrey. Maloney helped modernize the Islanders' scouting system—his draft picks included Darius Kasparaitis, Todd Bertuzzi, Bryan McCabe, and Zigmund Palffy—and was promoted to GM in 1992 when new ownership took over and Torrey departed. The Isles went to the Stanley Cup semifinals in Maloney's first season as GM, but the team retrogressed, and Maloney was let go on December 2, 1995.

Maloney wasn't out of work long. One of Dean Lombardi's first moves after being hired as general manager of the San Jose Sharks after the 1995-96 season was to bring in Maloney, who had developed the reputation as a good evaluator of talent.

But one year later, Maloney came back home when Rangers GM Neil Smith brought him back to Broadway as assistant GM in 1997. As in San Jose, Maloney's primary focus was the draft and player development. Glen Sather replaced Smith as general manager in the summer of 2000, but he kept Maloney as his assistant.

Maloney got a sizeable share of the credit for the Rangers' revival in 2005-06, when many of the young players he helped draft and develop stepped into key roles as the Rangers returned to the playoffs.

"It finally hit us that what we were doing wasn't working," he says of the shift from relying on older players to making the lineup younger and faster. The lockout that wiped out the 2004-05 season, he adds, proved to be beneficial in the development of young players like Henrik Lundqvist, Dominic Moore, and Petr Prucha—as was the decision to focus more on team chemistry by surrounding star forward Jaromir Jagr with a half-dozen fellow Czechs. "Nobody knew it would jell this fast," Maloney says of the way the Rangers came together. "And we have a lot of good young talent coming along. The future here is bright."

CHAPTER 14

JOHN DAVIDSON

The Skinny

Today's generation of Rangers fans knows John Davidson as "JD," the popular, erudite analyst who teamed with Sam Rosen for two decades to provide New York hockey watchers with unmatched coverage of their favorite team. But it's easy to forget that Davidson had another career, too—one in which he was the key figure in one of the great victories in Rangers history.

These days, it's not unusual for teams to take a goalie with a high draft pick—even the No. 1 overall selection. But three decades ago, teams were unwilling to take that kind of risk on a young goaltender and equally unwilling to move one right into the NHL. Davidson defied both trends when he was selected with the fifth overall pick in the 1973 Amateur Draft by the St. Louis Blues after starring with Calgary of the Western Hockey League, then went right from junior hockey into the NHL—the first goalie in history to do so.

Davidson impressed everyone by posting a 3.08 goals-against average in 39 games as a 20-year-old (the draft age was still 20 back then) for a weak Blues team in 1973-74, then played 40 games in 1974-75, posting a 3.66 goals-against average.

One of the people impressed with Davidson was Rangers general manager Emile Francis, whose team had lost in the preliminary round to the New York Islanders in the spring of 1975. With goaltenders Ed Giacomin

131

and Gilles Villemure both well into their thirties, Francis was looking for a young goaltender to build around. He decided Davidson was his man, and in June 1975, "The Cat" dealt veteran left wing Ted Irvine and youngsters Jerry Butler and Bert Wilson to the Blues for Davidson, then 22, and veteran forward Bill Collins.

Francis traded Villemure to Chicago, leaving the Rangers with a veteran (Giacomin) and a youngster (Davidson). The 22-year-old was looking forward to learning from arguably the greatest goaltender in team history. Little did he know that the apprenticeship would last only a couple of weeks.

"I played two years in St. Louis, which I really enjoyed, and then I was traded here," Davidson says of his start with the Rangers. "I still remember being on an airplane, flying to a game early in the season and turning to Frank Paice, who was the trainer, and asking, 'Where's Eddie?' Frank told me, 'He went to Detroit on waivers.' I just about fainted. I had expected to work with Eddie that year and learn from one of the masters."

In a move that stunned Rangers fans, Francis put Giacomin on waivers on October 31, 1975, and saw him snapped up by Detroit. Three days later, on November 2, Davidson was wearing a Rangers jersey while Giacomin wore a Red Wing jersey with No. 31 on it (not No. 1, which would later be retired by the Rangers). Davidson had a bird's-eye view as Giacomin beat his former team 6–4, with Madison Square Garden fans cheering, "Eddie, Eddie."

"Detroit came in, and I was at the other end of the ice," Davidson remembers. "He stopped about 45 shots and they knocked us off. I was a wreck. Eddie came to me after the game and wished me well—that was pretty classy of him. I'll remember that until I die. It was really an important thing for me to have him do that."

Davidson had his revenge two weeks later, when the Red Wings returned to the Garden and Davidson notched his first NHL shutout, beating Detroit 3–0. He wound up playing a career-high 56 games, posting a 3.97 goals-against average and his first three NHL shutouts for a defensively challenged team that missed the playoffs for the first time in a decade.

"The whole organization was going through a complete rebuild, kind of like they are now, in some ways," Davidson says of his early years in New York. "The Rangers had made the playoffs all those years and had gotten

Notes on John Davidson

Name:	John Davidson
Born:	February 27, 1953 (Ottawa, Ontario)
Position:	Goaltender
Height:	6-foot-3
Playing Weight:	205 lbs
How Acquired:	From St. Louis with Bill Collins for Ted Irvine, Jerry Butler, and Bert Wilson— June 1975
Years with Rangers:	1975-76 to 1982-83
Stats as Ranger:	222 games, 93 wins, 90 losses, 25 ties, 3.58 goals-against average, 7 shutouts
Uniform Numbers:	35, 00, 30
Accomplishments:	Players' Player Award 1975-76, 1976-77, 1977-78
	Good Guy Award 1976-77

close but never won. But then they decided to change the whole thing—they brought in John Ferguson [in 1976, to replace Francis]. That's what we went through. I was young, and we had a young defense—Dave Maloney and Ron Greschner. Up front we had young guys like Don Maloney and Don Murdoch—he was a great player for a while."

In the high-scoring NHL of the late 1970s, teams rarely worked their top goaltenders more than 40 or 50 games a season. Davidson split the goaltending with Gilles Gratton in 1976-77 and with Wayne Thomas in 1977-78. His goals-against average kept coming down, to 3.54 in 34 games in 1976-77 and to 3.18 in 39 games in 1977-78.

The Rangers missed the playoffs in 1976-77 and lost in a three-game preliminary round in 1977-78. That convinced team management that changes needed to be made at the top. Fred Shero, the architect of Philadelphia's Cup champs in 1974 and 1975, was brought in as coach and general manager.

The change proved to be good for the team and Davidson. With newcomers Anders Hedberg and Ulf Nilsson providing a boost to the offense, Davidson assumed the No. 1 job and posted his most successful season, with a 20-12-5 record. The Rangers jumped from 78 points to 91 and finished third in the Patrick Division.

"With the Rangers, we had gone through a couple of draft years where we brought in some really good young players," says Davidson. "That gave us a lot more depth than we'd had. We also had a couple of older players like Phil Esposito and Carol Vadnais, who had been through quite a few wars in the playoffs and really elevated their games in the playoffs. We also had Ulf [Nilsson] and Anders [Hedberg], the two Swedish guys. Ulf was hurt, but they were both good players, as were young guys like Don Maloney [then a rookie who had been called up in February].

Despite an ankle injury that KO'd Nilsson, the Rangers rolled to their first playoff series victories in five years. They polished off the Los Angeles Kings in two straight games in the preliminary round, then followed a series-opening loss in Philadelphia by demolishing the Flyers in four straight games. Davidson earned his first (and only) career playoff shutout in Game 4, a 6–0 victory at the Garden, and the Rangers completed the wipeout with an 8–3 victory at the Spectrum in Game 5.

That set up a semifinal meeting with the Islanders, whose victory in the 1975 preliminary round triggered Davidson's arrival in New York. In 1975, the Rangers were still among the NHL's elite, and the Islanders were the pesky outsiders. Now the roles were reversed: the Islanders had dethroned Montreal as regular-season champs and were favored to end the Canadiens' three-year reign as Stanley Cup titleholders, whereas the Rangers were decided underdogs.

The Setting

With Davidson playing the best goal of his career, the Rangers entered the semis with a confidence they hadn't shown in years. Much to the surprise of the Nassau Coliseum crowd, the Rangers won the opener handily, 4–1. They nearly went home up two wins, but the Isles evened the series with a 4–3 win in overtime.

John Davidson. *Courtesy of the John Halligan Collection*

The teams kept alternating victories. The Rangers were 3–1 winners in Game 3, as Davidson again excelled behind a spirited defense and swift, hard-checking forwards who shut down the Isles' top unit of Bryan Trottier, Mike Bossy, and Clark Gillies. But the Islanders evened the series in Game 4, winning 3–2 in overtime on a goal by Bob Nystrom.

"I got caught out of the net when Nystrom scored," Davidson says. "We raced for a loose puck and tied—the puck went way up in the air, but the momentum of the puck landed it near the net, and he tapped it in to win in overtime."

The Rangers weren't discouraged, though. They battled the Islanders on even terms late into Game 5 at the Coliseum before Hedberg's goal gave them a 4–3 victory and a 3–2 lead in the series. "We went back to the Island, and our guys really battled. Anders scored late, and we won."

That sent the series back to the Garden, where a raucous sellout crowd turned out to see if the Rangers could make the Stanley Cup Finals for the first time since 1972.

The Game of My Life
1979 STANLEY CUP SEMIFINALS, GAME 6
RANGERS VS. NEW YORK ISLANDERS—MAY 8, 1979

"The rivalry was really, really intense," Davidson remembers of that spring, one of the few times when the Rangers and Islanders were on the top of their games at the same time. "It meant a lot to the fans, and there were a lot of really talented people playing in it. These were two teams that could play many different ways—with toughness, with speed, with power plays or pure goal scoring.

"It was great hockey, very intense. There were guys that knew how to play hard. It wasn't a cheap series—not a series of fighting and sticks to the throat. It was really hard, honest, pure hockey—the way the game was meant to be played. It wasn't about referees and suspensions—it was about guys playing really intense hockey. There was a little bit of everything—hitting, goaltending, great players trying to score, leadership on both sides. There was great coaching: it was Freddie's first year, but [assistant coach] Mike Nykoluk did a lot for the team. Freddie was kind of a bench coach, and Mike did a lot of the other stuff. Of course, the Islanders had Al Arbour, who's a Hall of Famer.

"The fans were into this. I remember waking up one morning and there were gifts on my doorstep. It was incredibly intense. All the columnists were writing about it. It was a special time.

"We came home with a chance to put them away. I wasn't really busy in that game. Bossy scored in the first period—it was his only goal in the series. But I don't remember being very busy as the game went on. Our guys were really good—we had some really competitive guys. Don Murdoch and Ron Greschner scored in the second period, and I think [the Islanders] only had a couple of shots [actually three] in the third period.

"What we tried to do most of the time during the series and in Game 6 was [dump] the puck to Denis Potvin's side most of the time and make him move it. We'd play the puck to his corner. He would have to get to the puck to make a play, and essentially that was a way of stopping him, because he wasn't part of the play as much. It was a really hard thing to do, but we did it. Also, if I remember correctly, Steve Vickers played a lot against Mike Bossy. Steve held him to one goal in that last game. He played on a line with Walter Tkaczuk, and they were really smart players.

"As the final seconds were counting down, it was the loudest I remember the Garden. I know the players who won [the Stanley Cup] in 1994 probably feel that was the loudest they ever heard the Garden, but for me, this was the loudest. It was kind of unexpected. The Rangers went into the playoffs as underdogs. I had been hurt and didn't know how I was going to play and didn't finish the season strong. Then we got on a bit of a roll. We beat L.A. in the first round and Philly in the second round and ended up against the Islanders.

"Without question, it's my fondest memory of the place. I remember the look of some of the Islanders, like Denis Potvin on one knee. Both teams gave it everything they had. It was so taxing and hard and intense—not mean, but very tough, which is exactly the way the game is supposed to be played."

Afterword

The euphoria that surrounded the Rangers continued into the Stanley Cup Finals. With Davidson again at the top of his game, the Rangers opened the finals by beating the Canadiens 4–1 before a stunned crowd at the Forum.

Montreal was so shocked that coach Scotty Bowman planned to change goaltenders for Game 2, benching Ken Dryden in favor of Michel Larocque. But Larocque took a shot in the mask from Doug Risebrough during warm-ups, giving Dryden a second chance. The Rangers grabbed an early 2–0 lead, but the Canadiens regrouped, won the game 6–2, then beat the Rangers twice at the Garden and 4–1 again at the Forum to wrap up their fourth title in a row.

"We were up 2–0 in the second game, but they had a team that had something like 10 Hall of Famers on it," Davidson says. "Guy Lafleur had 13 shots on goal in one game. The Islander series was good for hockey in New York, but not winning the Final after winning Game 1 and leading in

Game 2—no matter how great Montreal was, and they were a great team. It's haunting, even to this day. I've been to so many Stanley Cup Finals, almost every one since then, and you see teams win and you say, 'We were close but not there.' It's tough being second."

There was already talk that Davidson had been playing the Finals with an injured knee. Unfortunately for the Rangers, it proved to be more than talk.

"My knee had started to be a problem," Davidson says. "That happened primarily in the Islanders series. It wasn't one serious injury. It was a knee that was worn out, bone on bone—just the wear and tear of being an athlete. When I went down, I couldn't get up."

Despite the knee problems, Davidson had a good season in 1979-80, playing 41 games with a 20-15-4 record, a career-best 3.17 goals-against average, and his last two career shutouts. He also played all nine playoff games as the Rangers beat Atlanta 3-1 in the first round before the Flyers avenged the previous year's loss by knocking off the Rangers in five games.

But though Davidson was only 27 and theoretically entering his prime, he was never the same again. He played only 10 games in 1980-81, going 1-7-1 with a 5.14 goals-against average, then managed to play just three games over the next two seasons before finally calling it a career as a player.

Little did he know that he was about to become even more popular as an announcer than he had been as a playoff hero.

"I got into broadcasting right after I finished playing," says Davidson, who became a full-time broadcaster in 1986. "I was kind of a third guy in there, along with Jim Gordon and Phil Esposito. I also did some interviews, which I was a wreck doing. After my first year doing that, I moved back to Canada and worked there for two years with John Shannon, who was just given a new job [with the NHL]. Then I came back to New York when Espo decided to leave the booth. I've been there ever since, working with Sam Rosen.

I've been very lucky. When you finish as a player, you're used to a team concept. Getting into television, it's the same thing. We're not in the trenches like the players are, but we're there as a team. You've got all kinds of different people involved, and if they don't all do their jobs, it doesn't work—same as a hockey team. It's really been good that way."

Fifteen years after Davidson and his 1979 teammates came up short in the Finals against Montreal, he was on hand to see the team end its 54-year championship drought. It's still one of the biggest thrills of his career.

"Being there and broadcasting [Game 7] in 1994 was fabulous," he says. "The team was a good team, very professional, carried itself very well. It was an easy team to like. It was good for hockey, good for the city. The series with the Devils and with Vancouver were such great series—they were just magical. So close, so many twists and turns. Each game was like a book in itself."

On March 16, 2004, Davidson was honored in New York with one of hockey's most prestigious awards, the Lester Patrick Trophy for "outstanding service to hockey in the United States." He continued as the cream of the crop among hockey analysts, working for NBC's coverage of the NHL and the Olympics. But first and foremost, he was the link between the Rangers and their fans—and he's optimistic that the Rangers' breakthrough in 2005-06 is the start of many good years to come.

"Ranger fans are great. There are a lot of passionate people, and they drive us along," Davidson says. "The culture of the organization has changed. Glen hired some good people, including [coach] Tom Renney, and [assistant GM] Don Maloney has worked his tail off. The whole culture has changed. They're in a very good place to springboard ahead. It's all just starting."

But after two decades behind the microphone, Davidson is beginning a new career. When former Madison Square Garden president Dave Checketts bought the Blues in June 2006, he wasted no time in naming JD the team president.

"It's a gigantic move, and it's one that had to be perfect for me," Davidson told reporters. "It is because the owners are people I know and have known for a long time. And I know St. Louis. I loved my two years here. Now the circle goes around, and I'm thrilled about it."

CHAPTER 15

JOHN VANBIESBROUCK

The Skinny

Despite a sub-.500 season in 1980-81, the Rangers had made the Stanley Cup semifinals in the spring of 1981 before being swept by the New York Islanders, who were on their way to successfully defending their Stanley Cup championship. Though they had some playoff success, the Rangers were still a jumble of parts, especially in goal where they used five netminders in 1980-81. The expected starter, John Davidson, had played only 10 games as he struggled to cope with a knee injury that ultimately forced him into retirement (and eventually into the broadcast booth, where's made an even bigger mark than he did as a player).

With no clear long-term starter in goal, the Rangers chose a goaltender from Sault Ste. Marie of the Ontario Hockey League in the fourth round of the entry draft. At 18, John Vanbiesbrouck was regarded as a project, someone who might help the Rangers several years down the road. He had posted a 31-16-1 record in the OHL in 1980-81 with a 4.14 goals-against average (not a bad showing in the highest-scoring era in hockey history).

The Setting

The future came faster than expected for Vanbiesbrouck. With Davidson playing only one game all season, the Rangers were left with a pair of rookies, Steve Weeks and Steve Baker, as their two netminders. But Baker pulled a groin muscle in a game against Boston on October 31, leaving the 23-year-old Weeks as the lone "experienced" goaltender. (He had played one game in 1980-81.)

With nowhere else to turn, the Rangers recalled Vanbiesbrouck from Sault Ste. Marie and dressed him as the backup goaltender for 14 consecutive games. Weeks started and finished all 14 games, going 6-5-3, while Vanbiesbrouck impressed his new teammates in practice with his quick hands and feet while playing a solid standup style.

With Baker still sidelined and a weekend that included a game in Denver on Saturday and a home game against the Hartford Whalers the next night, coach Herb Brooks decided that the game against the Rockies, one of the NHL's perennial losers, was a good place for his 18-year-old goaltender to make his NHL debut. The Rockies came into the first weekend of December 1981 with a league-worst 4-17-5 record; the Rangers were 9-13-3.

Brooks made the announcement the day before the game, and after practice at the University of Denver, Vanbiesbrouck got encouragement from his teammates, who called him "Beanbag."

"They wouldn't put me in if they didn't think I had the ability," the 18-year-old told the assembled media. "I don't think of myself as cocky, but confident and friendly."

For his part, Brooks said letting Vanbiesbrouck play was the only logical thing to do, owing to the team's injury situation.

"He's a very self-confident kid," Brooks told the media. "He's the youngest player in the league. But it was the only logical thing to do, to let Steve Weeks go home and have a good rest. We're concerned that John hasn't had any game competition for a month, but we hope that the euphoria of the first start will overcome that. Also, the guys will be taking the extra step for him."

Brooks was taking a real gamble—not only was he playing a kid right out of juniors, but Vanbiesbrouck's backup was Rick Strack, the goaltender with the Rangers' AHL affiliate in Springfield. He, too, had never played an NHL game.

At 18 years, three months, and one day old, Vanbiesbrouck was set to become the youngest goalie in Rangers history (except for 17-year-old Harry

Notes on John Vanbiesbrouck

Name:	John Vanbiesbrouck
Born:	September 4, 1963 (Detroit, Michigan)
Position:	Goaltender
Height:	5-foot-8
Playing Weight:	175 lbs
How Acquired:	Chosen by the Rangers in the fourth round of the 1981 Entry Draft
Years with Rangers:	1981-82; 1983-84 to 1992-93
Stats as a Ranger:	449 games, 200-177-47, 3.45 goals-against average, 16 shutouts
Nickname:	Beezer
Accomplishments:	Vezina Trophy 1985-86
	First-Team All-Star 1985-86
	Rangers Team MVP 1985-86
	Players' Player Award 1985-86

Lumley, who played one period of one game as an emergency replacement for injured Ken McAuley during the 1943-44 season).

As an oddity, not only was Vanbiesbrouck ready to become the youngest goaltender in team history, he was also set to be the only player in the history of the NHL to have all five vowels in his name.

The Game of My Life

RANGERS AT COLORADO ROCKIES—DECEMBER 5, 1981

"I had been up with the team for most of the month before the game. It wasn't like they just called me up for that one game. But they wanted to give Steve Weeks a night off. He'd played every game for about a month—he'd played well too. But we had played in Los Angeles, and then we were going to Denver and then home to play the next night. We had lost a couple of guys with injuries; JD [John Davidson] was out, and Steve Baker was out, so they decided to give me a start.

"I wasn't really nervous before the game. I had been trying to go over their team. I didn't know too many of their players. I knew a couple—guys like Don Lever, who were veterans. But the rest of them, I really didn't know a lot about them. One guy I did know was Chico Resch, who was in the goal at the other end. I was really excited to play against him.

"We gave up the first goal—Paul Gagne, who I remembered from the Windsor Spitfires, beat me. I remember because Nick Fotiu came up to me and kept saying, 'I'm sorry. I lost my man. I'm sorry.'

"We scored a couple of goals in the second period, and the guys worked hard in front of me. We wound up winning 2–1. When the buzzer went off, all the guys came over and congratulated me. I think they were happy for me, for winning my first game, but they were also happy because they had stepped up to help me out. It's still a night I'll never forget.

"We flew home that night and I dressed as the backup for Steve Weeks. But by the next week, I was back in juniors."

Afterword

Despite Vanbiesbrouck's fine showing, the Rangers were still in the market for a veteran goaltender. They landed one six days later, acquiring Ed Mio from the Edmonton Oilers in exchange for Lance Nethery. Mio's arrival signaled Vanbiesbrouck's return to junior hockey.

"I really didn't know what their plans were, and it was probably better that way," Vanbiesbrouck said. "I knew we had a lot of injuries. They never told me they were looking for a backup goalie. It wasn't really a surprise that I went back down. But I had never thought about it."

Vanbiesbrouck went back to Sault Ste. Marie and finished the season there with a 12-12-2 record and a 3.63 goals-against average. He spent all of 1982-83 with the Greyhounds and had a banner season, going 39-21-1 with a 3.61 goals-against average in a league-high 62 games.

The Rangers were reluctant to bring Vanbiesbrouck straight to the NHL from junior hockey. Instead, they sent him to Tulsa of the Central Hockey League, their top developmental team. The Oilers wound up winning the CHL championship, but not before being evicted from their home rink in February and being forced to play the rest of their season on the road. When the team was at "home," it practiced in a small suburban

John Vanbiesbrouck. *Courtesy of the John Halligan Collection*

rink, and coach Tom Webster took Vanbiesbrouck and Ron Scott out to the parking lot and shot tennis balls at them to keep them sharp. Despite all the problems, Vanbiesbrouck went 20-13-1 with a 3.46 goals-against average and then won all four of his playoff starts.

He also earned a trip back to the Rangers, for whom he went 2-1-0 with a 3.33 goals-against average. By the following fall, he was a Ranger for good. Though he split time almost equally with Glen Hanlon, a 12-24-3 record and 4.22 goals-against average earned him a seat on the bench for all but one minute of the playoffs.

But the 1985-86 season belonged to Vanbiesbrouck. At age 22, he became the first Ranger since Dave Kerr in 1939-40 to win the Vezina Trophy by himself (Ed Giacomin and Gilles Villemure shared it in 1970-71). He went 31-21-5 with a 3.32 goals-against average and three shutouts, and helped the Rangers finish with their lowest goals-against total since 1974-75. He was even better in the playoffs, leading the Rangers past Philadelphia and Washington to the Patrick Division title before a loss to the Montreal Canadiens ended their Cup hopes.

"It was a really consistent year for me," Vanbiesbrouck said. "Ted Sator came in as coach and he had a lot of confidence in me. He got rid of the older guys, like Glen Hanlon, and showed confidence in me and some of the other young guys like Mike Ridley, Kelly Miller, Bob Brooke, and George McPhee. We finished fourth in the regular season [and] then took down a couple of the big boys in the playoffs."

But for whatever reason, management decided the next season that the goaltending job should be divided. Defensemen Kjell Samuelsson was sent to Philadelphia for Bob Froese. Vanbiesbrouck still saw the lion's share of the action and led the team to the playoffs in 1986-87 and 1988-89.

By then, though, there was another goaltender on the horizon. The Rangers had drafted Mike Richter, a Philadelphia-area native who was headed for the University of Wisconsin, in the second round of the 1985 entry draft. After two seasons at Wisconsin and one with the U.S. Olympic team (he and future Rangers teammate Brian Leetch were teammates as Olympians, too), Richter turned pro after the 1988 Calgary Games. He spent one season with Denver, then in the CHL, and wound up making his NHL debut in the 1989 playoffs, where he started (and lost) Game 4 as the Pittsburgh Penguins completed a four-game sweep.

A new general manager, Neil Smith, and new coach, Roger Neilson, took control of the Rangers for the 1989-90 season. Vanbiesbrouck was again the No. 1 goaltender, but by the end of the season, he was starting to split time with Richter, who had supplanted Froese as the other goaltender. The combination worked: The Rangers won their first division title of any kind in 48 years.

(It wasn't the first time in Rangers history that the team had faced the dilemma of having two star-caliber goalies at the same time. Chuck Rayner and Jim Henry faced the same situation in the 1940s, and Gump Worsley and Johnny Bower did the same in the 1950s.)

"Young guys always push older guys, and Mike pushed me," Vanbiesbrouck says. "It was a good thing for me, and it made me a better player."

Beezer and Richter spent the next three seasons forming the Rangers' most effective netminding combination since Giacomin and Villemure in the early 1970s. The duo, dubbed "VanRichterBrouck," led the Rangers to a second-place finish in 1990-91 and then backstopped the team to the Presidents' Trophy in 1991-92—the first time since 1941-42 that the Rangers finished first overall in the regular-season standings. Neilson alternated his goaltenders through the first 76 games, an NHL record that may never be broken, and Vanbiesbrouck responded with a stellar season, going 27-13-3 with a career-low 2.83 goals-against average.

The Rangers outlasted New Jersey in the opening round, but were upended by Pittsburgh in the division finals. Things fell apart the next season, and the Rangers missed the playoffs. With expansion coming, the Rangers were doomed to lose a goaltender (they were allowed to protect only one), and Vanbiesbrouck wound up being the odd man out.

Technically, the Rangers dealt him to Vancouver for defenseman Doug Lidster, and the Florida Panthers technically selected him off the Canucks roster. That reunited him with Neilson, who had been hired to coach the new franchise and made bringing Beezer to South Florida a priority.

"I don't know why they made the decision the way they did. I was really disappointed to leave New York," Vanbiesbrouck said more than a decade after his departure. But it turned out to be a boon for his career. "I didn't know it at the time, but Roger really wanted me. Things turned out for the best."

Though Vanbiesbrouck wound up missing out on the Rangers' 1994 Stanley Cup bid ("that was a tremendous disappointment, missing out on the run to the Stanley Cup"), he played the best hockey of his career with the Panthers. He was even reunited with Richter for a day at the Garden when they shared the net for the Eastern Conference team at the 1994 All-Star Game.

Two years later, Vanbiesbrouck had his most successful season, leading the Panthers, then in only their third season, to the Stanley Cup Finals. He won 12 playoff games and posted a 2.25 goals-against average in postseason play.

"Coming to Florida and knowing I was the No. 1 guy meant a great deal to me," Vanbiesbrouck told a reporter in the fall of 1995, as he was leading the Panthers to what's still the best season in their history. "Everyone handled things so well that it was easy for me."

Vanbiesbrouck became so popular that the Panthers centered much of their marketing campaign around him. Fans in Miami cheered when the Panthers were introduced to the strains of "Leave It to Beaver," because "Leave It to Beezer" was the young team's ticket to success.

He carried that success over to 1996-97, posting 27 wins and a 2.29 goals-against average. But though he posted his 300th NHL victory (6–2 over the Islanders on December 27, 1997), Vanbiesbrouck and the Panthers both struggled in 1997-98. Florida let him go, and he signed as a free agent with the Philadelphia Flyers.

Beezer posted a team-record 2.18 goals-against average in his first season in Philadelphia and allowed just nine goals in six playoff games. But his 1.46 goals-against average wasn't enough to get the Flyers past the first round. Despite 25 wins and a 2.20 goals-against average in 1999-2000, Vanbiesbrouck rode the bench during the playoffs and was traded to the Islanders during the summer.

He and the struggling Islanders weren't a good match, and the Isles sent him to New Jersey at the trading deadline. Vanbiesbrouck won all four of his appearances and watched Martin Brodeur lead the Devils to Game 7 of the finals before losing to Colorado.

Vanbiesbrouck announced his retirement that summer, but came back late in 2001-02 when the Devils needed an experienced backup. His last

NHL appearance was a 4–3 overtime victory at Washington on April 13, 2002.

Beezer was always one of the more willing Rangers when it came to talking to the media—and now he's a member. In addition to enjoying time with his family, which includes four boys, Vanbiesbrouck serves as an analyst with NHL Radio and HDNet, which televises NHL games in high definition.

"It keeps me up with what's going on with the game," he said.

Vanbiesbrouck was always a crowd favorite. As fans at Madison Square Garden had chanted "Eddie! Eddie!" for Ed Giacomin a generation earlier, they now chanted "Beezer" in honor of Vanbiesbrouck. He's retired now, but the love the fans felt for him is still fresh in his mind.

"I really liked the fans," he said. "I know they appreciated me. I think New York fans have a thing for goaltenders."

CHAPTER 16

MIKE GARTNER

The Skinny

No matter where he went, Mike Gartner never failed to bring his scoring touch with him. That included New York, where he was among the most potent snipers in team history during three full seasons and parts of two others. For these reasons, among others, Gartner was voted into the Hockey Hall of Fame in 2001 in the first year he was eligible—a fitting honor for one of the most consistent goal scorers in NHL history.

Gartner was drafted by the Cincinnati Stingers of the World Hockey Association as a 19-year-old after a 41-goal season in juniors with Niagara Falls. He scored 27 goals for Cincinnati in his first pro season, and it would be 19 years later before Gartner would score so few goals in a full season again. Gartner was runner-up in the voting for WHA rookie of the year to a skinny kid from Brantford, Ontario, named Wayne Gretzky.

The Stingers were one of the three WHA teams that were not invited to join the NHL as part of the 1979 merger. Because no NHL team held his rights, Gartner was available in the Entry Draft, and the lowly Washington Capitals tabbed him with their first pick (No. 4 overall).

The Caps were still among the NHL's weakest teams, but Gartner gave their offense a boost. He quickly showed he was one of the fastest players in the league, and his speed and booming shot helped him score 36 goals and 68 points, both team highs, as a rookie in 1979-80. The next season was even better: Gartner fired home 48 goals (and added 46 assists). Gartner kept piling up the goals, scoring 38, 35, and 40 in 1983-84, when the Caps made the playoffs for the first time. In 1984-85, he rang up 50 goals and 52 assists for 102 points, all career highs, as the Capitals made the playoffs again. (They lost to the New York Islanders in the first round both times, the second after leading a best-of-five series 2–0.)

Gartner continued to put the puck in the net, scoring 35 goals in 1985-86, 41 in 1986-87, and 48 in 1987-88. It was a level of consistent production seldom seen in the NHL. Although the Caps had outgrown the losing ways of their early years to become one of the NHL's best regular-season teams, they were never able to get past the second round of the playoffs—and Gartner, as one of the team's leaders, was singled out by many as one of the reasons the Caps couldn't get further.

When Gartner had only 26 goals in 56 games in 1988-89, the Caps decided it was time for a change. They dealt Gartner and defenseman Larry Murphy (who, like Gartner, would wind up in the Hall of Fame) to Minnesota for Dino Ciccarelli. Gartner left the Caps as their all-time leader in goals (397) and points (789).

Gartner had seven goals in 13 games as a North Star, giving him 33 for the season and extending his streak of 30-goal seasons to 10. He kept lighting the red light in his first full season in Minnesota, but as the trading deadline approached, he had the feeling he might be on the move again.

"I was in Washington for 10 years and got traded to Minnesota," Gartner says. "I was there for about a year, but I was having contract troubles in Minnesota, and I had heard a couple of weeks before the trade deadline that there was a chance they were going to be moving me. I started to hear a lot of rumors about New York, and I actually got pretty excited about it when I heard the Rangers were trying to acquire my rights. When I was traded to New York, it wasn't as much of a shock because I had had a feeling I was going to be traded. It was a pretty big thrill."

Gartner certainly played like a man who was thrilled to be in the Big Apple. He scored 11 times in 12 games after the deal, helping the Rangers to their first division title in 48 years. The only bad part was that the Caps, his old team, knocked the Rangers out of the playoffs in the second round.

One thing Gartner enjoyed about New York was playing for Roger Neilson.

Notes on Mike Gartner

Name:	Mike Gartner
Born:	October 29, 1959 (Ottawa, Ontario)
Position:	Right wing
Height:	6 feet
Playing Weight:	190 pounds
How Acquired:	From Minnesota for Ulf Dahlen and a fourth-round draft choice—March 6, 1990
Years with Rangers:	1989-90 to 1993-94
Stats as Ranger:	322 games, 173 goals, 113 assists, 286 points, 231 PIM
Uniform Number:	22
Accomplishments:	Team record for goals by a right wing (49), 1990-91
	Hall of Fame, 2001

"Roger and I got along great. He was a terrific coach for the three years we were together in New York," says Gartner, who, like Neilson, was a devout Christian. "I've often said that Roger was the best coach I ever had, and I had some good coaches. I had Pat Burns, who I thought was also an excellent coach, and Bryan Murray. There were some different guys over the years. But Roger was always a really good fit for me, and I think, me for him."

Gartner's combination of speed and skill enabled him to fill the net in New York just as he had in Washington. It didn't seem to matter who he played with—the red light kept going on.

"A couple of the more successful years I had with the Rangers—I think I had 45 and 48 goals [actually 49 in 1990-91, 41 in 1991-92, and 45 in 1992-93]—were with Sergei Nemchinov as my center and Jan Erixon [a defensive specialist] as my left wing," he says. "I also had good years with Darren Turcotte as my center and [enforcer/checker] Kris King as my left wing. I was able to play with a lot of different players, and it worked out well."

The 49 goals in 1990-91 left Gartner one short of Vic Hadfield's single-season team record at the time, but the team finished a disappointing second and was eliminated in the first round of the playoffs. By this time, though, Gartner was approaching a milestone.

The Setting

Gartner began the 1991-92 season with 498 career goals. He also was on a team that had been reshaped by the addition of Mark Messier, who came from the Edmonton Oilers during the first week of the season in one of the biggest deals in team history. Goal No. 499 came on October 7, when he scored the game-winner in the home opener, a 2–1 victory over Boston. Then … nothing. Gartner went scoreless during the next three games.

But with his former club, the Washington Capitals, coming to town on October 14, Gartner was ready to make history.

The Game of My Life (Part I)
RANGERS VS. WASHINGTON CAPITALS—OCTOBER 14, 1991

"When I was at 499, obviously 500 is a big milestone to get for any player, and I think I was stuck on 499 for several games," he says. "You try not to think about it too much. You know it's going to happen, but you always have that thought in the back of your mind, 'Am I going to get hurt and never be able to get that 500th goal?' I remember that I thought going into the game that this would be a great time to do it, because we were playing Washington, my former team. I had played there for parts of 10 seasons, so it was kind of ironic that I did get it against Washington.

"The goal itself was pretty nondescript. It came early in the game [3:27 into the first period]. I was driving to the net, and I'm not sure who [Mark Messier] threw the puck across as I was going to the net. I was just stopping, and I got my stick on it, and it kind of squirted underneath Mike Liut. It took a couple of seconds before it even crossed the goal line, but it was in.

"The one bad part was that we lost the game [5–3]. We had a 3–2 lead after two periods, but they scored three times in the third."

Mike Gartner. *Courtesy of John Kreiser*

Intermission

Goal No. 500 was the first of four milestones that Gartner reached in 1991-92. He recorded his 1,000th career point with a goal on January 4 against New Jersey, played in his 1,000th game on March 20 against Detroit, and reached the 500-assist mark by setting up a pair of goals against Pittsburgh in the season finale on April 16. No player before or since has reached the 500-goal, 500-assist, and 1,000-point milestones in the same season.

The Rangers hit the heights as well, at least during the regular season. Gartner's 40 goals helped the Blueshirts win the Presidents' Trophy as the regular-season champion—the first time they had finished on top during the regular season since 1941-42. But after outlasting the Devils in the first round, the Rangers couldn't beat the defending-champion Penguins in the Patrick Division finals, losing in six games.

"We had good teams for three to four years in a row—I think we finished first or second in our division," says Gartner. "That was a disappointing year. Mark Messier came over from Edmonton for Bernie Nicholls, and we had a great team that one playoff run with Mark and Adam Graves, Mike Richter—basically, the whole group that was together when they won the Cup in 1994. We lost to Pittsburgh in the second round of the playoffs; we were up two games to one and wound up losing that series—and Pittsburgh went on to win eight straight games. They didn't lose again for the rest of the playoffs."

Even more disappointing was that the team didn't even make the playoffs in 1992-93, although Gartner's 45 goals made him the first player in Ranger history to hit the 40-goal mark in three consecutive seasons. He also scored four goals in the All-Star Game at Montreal, earning the Most Valuable Player Award.

With a revamped roster and a new coach, Mike Keenan, the Rangers started 1993-94 on a roll and kept winning. Gartner kept scoring too. He reached the Christmas break nearing another milestone. On December 19, he notched goal No. 599 to cap off a 6–3 victory over the Ottawa Senators at the Garden. As with No. 500, the historic goal came a week later, when New Jersey came to town on the night after Christmas.

The Game of My Life (Part II)
RANGERS VS. NEW JERSEY DEVILS—DECEMBER 26, 1993

"What I recall about both of them is that they were fairly similar in that I was stuck on 599 for several games before that. No. 600 was even a little bit different, though. We were playing against New Jersey, and I loved playing against New Jersey. For whatever reason, I always had great success against New Jersey, putting the puck in the net against the Devils.

"It was the same in one way—I got my pass on a stick and just touched the puck and it went into the net. [The goal was reviewed because Gartner had played the puck with his foot before getting his stick on it, but it was upheld.]

"This time, there was a celebration. All my teammates knew where things stood, and I remember at that time, [the Rangers] asked for permission to leave the bench. At that time, you couldn't empty the benches—you had to ask permission. I remember for the 600th, they had asked for permission from the league that if it did happen, they [his teammates] could come on the ice without being penalized.

"It's funny, because 500 was the big milestone, but to get into the 600-goal club—that was a little more exclusive. I kind of valued that a little more.

"And a good thing is that this time, we won the game [8–3]."

Afterword

Gartner kept scoring—he got No. 601 just 67 seconds after the milestone goal. But although the Rangers were still leading the overall standings as the trade deadline approached, Gartner had only 28 goals in 71 games, his lowest total as a Ranger, and Keenan and GM Neil Smith wanted to make some changes. One of them involved bringing in former Edmonton star Glenn Anderson, who was now with Toronto. The price: Gartner, who didn't want to go, even if it meant returning to his native Ontario.

"It was disappointing to leave the team at the trading deadline in 1994," he says. "We had a great feeling that whole year. We were in first place overall, and we had a feeling that this could be the year. To be with the team for a number of years before that and see it build to that point, and then get traded and watch that same team that I'd been playing with go on to win the Stanley Cup was obviously a tough thing to watch."

Gartner almost didn't have to watch: he came within a few games of getting a chance to play against his former teammates in the Stanley Cup finals. The Leafs won their first two rounds before losing to Vancouver in the Western Conference finals.

"There was actually a chance we could have played New York in the finals," he says. "We lost to Vancouver in the semis, but it was almost looking [like we'd get to play the Rangers in the finals] for a while. That would have been pretty strange."

Gartner had only 12 goals in the lockout-shortened 1994-95 season, but pumped home 35 in 1995-96, making the All-Star Game and winning the fastest skater competition for the third time—at age 36. However, the Leafs sent him to Phoenix in the off-season.

Despite the new team and new surroundings, Gartner kept scoring. He lit the red light 32 times in 1996-97, giving him an NHL-record 17 30-goal seasons—one for every full season he had played in the league. Though he scored just 12 times in 1997-98, there was one more milestone: goal No. 700. "The 700-goal club is even more exclusive [than the 600-goal club]" he says with a chuckle, "and I got into that one too." He finished his career in April 1998 with 708 goals, fifth on the all-time list.

It was a remarkably consistent performance by a player who was always able to adapt to the way the game was played and put the puck in the net.

"I always felt that I needed to find different ways to score," Gartner says of his scoring prowess. "Early in my career, I was able to use my speed and my shot down the [right] side, breaking down the wing. Then the game changed a little bit, and I had to find different ways to score. In the last half of my career, I spent a lot of time in front of the net. I got beat up pretty good, but I found ways to score. I found that there were very few players that I couldn't play with. I could adapt and play with whomever my center and my left winger were."

Gartner moved back to Toronto after his playing career was done, working with the NHL Players Association (NHLPA). He was named its director of hockey operations in February 2006. "I've got a few more responsibilities now as director of hockey operations for the players association," he says of his new job. "It keeps me busy."

V

TO THE CUP...
AND BEYOND

The Rangers won the Presidents' Trophy in 1991-92, but stumbled against Pittsburgh in the second round of the playoffs. After a disappointing season in 1992-93, general manager **Neil Smith** hired coach Mike Keenan, and the two combined to produce the team that finally ended a 54-year Stanley Cup drought.

The 1993-94 season was full of memorable games, as recounted by memorable names. **Adam Graves**, a favorite of Garden fans almost from the moment he arrived in 1991, broke Vic Hadfield's team goal-scoring record by scoring his 50th and 51st goals—ironically, against the Edmonton Oilers, his former team. **Mark Messier**, who guaranteed victory in Game 6 of the 1994 Eastern Conference finals, backed up his words with one of the greatest one-man performances in hockey history. **Stephane Matteau**, a young forward acquired at the trading deadline in March 1994, sent the Rangers into the Stanley Cup Finals for the first time since 1979 when he scored a double-overtime winner in Game 7 of the Eastern Conference finals against New Jersey.

Goaltender **Mike Richter**, who had finally taken the starting job after splitting time with Vanbiesbrouck for several years, made one of the most famous saves in Rangers history in Game 4 of the Finals. He talks about halting Pavel Bure on a penalty shot in Game 4, giving the Rangers a chance to rally for a victory. One week later, **Brian Leetch** wrapped up the Conn Smythe Trophy as playoff MVP by leading the Rangers to victory in Game 7, capping the five-year rebuilding project by Smith, who discusses how the championship team was built and what it felt like to see the fruits of his efforts turn into the Rangers' first Stanley Cup since 1940.

The Rangers hosted one of the most famous farewells in NHL history, and **Wayne Gretzky** tells the story of his final NHL game and the events surrounding it. After seven seasons of missing the playoffs from 1997 to 2004 (and another season lost to the lockout), the Rangers returned to the playoffs in the spring of 2006, largely thanks to the scoring of **Jaromir Jagr**, who talks about the night he broke the team single-season scoring record.

CHAPTER 17

ADAM GRAVES

The Skinny

On the ice or off it, few players have given Rangers fans more to be proud of than Adam Graves. As a player, a leader, and a citizen, Graves was a champion—one of those players who would do whatever needed to be done and do it to the best of his ability. As good as he was as a player, Graves was (and is) an even better human being, whose efforts for the good of others are unsurpassed.

Graves was a highly regarded talent when he joined the Windsor Spitfires of the Ontario Hockey League. NHL scouts started buzzing around in Graves' rookie season in junior hockey, when he put up 64 points in 62 games. The Detroit Red Wings made Graves the first pick in the second round, 22nd overall, in the 1986 Entry Draft.

The Wings left Graves in junior hockey, much to the delight of the Spitfires and their fans. Graves piled up 45 goals and 55 assists for 100 points for the top-rated junior team in Canada, though the Spitfires were upset by Medicine Hat in the finals of the Memorial Cup.

Graves returned to juniors in 1987-88, piling up 60 points in 37 games while working around a trip to the World Junior Championship and his first exposure to the NHL—nine games with the Wings, in which he had one assist.

Graves spent most of his first pro season with the Wings, going 7-5-12 in 60 games as a checker and role player. It looked like he would do more of the same in 1989-90, but fate intervened: Graves was part of the package that was sent to Edmonton by the Wings to bring back hometown boy Jimmy Carson (a 50-goal scorer as a rookie). The Oilers paired him with former Detroit teammate Joe Murphy and Martin Gelinas on the "Kid Line," a high-energy trio that gave the Oilers a lift. Graves finished the regular season with 21 points in 63 games with Edmonton, then added five goals and 11 points in 22 playoff games as the Oilers won their fifth Stanley Cup in seven years.

"Winning the Cup in Edmonton and having the opportunity for my mom and dad, and my dad in particular, to drink out of the Stanley Cup in the dressing room at the Boston Garden, was special," says Graves. "Standing on the bench with 10 seconds to go, we're up 4–1, and thinking to myself, 'It can't be true. It can't be true. I'm going to win the Stanley Cup.' It was outstanding."

Graves went 7-18-25 in 1990-91, then became a Group I free agent— eligible to be signed by anyone, with compensation to be agreed upon by the teams (or by the league, if no agreement could be reached). Rangers GM Neil Smith, looking for young legs, speed, and grit, signed Graves, who ultimately cost them checker Troy Mallette.

"The two years that I spent in Edmonton were outstanding, and the friendships you make along the way are as big a part of it as the on-ice factor," Graves says of his time with the Oilers. "Then to come to New York and to get the opportunity to play and be in a position to score what in hockey is a milestone goal is certainly a privilege."

With the Rangers, Graves found himself in a new role: two-way power forward, usually on the left side of Mark Messier, who came to New York just a few weeks after Graves. The move worked better than Rangers fans could have dreamed: Graves had more goals in his first season in the Big Apple (26) than he'd had points the previous season.

"My first couple of years in Detroit and Edmonton were building years," Graves says. "When I came to New York, I got to play more on the power play and started to play more—and like anything else, once you get an opportunity and you're fortunate enough to be surrounded by great players, which I was, you get into a groove and find out where you have to be on the ice. Experience is a great teacher, and when you have a team like

Notes on Adam Graves

Name:	Adam Graves
Born:	April 12, 1968 (Toronto, Ontario)
Position:	Left wing
Height:	6 feet
Playing Weight:	205 pounds
How Acquired:	Signed as Group I free agent by Rangers—September 3, 1991
Years with Rangers:	1991-92 to 2000-01
Stats as Ranger:	772 games, 280 goals 227 assists, 507 points, 810 PIM
Uniform Number:	9
Accomplishments:	Second-Team All-Star 1994
	King Clancy Memorial Trophy 1994
	Bill Masterton Memorial Trophy 2001
	All-Star Game 1994

we did and the players that I got to play with, confidence comes from the other players as well."

The Rangers won the Presidents' Trophy in 1991-92, but were ousted in the Patrick Division finals by the defending NHL champion Pittsburgh Penguins. The team fell out of the playoffs in 1992-93, but not because of Graves, who improved to 36 goals and 62 points.

While Graves was earning a reputation as one of the NHL's toughest two-way forwards on the ice, he was also earning a different kind of notoriety as someone who gave unstintingly of his time for charity, especially when it involved kids.

The Setting

The Rangers regrouped after their disappointing showing in 1992-93. They hired Mike Keenan as coach, made Mick Richter their No. 1

goaltender after losing John Vanbiesbrouck in the expansion draft, and added support players like Glenn Healy and Steve Larmer.

The Blueshirts started fast and kept going. One reason was the play of Graves, who piled up goals at a pace no Ranger left wing had managed since Vic Hadfield set the team record of 50 in 1971-72. Graves didn't have Hadfield's big slap shot, but he did have the same willingness to pay the price in front of the net, outbattling defenders to convert rebounds and get himself open for quick wrist shots from the slot. Graves also stuck up for his teammates, keeping opponents from taking liberties with players like Messier and Brian Leetch without spending too much time in the penalty box. That kind of effort made Graves a favorite among Garden fans.

The goals kept piling up for Graves. He passed his personal high of 36 and kept going—past 40, past 45, and up to 49, the number he took to the Northlands Coliseum when the Rangers made their annual visit to Graves' former home on March 23, 1994.

The Game of My Life

RANGERS AT EDMONTON OILERS—MARCH 23, 1994

"I couldn't say I exactly what I was thinking," Graves says of going onto the ice with the chance to score No. 50. "My whole premise, the way I played and approached everything, was just to focus on the meat and potatoes parts of the game—going into the corners, getting to the net on every play, playing strong along the boards, putting yourself in a position to get loose pucks. The game has changed completely now, but back then, my whole game was in front of the net. You knew that when you got into a game that you had to battle. Many times it was a war zone in front of the net. It was something that I had a passion for. I loved battling, and I loved getting in front of the net. You really had to battle for your ice and get position. Looking at today's game, it's the one huge difference now.

"My whole mind-set was 'that was my ice, and I wanted that ice.' Because of playing with the guys I was fortunate enough to play with, I knew that if I got to the front of the net and fought, battled for that ice, that I would have opportunities. I wasn't the type of player, like Brian Leetch, who was going to grab the puck and skate from end to end. That wasn't my skill set. Mine was trying to be strong, doing the simple things, the basic parts of

Adam Graves. *Courtesy of the John Halligan Collection*

the game, and doing them with strength and tenacity and battling. That's something I enjoyed. The front of the net was something that I had a great deal of passion for, but I knew I had to get there on every play—get there, get in position, and locate loose pucks.

"The 50th goal [at 14:32 of the first period] came off a turnover. Glenn Anderson threw it over to Mess, and we came in 2-on-1. Mess put the pass across the slot, and I was fortunate enough to one-time it past Billy Ranford. That was kind of ironic because Billy and I had been good friends for a long time. We won a Cup together in Edmonton, and he was a great goalie in his time. I think that was a special opportunity to score your 50th on someone you have such a great deal of respect for. It was a big thrill, and it was fitting that Mark passed me the puck.

"The 51st came off a point shot, I believe. I got to the front of the net and knocked the puck past Billy [at 17:26 of the opening period]. I could see everyone was kind of looking around, and [the puck] got caught in my skates, and I kind of hacked it in.

"I can't say that I've watched [the goal] a lot. But that's the great part of the game—the memories. You kind of remember those key moments where you don't have to watch a tape or a DVD to recapture and remember how it went in and how you felt. I said after the goal that because of the way I played and the fortune of playing with the teammates I played with, that scoring the 50th goal was as much a team achievement as it was my achievement."

Afterword

The pounding Graves took staking out territory in front of the net began to catch up with him as the season wound down. He scored just once the rest of the way, finishing the season with 52 goals, a team record that stood until Jaromir Jagr broke it on April 8, 2006.

Despite a sore back, Graves kept filling the net during the playoffs. The biggest of his 10 postseason goals was the last one—a typical Graves conversion from right in front that gave the Rangers a 2–0 lead late in the first period of Game 7 of the Stanley Cup Finals against the Vancouver Canucks. The Rangers won the game 3–2, triggering a celebration the likes of which New York hockey fans had never seen.

"To win it in New York, after 54 years, there's absolutely not a better place, not a more appreciative place—and I'll say it for as long as anyone will listen—the red, white and blue runs deep in my body," Graves says. "That was a special, special time, and it's something I'll cherish forever. It was a privilege to be part of it. It wasn't just our team. It was everyone's team. It was the city's team, and everyone felt a part of it. I think everyone knew at that time where they were when the team won—what they were doing, what they were wearing. That's what made it so special, especially after 54 years. That whole factor united Rangers fans everywhere. Everyone felt like it was 'our' team."

Graves' off-ice work also was recognized in 1994, when he was awarded the King Clancy Trophy for his charitable and humanitarian efforts.

Graves never came close to scoring 50 goals again, but he was a solid contributor through the rest of the decade, twice breaking the 30-goal mark while still providing toughness and leadership. His biggest goal came in Game 5 of the 1997 Eastern Conference semifinals, when he scored in overtime to eliminate New Jersey and send the Rangers to the conference finals.

Graves' leadership on and off the ice was recognized in 2001, when he was awarded the Bill Masterton Trophy. But not long after winning the trophy, he found himself in San Jose.

"It was tough, but I'm a realist," he says of being traded. "You have to be humble enough and smart enough to know that there's a beginning and an end to everything. The glass with me is always half-full. That's the way I look at things. I was very fortunate to have had the chance to play an entire decade in a city that I absolutely adored, and to play for a team that will eternally be my team. I was very lucky."

Graves played two seasons with the Sharks before stepping aside as a player. The Rangers wasted little time bringing him back to New York.

"I guess I'm an ambassador for the Rangers, on and off the ice," he says of his function with the team. "But I'd like to describe it by saying I'm a father first for my three children, and then an ambassador for the Rangers."

For Rangers fans, though, he'll always be "Gravy," part of a special team—one that's still special to him.

"*Chemistry* and *camaraderie* and *teamwork* and all those adjectives that you can use to describe a team certainly were appropriate for the 1993-94 team," he says. "You don't win without having that, both on and off the ice. It was a tight-knit group whose members cared about each other. It was family in many ways, and even through time, guys can see each other for the first time in five or six years and not miss a beat. It's because we have that connection. We've battled, we've gone to war, and we've accomplished something that is very special and unites us for the rest of our lives."

CHAPTER 18

MARK MESSIER

The Skinny

Twenty-three men served as captain of the New York Rangers during the franchise's first eight decades in the NHL. Any Ranger fan will tell you, however, that there's only one man who's been worthy of being *The Captain*. Mark Messier won five of his six Stanley Cup rings with the Edmonton Oilers, but it was the one he won with the Rangers in 1994 that secured his place among hockey's pantheon of immortals.

Messier got an early start in hockey. By age four, he was attending his father Doug's minor-league practices. By age 11, he was a stickboy with the Spruce Grove Mets in the Alberta junior leagues. He would go on to be a star with that same team a few years later.

At age 16, Messier was already on the path to stardom. His talent was apparent enough that he skipped both major junior and college hockey. In the fall of 1978, at the age of 17, he had a five-game tryout with the Indianapolis Racers of the World Hockey Association. Though Messier went scoreless in the five games and was let go by the Racers (who crashed into bankruptcy soon after), he was quickly picked up by the WHA's Cincinnati Stingers and played 47 games, scoring one goal and 10 assists.

The NHL and WHA made peace that summer, and four WHA teams bought their way into the more established league. The Stingers didn't make the cut, so Messier found himself eligible for the Entry Draft. He wound up being taken by his hometown team, the Edmonton Oilers, with the 48th overall pick.

Messier started the season with the Oilers, but he was still a raw 18-year-old learning to play the game at the pro level and actually spent a few games in the minors. He ended up playing 75 NHL games, scoring 12 goals and adding 21 assists while switching between center and left wing, then adding another goal and two assists in his first three NHL playoff games.

Messier improved by leaps and bounds, notching 23 goals in 1980-81 as the Oilers advanced to the second round of the playoffs and hitting the 50-goal mark in 1981-82, when he was named a First-Team All-Star. He had 48 goals and 106 points in 1982-83, when the Oilers advanced to the Finals for the first time.

Messier stepped to the fore in 1983-84, when he notched 101 points, leading the Oilers back to the Finals for a rematch with the New York Islanders. On a team with stars such as Wayne Gretzky, Jari Kurri, and Paul Coffey, it was Messier who took command of the series. In Game 3, he scored a spectacular goal late in the second period that turned the momentum completely in the Oilers' favor. They completed a five-game blitz of the Islanders, and Messier won the Conn Smythe Trophy as play-off MVP.

"Mark was like a pit bull," teammate Dave Hunter remembered two decades later. "He was a great leader who led by example. When someone makes a play like Mark did on that goal, it pumped up the whole bench."

The Oilers won again in 1985, 1987, and 1988, putting them among the NHL's great dynasties. But they traded Gretzky to Los Angeles after winning the 1988 Cup, beginning the breakup of what could have been the greatest team of all time. With Gretzky gone, Messier inherited the captain's *C* and became the unquestioned leader of the Oilers.

Gretzky and his new team ended the Oilers' hopes for a repeat in 1989, rallying for a seven-game victory in the opening round of the playoffs. But Messier stepped to the fore again in 1989-90, finishing second to Gretzky in the scoring race with 129 points and winning the Hart Trophy as the regular-season MVP.

But it was in the playoffs that Messier's legend as one of hockey's great leaders was permanently established. With Edmonton trailing 2-1 in games to Chicago in the semifinals, Messier put the Oilers on his back, scoring

Notes on Mark Messier

Name:	Mark Messier
Born:	January 18, 1961 (Edmonton, Alberta)
Position:	Center
Height	6-foot-1
Playing Weight:	210 lbs
How Acquired:	From Edmonton with Jeff Beukeboom for Bernie Nicholls, Steven Rice, and Louie DeBrusk—October 4, 1991; Signed as a free agent—July 13, 2000
Years with Rangers:	1991-92 to 1996-97; 2000-01 to 2003-04
Stats as Ranger:	698 games, 250 goals, 441 assists, 691 points, 667 PIM
Accomplishments:	Hart Trophy 1991-92
	First-Team All-Star 1991-92
	All-Star Game 1991-92, 1992-93, 1993-94, 1995-96, 1996-97, 2003-2004
	Rangers MVP 1991-92, 1994-95, 1995-96
	Players' Player Award 1995-96
	Frank Boucher Trophy 1991-92, 1994-95, 1995-96, 1996-97

twice and setting up two other goals in a 4–2 victory that took the life out of the Blackhawks. The Oilers won the next two games, then beat Boston in five games for their fifth Cup in seven years. In Game 4, Messier had three assists in a 5–1 victory that all but clinched the win.

Stopping Messier "was like trying to catch a tiger by the tail," Boston center Bobby Carpenter told reporters.

The Oilers made it to the semifinals in 1991 before being ousted by Minnesota, but by then, the end of the Oilers' time among the NHL's elite teams was visible. Rangers general manager Neil Smith, seeking to end his franchise's then-50 years without a championship, targeted Messier as the man who could end the drought.

"Losing is a culture, and it's a hard thing to change," Smith said of his reasons for wanting Messier. "That's why I brought Mark to the Rangers. Mark really changed the culture."

The deal was made on October 4, 1991, and the cost turned out to be surprisingly low: Bernie Nicholls, a talented but expendable scorer, plus youngsters Steven Rice and Louie DeBrusk (as a bonus, the Rangers also got Jeff Beukeboom, a solid defenseman).

Messier wasted little time changing the atmosphere around the Rangers. On the ice, he rang up 107 points and became the first Ranger since Andy Bathgate in 1958-59 to win the Hart Trophy. More important, he became the leader Smith wanted—the kind of player teammates respect and follow and opponents fear. Other Rangers, even a handful of Hall of Famers, had worn the captain's C—but Messier was the first to be known as the Captain.

His leadership formula was simple.

"I think in the end, it's just trying to help people realize their potential and figure out how to motivate them, because everybody grew up in a different lifestyle, with a different set of circumstances," he says. "Everybody's got a different trigger point. You have to get to know the players on a much deeper level than just hockey. I think that ultimately will let you tap into what motivates them. Without that, you're just another teammate; you're just another hockey player who doesn't really understand them, and they're probably not going to listen to what you have to say very often. In the end, they have to know that the only thing that matters to both of you is ultimately trying to find a way to win and that you don't have any ulterior motives against them. You're just trying to find out how to get the best out of them, and they respect that."

With Messier leading the way, the Rangers finished first overall for the first time in 50 years. But after beating New Jersey in seven games in the opening round, the Rangers stumbled against the defending-champion Pittsburgh Penguins, losing a 2–1 lead and dropping the division final series in six games.

Mark Messier. *Courtesy of the John Halligan Collection*

The disappointment of the 1992 playoffs carried over into the following season. After a good start, injuries started to take a toll, and the Rangers wound up missing the playoffs.

Smith brought in Mike Keenan as coach for 1993-94, and the fog of losing from the previous season quickly blew away. The Rangers started fast and never faltered, winning the Presidents' Trophy for the second time in three years. Messier finished with only 26 goals but had 58 assists and 84 points, helping linemate Adam Graves to the greatest season by a Ranger goal-scorer.

"I'm not as worried about scoring goals, because I've done a lot of playmaking that has led to a lot of other goals," he told reporters late in the season. "Look at Adam Graves. I'm proud of the fact that he has 51 goals this season." Graves finished with 52, a record not broken until Jaromir Jagr scored 54 in 2005-06.

There was still no question about what Messier meant to the Rangers.

"He wouldn't have to score a goal all year long and he'd still probably be the MVP of this team," Graves said. "He's a great playmaker and sets up plays, kills penalties—he does everything. He raises his play at the key time."

That key time was coming.

The Setting

Many experts expected the Rangers to struggle in the first round against the Islanders, who had made the playoffs thanks to a late-season hot streak, and were one of the few teams that had played them tough during the regular season. Instead, the Blueshirts polished off their suburban rivals in four easy games, with Messier putting the capper on the series with the clinching goal in Game 4 at the Nassau Coliseum.

But unlike in past years, the 1994 Rangers knew just winning a playoff series wasn't enough. "It's a first step," Messier told the assembled media after the sweep. "We know what our goal is, and we're not going to get ahead of ourselves."

Next up was Washington, which had eliminated the Rangers four years earlier. This time, though, the Rangers made short work of the Caps, winning the first three games and taking the series in five. That put the Rangers into the Eastern Conference finals, the first time they had made the final four since 1986. But that team was a playoff surprise, and an underdog. This Ranger team was the reigning Presidents' Cup winner and the favorite to win the Cup.

Their opponents, the New Jersey Devils, weren't impressed. Although the Rangers had swept all six games against the Devils during the regular season, New Jersey stunned the Garden crowd in the series opener, scoring with 43 seconds remaining in regulation to force overtime, then winning 4–3 on Stephane Richer's overtime goal.

Messier wasted no time putting his stamp on Game 2. He scored 1:13 into the game to give the Rangers an early lead, and they added three goals in the third period for a 4–0 victory. Stephane Matteau's goal 6:13 into the second overtime won Game 3 and gave the Rangers a 2-1 lead in the series, but the Devils pulled even with a 3–1 win at the Meadowlands, then silenced the Garden crowd in Game 5 with a thorough 4–1 victory.

As the Rangers prepared for Game 6 at the Meadowlands, Messier knew that their season was on the line. Like Joe Namath 25 years earlier, the Captain put his neck on the line and guaranteed victory. And like Namath, he backed up his words.

The Game of My Life
1994 EASTERN CONFERENCE FINALS, GAME 6
RANGERS AT NEW JERSEY DEVILS—MAY 25, 1994

"We had had an unbelievable season that year," Messier says when asked to describe the atmosphere before Game 6. "The only thing that separated us from New Jersey was the six victories we had against them during the regular season. We beat them all six times we played them. For us, that was a big confidence booster going into the series—we knew that we could beat them because we *had* beaten them.

"When we got down in the series, and especially when we went back to New Jersey for Game 6, I was trying to figure out a way to instill the confidence we had shown all year against New Jersey. I felt that it [guaranteeing a win] would be a great way to let my players know that I believed we could go in there and win Game 6, because we had beaten them six times during the regular season—three times in their building. I thought that if they got up in the morning and saw that I believed we could beat them, that it would be a great way to help us with our confidence.

"But it was a little underestimation on my part that 20 million other New Yorkers and the New Jersey Devils would read it too.

"I was so focused on our team and what we needed to do that it really didn't matter to me at that point. I got so locked in and so focused that I didn't think about that. When I got up the next morning and saw the guarantee in the paper, at that point it didn't matter, because our chances of winning the Stanley Cup were so close, and we really needed to win that game to avoid elimination. But more importantly, I thought we had the team that could win it that year. I thought we were able to win that year, and I thought we were the best team still left playing—and we needed to figure out a way to win that game.

"Everybody remembers the hat trick and the guarantee, but without Mike Richter's goaltending early, we probably don't win that game. Mike was great all through the game, but especially early on. The Devils came out flying and took a 2–0 lead, but Mike gave us a chance to win. The Devils were a great team, and they were playing as well as or better than us at that particular point, and we had to figure out a way to play better. It wasn't that we were playing poorly; it was that the Devils were playing really, really well. They really had us under the gun, and they came out in Game 6 and played unbelievable hockey, but Richter held us in there until we were able to score late in the second period [on a goal by Alexei Kovalev that Messier set up]— to at least make it 2–1 going into the third period and give us some life going into the locker room. That's exactly what happened.

"We realized that we had been outplayed severely to that point, and to be down only 2–1 was a real big turning point. Playing with a 2–1 lead and trying to close out a team can be a really tough position to be in, especially for a team like New Jersey that didn't have a lot of experience. They maybe tried to protect [the lead] a little too much. We had to throw everything we had at them, and the momentum of the game changed. They were a very young team, and Martin Brodeur was a very young goalie.

"They had a few guys with some experience, but I'm not sure if they had anyone who had won a Stanley Cup. Experience is certainly one element of a team that's important, but it isn't everything—you can see that in today's game. But we did have the experience to handle some of the adversity we had gone thorough. And we got lucky—we got some unbelievable goaltending, and because of the experience we had, we were able to keep our focus and do what we had to do.

"We came out in the third period and knew we had to put more pressure on them. Brodeur was playing great, so we knew we needed to drive to the net and hopefully create some rebounds. That's just what we started to do. Their defense was keeping us out on the perimeter, so we wanted to penetrate a little deeper and throw the puck at the net from any angle that we could and make sure we had other people going to the net. My first goal was perhaps a little bit lucky, I think [defenseman Ken] Daneyko had me angled going toward the boards, but I was able to slip a backhander through Brodeur's legs at a funny angle [2:48 into the period]. He might not have been expecting it.

"On the second goal [at 12:12], Alexei Kovalev came over the blue line and got the puck to the net, and I got the rebound, just like we had talked about between periods, and put it past Brodeur. The third one was an empty-netter at the end of the game.

"Winning the game was a good feeling—but we didn't have long to relish it. All we had done was send the series back to the Garden, and we knew that Game 7 was no sure thing. If that would have been the last game and we'd won the Stanley Cup, *that* would have been a great feeling. Other than the fact that we were going back home and we had lived to play another day, it was a pretty short-lived celebration. We knew they weren't going to roll over in Game 7—they probably felt like they had let one get away and were probably a little mad at themselves and probably a little more determined. We knew Game 7 was going to be a tough game, especially some of the guys who had a little more experience and had been there.

Afterword

Messier's heroics kept the Rangers' season alive, but there was another hurdle to climb before the Rangers could advance to their first Stanley Cup final since 1979. Two nights later, they climbed that hurdle with a 2–1 victory in Game 7 on Stephane Matteau's second double-overtime goal in the series.

The Vancouver Canucks, the Rangers' opponent in the finals, had struggled for much of the regular season before getting on a roll in the playoffs. They kept rolling in Game 1, tying the game with 60 seconds left in regulation time and winning on Greg Adams' goal with 32 seconds left in the first overtime.

The Rangers rebounded by winning Games 2, 3, and 4, moving them within one victory of their first Cup since 1940. But the Canucks wouldn't go quietly. They won Game 5 at the Garden, 6–3, and evened the series with a 4–1 victory at the Pacific Coliseum.

Game 7 was a night like New York hockey fans had never seen. Messier helped get the Garden rocking when he set up Brian Leetch's game-opening goal midway through the first period. The Rangers led 2–1 midway through the second period when Messier shoveled a rebound past Kirk McLean to put the Rangers ahead by two.

That goal proved to be the Cup-winner, as Vancouver scored in the third period but the Rangers held on for a 3–2 victory and an end to the longest Cup drought in NHL history. It was the culmination of what Messier had come to New York to do.

Looking back, Messier says, getting the Cup-winning goal himself didn't really matter. "I had enough experience to realize that if you don't have good people around you, if you don't have the support that you need, you're not going to win anyway. One of my messages has always been that if you win the game, there's going to be enough credit and enough praise to go around for everybody. It didn't matter who scored; it didn't matter who made a play or did this or that. We all felt that anything that happened was for the team, and so it was basically a footnote for all of us—the scoreboard or the statistics—because in the end, we had one thing in mind, and that was to win. I think everybody felt proud of the fact that we were able to do that."

Keenan, who had seen Messier take apart his Philadelphia Flyers in the 1987 Finals, had a front-row seat this time. "Mark Messier is the greatest leader in pro sports today," he said after Game 7. By this time, Messier had a handful of Stanley Cup rings and was the only player in NHL history to captain two franchises to a championship.

"It's hard to compare the Cup in New York with the five Cups in Edmonton because every year brings new challenges, different people, and a different set of circumstances," he says. "But ultimately, winning the Cup is what you play for. If I had to compare them, I'd probably compare the first Cup [in Edmonton] to the sixth Cup, because it was so new for everybody. An expansion team coming into the NHL and winning a Cup five years into their existence in front of fans that had been following the NHL for years and years and years without having a team of their own, who got to see them win the Cup in their hometown—it was an amazing feeling. That was a lot like it was in New York—although the Cup had been won in New York, it hadn't been won in a long time, so there were a lot of fathers and sons and grandfathers and grandsons who were able to share the experience they had talked about for many years prior. In a way they were so new and fresh for everybody, I felt that in a way they were very similar."

The picture of a grinning Messier hugging the Stanley Cup is a New York classic. He and his adopted city were in the middle of a love affair that continues to this day.

"I think everyone remembers that year like it was yesterday," he says. "It was a magical time for hockey fans in the New York area and around the country. It was a year that we had started out by winning a trophy over in England, the "Mustard Cup" [at a preseason event sponsored by French's]. There was a lot of good chemistry, a lot of great camaraderie, a lot of synergy. Because of the type of team we had and the type of players we had, we really seemed to encompass the fans into our year that year. The players were approachable, they were accessible, they did an unbelievable job in the community.

"What happened is that we really tied a bond with the fans in New York, and once that was established, to go out and win the Stanley Cup that year cemented anything that ever happened into the folklore of the area."

Messier, his teammates and their friend Stan (the Cup) were the toast of New York that summer, taking part in a ticker-tape parade, appearing with David Letterman, and celebrating in a way that few teams in sports history had ever done. It was something he was glad to be able to share with the fans of his adopted hometown.

"Sports is only one aspect of creating a relationship between a city and a sportsman," he says of the love affair he's enjoyed with New York fans for well over a decade. "Just playing the game—hockey or basketball or baseball—that won't do it. You have to have a consistent message so that people can really trust you. You have to handle the press with respect, because ultimately through the press, you're talking to the fans. That's their way of communicating with you, or you communicating with them. It's a way of them getting to know you and know that they can trust you. I think how you interact with the people in the community is very important—what kind of charity work you do, whether you're accessible off the ice, whether people can come up and talk to you and feel comfortable doing that. All those things are important to cement that relationship. It's something I would do no matter what, because of my upbringing.

"In the end, New York is really a blue-collar town. They like hard work—to do a hard day's work at the office and then go out and have a good time. We were able to share that with them."

The lockout that fall delayed the raising of the championship banner until January 1995, but when the season finally started, there was Messier, doing the honors.

The Rangers were unable to repeat the magic of 1994, finishing eighth in the Eastern Conference in the abbreviated regular season, though Messier led the team with 53 points in 46 games. They upset first-place Quebec in the opening round of the playoffs, but were swept by Philadelphia.

Messier turned 35 midway through the 1995-96 season, but showed he had lost none of his skills on the ice. He threatened Vic Hadfield's team record of 50 goals before ending up with 47, and topped the team with 99 points. He was the heart of the Rangers on the ice and off.

"There's no one on this team that he hasn't helped," goalie Mike Richter said. "He's a how-to book on success for hockey players. The reason he's so great is that he's probably the mentally strongest person I've ever been around."

By the 1995-96 season, Messier was recognized as the greatest leader in NHL history, if not in the history of sports. He was someone that teammates old and young looked up to.

"Anyone who gets a chance to play with Mark is going to learn from him," Graves said. "You don't become as great a player and as great a leader as Mark is without being a great person too. The thing that sets him apart from so many other superstars is how proficient he is at putting his teammates ahead of himself at all times. That's why he gets the respect he does. No one is forgotten—and he's very good at pulling everyone together."

The Rangers shocked their fans by dropping the first two games of the 1996 playoffs to Montreal at the Garden, then stunned the Canadiens by winning the next four. But after they lost in the second round to Pittsburgh, Smith decided to bring in some help for Messier—so he signed his long-time friend and running mate from Edmonton, a fellow named Wayne Gretzky.

Although the Messier-Gretzky combo gave the Rangers perhaps the best one-two punch at center in franchise history, the team finished fifth in the East in 1996-97 but ousted Florida and shocked New Jersey in the first two rounds. Messier started the play that led to Graves' series-winner in overtime in Game 5. But the Flyers ousted the Rangers in the Eastern Conference finals, cutting short the Rangers' dreams of another Cup.

Messier's contract expired after the 1996-97 season; however, most people assumed he and the Garden management wouldn't have any problems working out a new deal. But whereas MSG officials raced to sign Knicks' icon Patrick Ewing, they hemmed and hawed about a new deal with Messier. Much to the shock of Rangers fans (and players), the Vancouver Canucks swooped in and inked Messier to a three-year deal worth about $20 million.

The Canucks wanted Messier as much for his leadership as for his on-ice skills. While Messier's abilities in the locker room were as good as ever, his health wasn't—and neither was his supporting cast. After playing a full season in 1997-98 and finishing with 22 goals and 60 points, he was hampered by injuries in each of the next two seasons, missing a total of 39 games. The Canucks missed the playoffs all three seasons.

But so had the Rangers, who never recovered from the loss of their captain. When Glen Sather replaced Smith as general manager in June 2000, one of his first targets was Messier, who rejoined the Blueshirts six weeks later.

Coming back to the Rangers brought the Captain to tears.

"Once again, I've embarrassed myself in front of millions of people in America and Canada by crying," the always emotional Messier finally blurted out, along with an attempt at a laugh.

He came back to get the Rangers back to the playoffs.

"I'm not here to retire," Messier said. "I'm here to win, to play well, to do all the things I have done in the past."

Sather hoped bringing back Messier would help reverse the team's fortunes after three non-playoff seasons.

"In one conversation we had, Mark said to me he may not be able to carry a team to the Stanley Cup, but he can certainly lead," Sather told the assembled media. "And leading is what I'm looking for."

Messier, wearing the captain's *C* again, scored 24 goals and 67 points in 2000-01, his best offensive numbers since 1996-97. But injuries, especially to Richter, and a mix of veterans and kids that didn't click, kept the Rangers out of the playoffs again.

They stayed out of the playoffs in each of the next three seasons as well. Injuries cost Messier 41 games in 2001-02 and limited him to seven goals and 23 points. He stayed healthy in 2002-03 and 2003-04 and was a solid contributor, but as the 2003-04 season wound down and the team again dropped out of playoff contention, rumors of Messier's retirement began to swirl. He played what turned out to be his last NHL game on March 31, 2004, scoring a goal against Buffalo in a 4–3 loss at Madison Square Garden. After the game, he was saluted by the crowd, his teammates, and even the Sabres.

But the lack of success in his second stint with the Rangers still rankles Messier.

"I felt that we should have been able to compete better than we did, and that was a big disappointment," he says. "At the end of the day, nobody likes to be an underachiever, and I really felt we underachieved tremendously in those four years."

Messier officially retired in September 2005, and the Rangers wasted little time planning a suitable tribute to their captain. With the Oilers scheduled to come to the Garden that night, January 12, 2006, was designated Mark Messier Night.

"January 12 was a special night for me and my family," Messier says in looking back at the night No. 11 was raised to the Garden rafters. "It was basically the end of a chapter that was culminated with an on-ice celebration. When you try to condense 26 years of professional hockey into one night— it was pretty overwhelming. It was a tough night but a great night, one that none of us will ever forget."

As he was during his playing days, Messier is still very involved with charity work, especially in his support of the Tomorrow's Children's Fund for children with cancer and other serious blood disorders. He's been involved with Tomorrow's Children for more than 15 years, and on December 9,

2005, the Mark Messier Skyway opened at the Hackensack University Medical Center. It's an indoor hockey fantasyland complete with interactive games, Messier's personal memorabilia commemorating his career, and his personal video and photo libraries. It's intended to provide a brief distraction for the remarkable children of TCF and their families as they endure the everyday stresses associated with battling a life-threatening disease. He's also involved in planning the second edition of the Mark Messier Leadership Camp.

Hockey fans got to see Messier on TV during OLN's coverage of the 2006 Stanley Cup Finals, but he says he's not looking to be a full-time TV analyst.

"The NHL asked me to help OLN with their telecasts," he says of his appearances in the Finals. "It was a new venture for them, and so I felt I could help out the NHL for all they had done for me. I enjoyed it—it was a great experience to see that side of the game. It was fun. If I do any next year, it will be on a limited basis. I don't think I would want to do it full time. I have two small kids right now, and it would take a lot of time away from them.

"My older son, Lyon, is playing in a junior league in Texas. He's 19, and he's got a lot of talent—he's a right defenseman, like his grandfather. He's a great skater. He just has to learn how to play his position. If someone gives him that opportunity, I think he has a great shot to make the NHL."

Though Messier is also involved in planning the second edition of the Mark Messier Leadership Camp, it's not impossible that he could become involved in a different kind of leadership—following former teammates such as Wayne Gretzky and Kevin Lowe, who've found success coaching and managing NHL teams.

"There is some," he says of his ambitions to get back into hockey. "I'm not quite sure in what capacity right now. I expect within one more year, with the kids, I'm going to try to get back into the game in some regard, and I'll see what kind of opportunities there are out there."

The only problem for Messier the coach or Messier the general manager: There's only one Mark Messier, the Captain.

CHAPTER 19

STEPHANE MATTEAU

The Skinny

Stephane Matteau's first splash in sports came on the baseball field rather than on the ice. He was a member of the 1982 Rotary team that represented Canada in the Little League World Series. One of his teammates was future NHL star Pierre Turgeon.

But Matteau eventually turned to hockey, becoming a solid player with the Hull Olympiques of the Quebec Major Junior Hockey League. He scored 27 goals and 75 points with 113 penalty minutes in his second season with Hull, and the Calgary Flames selected him with the 25th overall pick in the 1987 Entry Draft.

The Flames were loaded with talent up front and were perfectly content to let Matteau continue to develop in junior hockey. He slipped to 17 goals and 57 points in an injury-filled 1987-88 season, but turned into a star in 1988-89, going 44-45-89 and piling up 202 penalty minutes, showing that he had both the skills and the grit to make it as a pro.

The Flames won the Stanley Cup in 1989 and had no burning need to bring up a rookie, even one with as much promise as Matteau. They sent him to Salt Lake City of the International League, where he had a solid pro debut season with 23 goals, 58 points, and 130 penalty minutes, showing again that he was more than willing to play a physical game and very capable of putting the puck in the net.

That combination was enough to earn Matteau a job with the Flames in 1990-91. Though he played mostly on the third and fourth lines, the first-year left wing had 15 goals and 18 assists in 78 games while contributing solid work as a checker. But he injured his thigh early in the 1991-92 season, and the Flames, still flush with forwards, traded him to Chicago in December.

The deal with Chicago turned out to be a boost for his career. Though Matteau played only 20 games after the deal because of the injury, coach Mike Keenan liked his grinding style of play enough to make him a regular during the Hawks' run to the Stanley Cup Finals. Matteau went 4-6-10 in 18 games while doing solid work as a checker and grinder. He had 15 goals for the Hawks in 79 games in 1992-93 and scored 15 in 60 contests as the 1993-94 season headed for the trading deadline.

Meanwhile, the Rangers led the Atlantic Division and were on top of the overall NHL standings, but straining to hold off New Jersey in both races. Keenan, now coaching the Rangers, wanted more grit, and GM Neil Smith made a number of deadline deals. Much to his surprise, one of the players headed for New York was Matteau.

"At first I was surprised [to be traded to New York] because the Rangers were in first place," he says. "We [the Blackhawks] had just played the Rangers about three weeks before I got traded. They looked to me like the best team at the time, and I didn't think they needed to make changes. When I first heard I was being traded to New York, I said, 'I'm just going to be a spare player. I'll be on the fifth line, just waiting in case someone gets hurt.'"

Matteau and Brian Noonan came to the Rangers from Chicago, but the price was steep: Talented young winger Tony Amonte headed to the Windy City. "I knew Keenan in Chicago," says Matteau. "I played for him when we lost the Stanley Cup Finals against Pittsburgh in 1992. I know Tony Amonte was the big prize for the Rangers at the time, but Keenan knew what type of players Brian Noonan and I were, and they paid a big price. But in the end, it benefited the Rangers at the time. Tony was having a great career at the time, and he's still playing. It worked perfectly for both teams."

Matteau didn't know many of his new teammates, but he wasted little time making an impression.

"In my first game, we were down a goal in Calgary, and we pulled the goalie," he remembers. "Coach Keenan sent me onto the ice, and I scored,

Notes on Stephane Matteau

Name:	Stephane Matteau
Born:	September 2, 1969 (Rouyn-Noranda, Quebec)
Position:	Left wing
Height:	6-foot-3
Playing Weight:	215 lbs
How Acquired:	From Chicago with Brian Noonan for Tony Amonte and the rights to Matt Oates—March 21, 1994
Years with Rangers:	1993-94 to 1995-96
Stats as Ranger:	85 games, 11 goals, 10 assists, 21 points, 49 PIM
Uniform Number:	32

so that was a pretty good debut for me and the Rangers. It made me feel a little more at home. I scored the next night too against the Oilers in Edmonton. After that, I was pretty much set on the team."

The Setting

The Rangers did hold off the Devils to win the division title and finished first overall, winning the Presidents' Trophy for the second time in three years. They swept the New York Islanders and wiped out the Washington Capitals in five games.

That set up a matchup against New Jersey in the Eastern Conference finals. The Devils, unlike the Rangers' two previous opponents, had no intention of going quietly. They stunned the Garden crowd by winning the series opener 4–3 in double overtime. The Rangers dominated Game 2, winning 4–0 before the series moved to the Meadowlands, where Matteau was again the hero.

"Everyone knew we and the Devils were probably the best two teams in the league at the time, and it was a shame that series wasn't the Stanley Cup

Finals," he remembers. "In the first game against New Jersey, I had probably the worst game of my life in the playoffs. I made a lot of mistakes, and we lost in double overtime. I felt pretty lousy for the next two games, so when I scored in New Jersey, that was a huge release. That put us up 2–1 in the series."

But the Devils rebounded, evening the series with a 3–1 win at home and shocking the Garden again with a convincing 4–1 win in Game 5.

That sent the series back to the Meadowlands for Game 6, and the Devils came out like a team that was headed for the Stanley Cup Finals, taking an early 2–0 lead. But the Rangers, despite being badly outplayed, managed to regroup.

"To me, Game 6 against New Jersey was the most thrilling game I ever experienced," Matteau says. "Knowing we were down 3–2 in the series and then 2–0 in the game, we were starting to realize that one game and our dreams of winning the Stanley Cup would be over. The whole thing seemed like it was falling apart, and it looked like we were ready to throw in the white towel. Then Mr. Messier–I call him Mr. Messier because I have the utmost respect for him—really took charge. It was incredible to watch and to be part of it."

Messier, who had publicly guaranteed a victory, backed up his words by scoring three goals and setting up another as the Rangers came from behind for a 4–2 victory that sent the series to a seventh game. It was a night Rangers fans will never forget. Neither will Matteau.

The Game of My Life
1994 EASTERN CONFERENCE FINALS, GAME 7
RANGERS VS. NEW JERSEY DEVILS—MAY 27, 1994

"The atmosphere had totally changed from Game 6, going from knowing we could lose, to Game 7 and knowing we could not lose," Matteau remembers more than a decade later. "The Devils had one chance to put us down, and there was no way that team was going to put us down on a second straight night. The atmosphere was great. We could smell the Stanley Cup.

"But we still had to beat the Devils. The advantage was on our side. The feeling was back on our side, but we still had to defeat them, and they were a great team. They didn't roll over. [Martin] Brodeur was a great young

Stephane Matteau. *Courtesy of Ernie Fitzsimmons*

goalie; tough, he was very calm, and the Devils rebounded well after such a huge loss. It's not easy to lose a game like that at home, but they came back strong and fought till the end.

"Brian Leetch scored in the second period, but as the minutes were counting down, I was thinking, 'It's not over.' We had blown a few leads in the third period, and when [Valeri] Zelepukin scored [with seven seconds left in regulation time], I was like, 'Here we go again—another dramatic ending.' But that's why the Rangers [management] had brought all those leaders to the team—Kevin Lowe, Craig MacTavish, Glenn Anderson—guys who had won four, five Stanley Cups. Usually you have one, but we had five or six guys who had been down that road before and had overcome a lot of adversity. They stood up—not only Mark Messier, but all those guys stood up and started talking, and we all bought into their motivational speech. It was a great feeling. Everyone realized how close we were to making the Stanley Cup Final, but we had a long way to go.

"The first overtime was crazy. There were a few 2-on-1s, 3-on-1s. Usually in overtime, you try to close the gap—2-on-2s, 3-on-3s. But there were a few 2-on-1s on both sides, and no one could score.

"Between the first and second overtimes—I usually took my skates off between periods and retaped my stick. I was retying my skates and one of my laces broke. So everyone was on the ice, and I was alone with Eddie Olczyk, who didn't play that night. In Game 3, when I scored my first double-overtime goal, he touched my stick and he kissed it. So with both of us sitting alone in the dressing room, I kind of panicked because I needed to go onto the ice. I said, 'Eddie, I need you to talk to my stick, and whatever it takes, do it.' He touched my stick, kissed it, and hugged it. I said, 'I'm going to score,' and sure enough, on my second shift, I scored again. I kind of had the feeling, like any other kid, that 'I'm going to score the big goal to get us into the Stanley Cup Final.' When it happened, I was shocked and surprised and overwhelmed.

"On my second shift, the puck went up in the air [into the Devils' zone], and someone lost track [of me], and I was facing the puck all the time. The puck went into the corner. I got it and tried to make one move on the short side. [Devils defenseman Scott] Niedermayer was hugging me, holding my arm. I kind of tried to put the puck in front of the net while I was along the far post, and it was one of the luckiest bounces ever on my part. I saw the puck going in very slowly. I was the first one to see the puck go into the net. It was one of the greatest feelings of my life.

"At the time, I didn't know who had scored—[Esa] Tikkanen [who had shot the puck into the zone] could have touched it. But I didn't care. We were going to go to the Stanley Cup Finals, and I was going to have a shot to win my first Stanley Cup."

Afterword

The Rangers faced the Vancouver Canucks in the Finals, and after four games, the series appeared to be all but over. Vancouver won the opener, but the Rangers took the next three games and came back to Madison Square Garden ready to end a 54-year championship drought.

"We were cruising, we were up 3–1 against Vancouver," Matteau says. "A lot of their fans, after we won the two games [Games 3 and 4] in Vancouver, their fans started throwing things on the ice. We were under control, and we were going to win Game 5 in New York. But we kind of took it easy—we were thinking about the parties afterward, and Vancouver won the next two to set up Game 7 in New York.

"The last 10 minutes [with the Rangers leading 3–2] felt like they were going to take 10 years. I was with Brian Noonan on the bench, and I told him with nine or 10 minutes left, 'After we win, let's take a picture—let's be next to each other in the team picture.' He said, 'Let's win the game first.' I said, 'You're right. There's still too much time to go.'

"When the final buzzer went off, it was a huge relief. After two months of hearing about the 54-year drought, you buy into the big drama of the New York fans, I was pleased first of all for the New York fans, to win their first Stanley Cup in so many years. Afterward, I realized it was my first Stanley Cup. It was a great, great feeling.

"The parties lasted into the summer."

Unfortunately, neither Matteau nor the Rangers were able to recapture the magic of 1994. The lockout shortened the season to 48 games, and the Rangers struggled to merely make the playoffs. Matteau struggled too.

"It was a different season the next year—we had the lockout, and we wound up finishing eighth," he says. "That's when I realized that they went out there to win the Stanley Cup for the first time in many years, and they paid a big price. We had an older team, and the following year the lockout didn't help. Keenan left, Colin Campbell came in [as coach], and things went wrong from the first day. I don't know if I was out of shape or took life for granted. I made a lot of mistakes, and things didn't go my way. After the playoffs, I didn't play as good as I could. I got traded."

The Rangers sent Matteau to St. Louis midway through the 1995-96 season, and the Blues sent him to San Jose in the summer of 1997. Matteau had five productive seasons with the Sharks before Keenan, who had taken over as coach of Florida, reacquired him after the 2001-02 season. After scoring just four goals in 52 games with Florida, he retired in the summer of 2003 after 13 seasons in the NHL.

Matteau, now a travel agent in Montreal, left the NHL with no regrets.

"I played 13 years, and I'm very proud of my career," he says. "I won the Stanley Cup. People in New York remember me—every time I go to New York, it's always a huge event. I know I didn't play a long time for the Rangers, but I think I left a big impact. I'm still a big hockey fan, and I have a lot of respect for all the teams I played for. The Rangers were great to me and my family, and I love going back to New York. I have only good memories of being a Ranger."

CHAPTER 20

MIKE
RICHTER

The Skinny

Mike Richter has more memorable moments in his career than any goaltender in Rangers history. He won a Stanley Cup, was the MVP of the 1996 World Cup, won the goalie skills competition at the 1992 All-Star Game and the MVP Award at the 1994 game, and played for the U.S. Olympic Team three times, winning a silver medal in 2002. That's quite a resume.

Richter was born in the Philadelphia suburb of Abington, Pennsylvania, and played for the Philadelphia Jr. Flyers. Luckily for the Rangers, he came to their attention while playing at Northwood Prep, a Lake Placid school known for its hockey teams. Two weeks after graduation in 1985, the Rangers grabbed him with their second pick in the NHL Entry Draft.

With John Vanbiesbrouck just starting to emerge as a top-flight NHL goaltender (he would win the Vezina Trophy in 1985-86), there was no pressure to rush Richter to the NHL. He had already decided to play at the University of Wisconsin, where he won 14 games as a freshman and made the All-WCHA Second Team as a sophomore.

Richter left school before the 1987-88 season to join the U.S. National Team in preparation for the 1998 Winter Olympics in Calgary. One of his Team USA teammates was a young defenseman named Brian Leetch, whose career would be intertwined with Richter's for well over a decade. The two would also become fast friends.

Richter split four decisions at the Olympics and turned pro after the Games, going 16-5-0 for the Colorado Rangers of the International League and winning five of eight playoff decisions. He was the No. 1 goaltender with the renamed Denver Rangers the following season, going 23-23-0 and impressing the Rangers enough to earn a start in Game 4 of the playoffs against Pittsburgh. The Rangers lost, but new GM Neil Smith and coach Roger Neilson must have been impressed because Richter came to the NHL to stay in 1989-90.

Richter went 12-5-5 as a rookie with a 3.00 goals-against average, gradually earning more time behind Vanbiesbrouck. By 1990-91, Neilson was alternating the two. The duo, tabbed "VanRichterBrouck" by the media, set an NHL record in 1991-92 when they alternated starts in 76 consecutive games.

The Rangers won the Presidents' Trophy that same season by finishing first overall for the first time in 50 years. Richter got the bulk of the work in the playoffs, and the Rangers appeared to be on the way to dethroning the defending the Cup-champion Pittsburgh Penguins until Ron Francis beat Richter with a 65-footer late in Game 4 to force overtime. Pittsburgh won the game in OT, and the Rangers never rebounded, losing the series in six games.

Richter and Vanbiesbrouck shared the crease again in 1992-93, but the team struggled down the stretch and missed the playoffs. With expansion coming that summer, Smith had to choose between his goaltenders; he knew he would only be able to keep one. Smith opted to keep Richter, giving him the No. 1 job for the first time.

With Richter getting the bulk of the work, the Rangers grabbed first place early in the season and never let go. The former crease mates were reunited as teammates with the Eastern Conference squad at the All-Star Game at Madison Square Garden, where Richter won the MVP award in a 9–8 victory with a spectacular second-period showing in which he made 18 saves, including four on Vancouver star Pavel Bure. "It's overwhelming," Richter said after the game. "I'm very, very happy. You play 20 minutes, that's all. I don't think it was a landslide victory for me to get the MVP."

Richter finished with a team-record 42 wins, and the Rangers finished first overall for the second time in three years, then swept the New York Islanders and beat the Washington Capitals in five games. That set up a

Notes on Mike Richter

Name:	Mike Richter
Born:	September 22, 1966 (Abington, Pennsylvania)
Position:	Goaltender
Height:	5-foot-11
Playing Weight:	185 pounds
How Acquired:	Selected in the second round, 28th overall, in the 1985 Entry Draft
Years with Rangers:	1987-88 to 2002-03
Stats as Ranger:	666 games, 2.89 goals-against average, 24 shutouts, 301-258-73
Uniform Number:	35
Accomplishments:	Played in NHL All-Star Game 1992, 1994 (MVP), 2000
	Rangers MVP Award 1999-2000, 2001-02
	Players' Player Award 1999-2000
	Crumb Bum Award 1996-97
	Frank Boucher Trophy 1998-99, 1999-2000, 2001-02
	Good Guy Award 1990-91
	Rangers Fan Club Rookie of the Year 1990-91

semifinal series against New Jersey, which had finished second to the Rangers in both the Atlantic Division and the Eastern Conference. New Jersey led the series 3–2 and appeared to be headed for the Finals when they took a 2-0 lead late into the second period of Game 6 at the Meadowlands. The only reason the game was close was Richter, who made fabulous save after fabulous save to keep his team alive. "He kept us in the game," said Messier, who rallied the Rangers with three goals and an assist for a 4–2 victory. Richter came within 7.7 seconds of a shutout in Game 7 before Valeri

Zelepukin tied the game at 1–1, but Stephane Matteau's game-winner in the second overtime sent the Rangers to the Stanley Cup Finals for the first time in 15 years.

The Setting

The Rangers and Vancouver split the first two games of the Finals at Madison Square Garden as Vancouver rallied for a 3–2 win in the opener, and the Rangers rebounded with a 3–1 win in Game 2.

The series moved to Vancouver for Game 3, and the Canucks started fast, with Bure scoring 62 seconds into the game. But Richter was flawless the rest of the way, finishing with 24 saves as the Rangers rode a two-goal performance by Brian Leetch to a 5–1 victory.

With the series now 2–1, Game 4 figured to be pivotal. A Ranger win would put them within a victory of ending the longest Stanley Cup drought in NHL history. A Vancouver victory would even the series and give the Canucks momentum.

The Game of My Life
1994 STANLEY CUP FINALS, GAME 4
RANGERS AT VANCOUVER CANUCKS—JUNE 7, 1994

"They got a couple of early goals on us. [Richter was beaten by Trevor Linden on a power play at 13:25 of the first period and by Cliff Ronning less than three minutes later.] They came out flying and were really putting a lot of pressure on us.

"The turning point of the game came early in the second period, when Bure came racing in and got hauled down—I don't know who did it. The ref [Terry Gregson] awarded him a penalty shot.

"Any situation in a game—any shift—can be a momentum-changer. I knew that this was a chance for a major change in momentum. They had the chance to give us a knockout blow—it would have been tough for us to come back after allowing another goal. At the same time, it would be a big boost for us if I could stop him.

"Bure was a great scorer having a great playoff. He had had a lot of chances—a lot of breakaways—and he scored against me in Game 3. Oddly

Mike Richter. *Courtesy of the John Halligan Collection*

enough, when I think about it, I wasn't thinking about having seen his breakaway moves in the All-Star Game. I knew he had a lot of speed and a number of moves.

"You can't predict what great players are going to do. You almost have to blank out your mind. He was too good a player for me to think that he would only have one move. He wanted to keep his options open, and so did I. I wanted to come out quickly to take his options away, because I knew he would come with a lot of speed. I had to match his speed going forward as I started going backward, and I knew I had to time it right.

"There was a lot of adrenaline flowing. I had to make sure to control myself and not react too quickly. I couldn't even see the puck as he was coming down the ice, but I could feel it. It seemed like the moment was suspended in time.

"He faked to his backhand, went to his forehand, and I got my right leg out and stopped him.

"The sound in the building was something else. Everything suddenly went quiet—it felt like there was a big gasp and a lot of the air went out of their fans. I could feel the energy boost in our guys too. We tied it late in the second period [on a goal by Sergei Zubov] and got a couple of goals in the third period [by Alexei Kovalev and Steve Larmer] to win the game 4–2.

"The funny thing was, I wasn't thinking of having faced Bure during the All-Star Game. JD [Rangers TV analyst John Davidson] told me later that Bure used the same move that he had tried at the All-Star Game.

"I don't know if it was the biggest save of my career. But it was a big one, and it was my contribution to the win."

Afterword

The Rangers went back to the Garden dreaming of winning the Cup at home, but allowed five goals in the third period and lost 6–3. "I think we were nervous," says Richter. "We might have been thinking about what it would be like to win the Cup before we won it. The fourth win is always the hardest."

Vancouver won Game 6, 4–1, but with Richter making 28 saves, the Rangers held on for a 3–2 win in Game 7 to win their first Stanley Cup since 1940.

Richter remembers hearing the final buzzer and realizing that the Rangers were Stanley Cup champions. "To realize that we had won, how hard we had worked, and that it had all come true—I've never seen anything like it. Marching down the Canyon of Heroes [in the ticker-tape parade that followed]—it was a special time and place."

Leetch got the Conn Smythe Trophy as playoff MVP, but Richter was every bit as much a hero. He and his teammates were looking forward to defending the Cup, but the 1994 lockout short-circuited everything. Instead of battling for first place, the Rangers barely finished eighth, and though they upset first-place Quebec in the first round, a second-round loss to Philadelphia left a bitter taste all-around.

"I think that was one of the biggest disappointments of my career—not being able to repeat," he says.

But any doubts about Richter's brilliance were pushed aside in September 1996, when he led Team USA to the championship in the first World Cup of Hockey, earning MVP honors after his play in goal helped the Americans beat Team Canada in the third and deciding game. That fall, he excelled again as the Rangers beat Florida and upset first-place New Jersey to make the Eastern Conference finals before losing to Philadelphia.

The Rangers hit the skids after the 1997 playoffs, but Richter continued to excel. He surpassed the 200-win mark in 1997-98; moved past Hall of Famer Ed Giacomin with his 272nd career win, a 2–1 overtime triumph over Toronto on January 18, 2001; led Team USA to the silver medal at the 2002 Winter Olympics; and earned his 300th career victory by making 29 saves in a 3–2 overtime victory over Phoenix on October 28, 2003.

However, that turned out to be the next-to-last victory of his career. Richter had survived surgery to both knees and returned without missing a beat. But he sustained a fractured skull and a serious concussion when he was hit in the head by a slap shot from Atlanta's Chris Tamer on March 22, 2002, ending his season.

Richter battled back and returned to the lineup in time for the 2002-03 season, hoping to lead the team back to the playoffs and help groom rookie Dan Blackburn as his eventual replacement. Though he was able to join the 300-win club, he sustained another concussion on November 5, 2002, when he was bumped in the head by Edmonton's Todd Marchant during a third-period scramble. Richter finished the game, recording his 301st career victory, but it also turned out to be his last. He suffered from postconcussion syndrome and never played again. "I really miss the competition," he says of being forced to leave the Rangers after 14 seasons.

Richter officially retired before the 2003-04 season and was honored on February 4, 2004, when his No. 35 was raised to the Garden rafters on Mike Richter Night. It's an honor he'll savor for the rest of his life. Dressed in a suit and tie, instead of his blue uniform, he led the Rangers onto the ice for one final time.

"It's really a special thing to walk into a building like the Garden and see a confirmation of what you were able to achieve as a player," he says today of seeing his number hanging next to those of Rod Gilbert, Ed Giacomin, and Mark Messier. "It's something I really cherish every time I see it."

These days, Richter is husband, a father, and a college student—he's a year away from getting his undergraduate degree at Yale. He served as an assistant coach for the Bulldogs in 2004-05—"I helped out with the goalies and really enjoyed it," he says.

He may be a Yalie now, but Richter will be a Ranger always.

CHAPTER 21

BRIAN LEETCH

The Skinny

The Rangers had to wait a little longer than they would have liked for Brian Leetch to arrive. He turned out to be well worth it. Then–general manager Craig Patrick drafted Leetch with the ninth overall pick in the 1986 draft. But Leetch decided he'd be better off playing in college and opted to attend Boston College.

Leetch played under legendary coach Len Ceglarski, whose only regret about having Leetch was that the young defenseman stayed only one season. But what a season: Leetch went 9-38-47 in 37 games for the Eagles, was the Hockey East Rookie of the Year and Player of the Year, and became the first freshman to be named a finalist for the Hobey Baker Award as college hockey's top player.

"He was always a great team player," Ceglarski remembered years later when asked about Leetch as a collegian. "He was probably the quietest guy in the locker room—he just went about his business. On the ice, he always had great vision. He had that innate sense of passing the puck to the right player at the right time, and he seldom missed the net with his shots."

After a season at Boston College, Leetch left to become the captain of the U.S. Olympic team for the 1988 games in Calgary. It's the same road his father, Jack, had taken before him—Jack Leetch was also an All-American at Boston College and played for the U.S. national team.

201

But Brian's road to NHL stardom still had a few potholes ahead. He had been on the ice for only about 20 seconds at the 1987 Olympic festival when he injured his left knee and wound up spending much of the pre-Olympic schedule on crutches.

Leetch finally arrived in the Big Apple after the Olympics ended. He was an immediate hit, scoring 14 points in 17 regular-season games, then winning the Calder Trophy in 1988-89 by putting up 23 goals and 71 points.

However, the injury bug bit Leetch again in 1989-90. While sparking the team to its first division title in 48 years, Leetch eluded two Toronto Maple Leafs with a nifty fake in the corner, only to have his left leg slide out from under him and into the boards. That snapped both his ankle and the team's playoff hopes—they lost to Washington in the second round.

Leetch rebounded with a 16-goal, 88-point season in 1990-91 and then blossomed into a 102-point scorer the following season, following the arrival of Mark Messier on Broadway.

"I think I learned a more businesslike approach on the ice from Mark," Leetch said years later. "I learned not to get too high when you win a game and that when you lose, hey, you're still a good player."

Leetch and Messier quickly developed the kind of chemistry that coaches dream of. Messier won the Hart Trophy as league MVP, while Leetch became the first Ranger since Harry Howell—25 years earlier—to take home the Norris Trophy as the NHL's top defenseman. The Rangers finished first in the regular-season standings for the first time in 50 years, but were beaten by the defending-champion Pittsburgh Penguins in the second round.

The 1992-93 season turned out to be a painful one. In December, Leetch went into the boards after missing a check and damaged nerves in his neck, shoulder, and arm. Three months later, he slipped and broke his right ankle in an away-from-the rink mishap. With their defensive leader out for more than half the season, the Rangers missed the playoffs.

But then-general manager Neil Smith said the broken ankle may have been a benefit to Leetch in the long run.

"I think it matured him some," Smith said. "I think he felt responsible for what happened in 1993 and that he was committed to being the best he could be the next year."

Notes on Brian Leetch

Name:	Brian Leetch
Born:	March 3, 1968 (Corpus Christi, Texas)
Position:	Defense
Height:	6-foot-1
Playing weight:	190 pounds
How acquired:	Rangers' first-round pick (ninth overall) in 1986 Entry Draft
Years with Rangers:	1987-88 through 2003-04
Stats as Ranger:	1,129 games played, 240 goals, 741 assists, 981 points, 525 PIM
Accomplishments:	Calder Trophy 1988-89
	Norris Trophy 1991-92, 1996-97
	Conn Smythe Trophy 1993-94
	First-Team All-Star 1991-92, 1996-97
	Second-Team All-Star 1993-94, 1995-96
	All-Star Game 1990, 1991, 1992, 1994, 1996, 1997, 1998, 2001, 2002 (unable to play due to injury in 1993 and 2003)

With new coach Mike Keenan behind the bench, Leetch blossomed into a more complete defenseman in 1993-94. His play in his own zone improved, and he and partner Jeff Beukeboom were one of the best defense combos in the NHL. The Rangers started fast and kept going, finishing first overall for the second time in three seasons. He finished with 23 goals and 79 points, but his contributions went far beyond his offensive numbers.

"He took his game to another level," Messier said of Leetch's play. "He can control the game like the greats of the past."

The Setting

The Rangers had no trouble in the first two rounds, sweeping the Islanders and polishing off Washington in five games. They had to rally to beat the Devils in seven games, winning Game 7 in double overtime. That left only the Vancouver Canucks standing between the Rangers and the end of the longest championship drought in NHL history.

Leetch set up two goals in the opener, but Vancouver tied the game with 60 seconds left in regulation and won in overtime. He scored an empty-netter to clinch a 3–1 win in the second game and then notched two goals in the Rangers' 5–1 victory in Game 3. But those performances were just a warm-up for Game 4. With his team down 2–0 after one period, Leetch scored at 4:03 in the second period, set up a goal by Messier with 16 seconds left in the middle period to tie the score, and assisted on Alexei Kovalev's go-ahead goal and Steve Larmer's insurance tally in the third for a 4–2 victory.

But with just one win separating them from the Cup, the Rangers suddenly went flat. With a sellout crowd at Madison Square Garden chanting, "We want the Cup!" the Canucks spoiled the party by holding Leetch scoreless and scoring five times in the third period for a 6–3 victory. Two nights later, they evened the series with a 4–1 win.

That sent the two teams back across the country for Game 7—the first time the Rangers had ever played a Game 7 in the finals at home. It was a night Leetch, his teammates, and every Rangers fan will never forget.

The Game of My Life

STANLEY CUP FINALS, GAME 7
VANCOUVER CANUCKS AT RANGERS—JUNE 14, 1994

"We led the series 3–1, we lost Game 5 at the Garden and Game 6 in Vancouver. But we were still confident. We had finished first overall and had worked hard all year for the home-ice advantage, and I thought we had played well in every game except Game 6. Having Game 7 at home was a big thing. I also heard the Canucks talking about how hard it was going to be to win three in a row. So I felt pretty confident.

"The easiest part of a game like that is going out on the ice for your shift—moving the puck and getting involved in the play. The hardest part is sitting on the bench between shifts. That's when you get nervous.

Brian Leetch. *Courtesy of John Kreiser*

"It helped a lot that we were able to score first. It's always easier playing with a lead. Sergei Zubov came down the middle, and (goalie) Kirk McLean went down, thinking that he would shoot. 'Gravy' (Adam Graves) was screening him, and I was on the left. Sergei fed me the puck, and I had a half a net to shoot into.

"Gravy scored again a few minutes later on the power play, so we had a two-goal lead after the first period. We led 3–1 going into the third, but Trevor Linden scored again for them to make it 3–2. Nothing came easy.

"Those last 10 minutes seemed to last forever—although I'm sure for them, it must have seemed like the time was flying. That's about when the impact—the fact that we were playing in Game 7 of the Stanley Cup Finals—really kicked in. Mike Richter made a bunch of great saves, and we got a couple of good bounces.

"In the final seconds, Steve Larmer dumped the puck down the ice. I started to celebrate—I jumped on Mike and gave him a hug. But then they called it icing and put some time back on the clock. When I saw it was just 1.1 seconds, though, I wasn't worried. I felt that wasn't enough time for them to do anything, and we had Craig MacTavish taking the draw.

"When they dropped the puck again and the buzzer went off, I went over to Mike again and said, 'This one really counts.'

"We had played so much hockey and had so much emotion—the semifinals and finals both went seven games—that the biggest thing I felt after the game was relief. I went home that night and went to bed feeling tired, but when I got up the next day, I began to feel the excitement. We spent the next few days celebrating."

Afterword

The days after the Rangers' first Stanley Cup triumph in 54 years were a whirlwind for the Blueshirts, and especially for Leetch, who became the first U.S.-born player to take home the Conn Smythe Trophy as playoff MVP after leading all postseason scorers with 34 points, including 11 goals. The Rangers were the toast of the town—Leetch even made an appearance on *Late Night with David Letterman* along with Messier, and the team was honored with a ticker-tape parade in the Canyon of Heroes.

The Rangers' defense of the Cup was delayed more than three months by the lockout that cut the 1994-95 season down to 48 games. The Rangers struggled for most of the season, finishing eighth in the Eastern Conference. An upset of the first-place Quebec Nordiques in the opening round gave the Rangers and their fans some hope for a repeat, but the Philadelphia Flyers quickly dashed those hopes. They swept the Rangers in four games, even though Leetch played one of the greatest individual games by a Ranger in Game 2, scoring all three of his team's goals, including one with 8:41 left in regulation that forced overtime. But the Flyers got the game-winner 25 seconds into the extra period and then cruised to wins in Games 3 and 4 at the Garden. After the season, Leetch was named to the second All-Star Team.

Leetch averaged more than a point a game in 1995-96 and then won his second Norris Trophy in 1996-97 by scoring 20 goals and 78 points while playing brilliant two-way hockey. The Rangers, with Wayne Gretzky joining Messier and Leetch, beat Florida and upset first-place New Jersey to advance to the Eastern Conference semifinals against the Flyers. But after splitting the first two games in Philadelphia, the Rangers dropped three straight to come up short in their bid to get back to the finals.

Messier left as a free agent after the season, and Leetch inherited the captain's C, but something was obviously missing. He fell off to 50 points in 1997-98 and 55 in 1998-99, after which Gretzky retired. Injuries limited Leetch to 50 games and 26 points in 1999-2000, and even though his offensive touch returned in 2000-01—he had 21 goals and 79 points—the Rangers continued to miss the playoffs. The memories of Leetch's accomplishments began to fade.

"When you have a good team, it's easier for an individual to get noticed," Leetch says. "I had personal success before and after 1994. But with a team that good, I got more notice."

Despite the return of Messier in 2000, the Rangers continued to struggle. With the team's playoff-less streak in its seventh season and the nucleus getting older every day, general manager Glen Sather started dealing off some of his veterans. That included Leetch, who was dealt to Toronto on March 3 for a prospect and a draft pick. If there was any doubt that Leetch could still play, he quickly dispelled it with the Leafs, averaging a point a game in 15 games.

When the lockout that wiped out the 2004-05 season was settled, Rangers fans were hopeful that the best defenseman in team history would come back home. Instead, he signed with the Boston Bruins. There's little doubt that when Leetch's career is over, his No. 2 jersey will join Rod Gilbert's No. 7, Ed Giacomin's No. 1, Messier's No. 11, and Richter's No. 35 in the Garden rafters. He's second in games played (1,129) and points (981), first in assists (741) and goals by a defenseman (240), and is still the only defenseman in team history to break the 100-point mark in a single season. And no Rangers fan will ever forget the sight of Leetch holding the Conn Smythe Trophy after the greatest night in New York hockey history.

CHAPTER 22

NEIL SMITH

The Skinny

The Rangers and New York Islanders have had few dealings over the years—they've never made a direct trade. But it was Islander-trained Neil Smith who did something no Ranger executive had done since the era of Lester Patrick and Frank Boucher: bring the Stanley Cup back to New York.

Smith starred as a defenseman at Western Michigan University, earning All-America honors as a freshman and being named team captain the next year.

The Islanders drafted Smith in the 13th round of the 1974 Amateur Draft and waited for him to finish school. But after a couple of years in the International Hockey League, Smith decided his path to the NHL would be smoother in the front office than on the ice. He joined the Isles' scouting department during the 1980-81 season.

Smith may have been young, but he learned a lot from general manager Bill Torrey and coach Al Arbour, the men behind the Isles' dynasty. Mostly, he learned the value of a winning environment.

"They had Al and Bill, and they really had a winning culture," Smith says of his days on the Island. "That's where I got it from, working for those guys for a couple of years. You learn what it takes."

Two years and two Stanley Cups later, Smith moved along with Isles' exec Jim Devellano to the Detroit Red Wings, then one of the NHL's weakest teams. He started as director of professional scouting, then became director of their farm system, then director of scouting and GM of the AHL's Adirondack Red Wings, who won two Calder Cups on Smith's watch.

At age 35, Smith was one of hockey's top young executive talents. But the Rangers stunned everyone when they named Smith as their general manager on July 17, 1989, not long after GM Phil Esposito had been let go after the team was swept by the Pittsburgh Penguins in the opening round of the playoffs.

Smith had a big task ahead of him.

"There was a lot of work to be done to build the organization back up," he says. "I was lucky because I was left with a number of really good players for the future. Brian Leetch and Tony Granato had just finished their rookie seasons—Leetch was the rookie of the year. John Vanbiesbrouck was a very good goaltender, and [Mike] Richter was on the horizon. We had Ulf Dahlen, who was a marketable guy and a really good player, and Tomas Sandstrom. Tony Amonte had already been drafted. So we had quite a bit of future talent there—maybe not at the time, you didn't know it was going to be that good, but it went on to be good. From a player personnel standpoint, it wasn't that bad. But what was needed—we had no coach, no assistant coaches, no farm team or coaches. A lot of changes had to be made."

Smith wasted no time making them. He hired Roger Neilson, who had led the Vancouver Canucks to the 1982 Stanley Cup Finals, as his new coach. The Smith-Neilson combination paid immediate dividends as the Rangers won their first division title in 48 years.

"Roger did a great job," says Smith. "But we were also lucky because the Patrick Division wasn't very strong. We won the title with 85 points—but still, we won it."

The Rangers beat the Islanders in the opening round, but the loss of Leetch, who broke his ankle in a late-season game at Toronto, proved to be too much as the Washington Capitals downed the Blueshirts in six games in the Patrick Division finals.

The division improved the next season. "We had the exact same record," Smith says, "but we finished second. Pittsburgh won the division and won the Cup."

Smith knew more changes had to be made, not only on the ice but in the locker room as well.

Notes on Neil Smith

Name:	Neil Smith
Born:	January 9, 1954 (Toronto, Ontario)
Position:	General manager (July 1989–June 1992); president and general manager (June 1992–June 2000)
Joined Rangers:	July 17, 1989
Years with Rangers:	1989-90 to March 28, 2000
Stats as Ranger:	857 games; 393 wins; 347 losses; 117 ties
Accomplishments:	Built first Ranger team to win Stanley Cup since 1940

"We made a lot of changes because I didn't like the attitude of the organization," he says. "The environment was like, 'We're used to this. It's OK to lose in the first or second round. I was [angry] because I wanted to keep moving ahead, and it seemed like losing didn't bother them that much. So I went out and made the changes."

The biggest change actually didn't take place until the 1991-92 season started. Smith wanted to bring a winning attitude to New York, so he went to the Edmonton Oilers, who still had many of the key members of their 1980s dynasty team on the roster and were looking to cut payroll. On October 4, 1991, Smith made one of the biggest trades in Rangers history by sending Bernie Nicholls, Steven Rice, and Louie DeBrusk to the Oilers for Mark Messier.

"Losing is a culture, and it's a hard thing to change," Smith says. "That's the reason I brought in Messier. We had to change the culture of the team—change what it means to be a Ranger and what the expectations are that are put upon the players. Mark really changed the culture."

But not only could Messier lead, he could still play, too. With The Captain in the middle of the top line, the Rangers started fast and never let up. The Rangers finished No. 1 in the overall standings for the first time since 1941-42, then outlasted New Jersey in seven games to advance to the division finals against Pittsburgh.

"That was a team we thought really had a great chance to go all the way, especially after [Mario] Lemieux was hurt," says Smith. "But then we had that horrible loss [a Game 4 loss in which Mike Richter muffed a 65-footer and the Penguins went on to win in overtime]. We just couldn't recover, and they went on to beat us and capture the Cup because they knew how to do it and we didn't at that time. That was very disappointing."

But not as disappointing as 1992-93, when the Rangers went from Presidents' Trophy winners to missing the playoffs.

"That year was probably the most disappointing of all the time I was there," says Smith, who added the title of team president to his GM portfolio after the 1991-92 season. "It was a team that was definitely a contender to win the Cup, and instead, we missed the playoffs."

Nothing went right. Leetch was injured twice and missed nearly half the season. Messier wasn't up to his Hart Trophy performance of the previous season, and the magic of 1991-92 was gone. Neilson was axed at midseason, but it didn't help.

"It was just a mess," Smith says. "There were a lot of injuries and a lot of dissension—with Roger, it was 'Did Messier want him, or didn't he?' and a lot of other crap going on.

"The next summer, we made a lot of changes again."

Smith actually started before the 1992-93 season ended. He brought in Mike Keenan as coach in April 1993. During the summer, backup goaltender Glenn Healy replaced Vanbiesbrouck, who Smith knew he would lose in the expansion draft, and Smith continued tinkering to find the right blend.

The Rangers did win a cup before the 1993-94 season even started; they went to London and took the "Mustard Cup" by knocking off the Toronto Maple Leafs twice in a tournament sponsored by French's. With Messier and Leetch healthy, Richter ensconced as the No. 1 goaltender, and Adam Graves enjoying a career season, the Rangers began the season on a tear and kept going.

"I think the players all wanted to redeem themselves from the year they had before," Smith says. "And with Keenan, the new sheriff, in town, they were really pushed, right from the get-go, to have a good year. I had to get someone like Keenan, because this was a star-studded veteran team that needed someone hard-nosed to run it."

Neil Smith. *Courtesy of John Kreiser*

The dealing continued. In November, Smith added Steve Larmer, a premier two-way forward, and banger Nick Kypreos at the cost of veteran defenseman James Patrick and forward Darren Turcotte in a three-way deal with Chicago and Hartford.

The Rangers stayed on top in the Patrick Division and battled for the overall NHL lead throughout the winter. But with the playoffs approaching, Smith knew more changes had to be made.

"There were a number of things that had to be done," Smith says. "We felt that the playoffs were different—that a different type of team would win the playoffs, as opposed to who would win in the regular season. I liked Amonte and Mike Gartner, but I wound up moving Gartner [to Toronto] for Glenn Anderson, because we wanted another experienced playoff guy. We used Amonte to get [Brian] Noonan and [Stephane] Matteau [from

Chicago]. I didn't like the trade at the time, but it gave us some experienced, veteran guys that Keenan liked. I also wanted [Craig] MacTavish because I didn't think we were strong on faceoffs. We sent [Todd] Marchant [to Edmonton] for him."

Matteau made an impression right away, getting the tying goal in his first game as a Ranger, giving New York a rare point in Calgary. With the cast now complete, the Rangers roared down the stretch, winning the division and capturing the Presidents' Trophy for the second time in three years.

But regular-season success was one thing—playoff success was another. The Cup drought was in its 54th season, and Smith thought he had the team to end it.

The Setting

The Rangers stampeded through the first two rounds, embarrassing the Islanders in four games and ripping through the Caps in five.

But the Eastern Conference finals were different. The Rangers had held off the Devils for the division title during the regular season by sweeping the season series from their trans-tunnel rivals. The Devils showed no signs of being intimidated, however; they won the series opener at the Garden in overtime, survived a double-overtime goal by Matteau in Game 3, and won the next two games to go back to the Meadowlands with a chance to go to the Finals for the first time in franchise history by winning the sixth game at home.

For most of the first two periods, it looked like they'd get there. The Devils led 2–0 late in the second period, but Messier, who had "guaranteed" victory in the papers, scored three goals and set up another to rally his team for a 4–2 victory. Matteau's second double-overtime goal of the series sent the Rangers to the Finals for the first time since 1979.

The Rangers were favored to beat Vancouver, the Western Conference champion. They started out on the wrong foot, blowing a 2–1 lead in the final minute of Game 1 and losing in overtime, but won the next three games to move within one victory of their first Cup since 1940.

"We had actually blown them out in all four games, even though we lost the first one," Smith says. "We had about 60 shots [actually 54]. They weren't really in it. There was every reason to think we'd win it in Game 5.

214

But the euphoria and the craziness got to everyone, and the Canucks came in with no pressure."

The Canucks blew a 3–0 lead in the third period of the fifth game, but regrouped and won, 6–3. The teams returned to Vancouver, and the Canucks played their best game of the series, dominating the Rangers on the way to a 4–1 victory. That left the Rangers' hopes of ending the drought hanging on one game.

The Game of My Life
1994 STANLEY CUP FINALS, GAME 7
RANGERS VS. VANCOUVER CANUCKS—JUNE 14, 1994

"The key to the whole thing was that we had an extra day off [Game 6 was on Saturday, June 11; Game 7 wasn't until June 14, giving the Rangers two days off instead of the usual one off day between games in the Finals]. We had an older team, and that really helped us. Plus, we didn't take the red-eye back. We stayed over in Vancouver on Saturday night and flew home during the daytime. That gave the players more rest.

"To be honest, I can't remember everything that went on that day [June 14], at work and when I left home. It's all a blur. I do remember it was very difficult sitting there for that game. We really didn't think about it going the other way. If we had, we'd have driven ourselves crazy. I thought from the moment I walked in the building that we were going to win—that there was no doubt we were going to win.

"We got up on them when Leetch scored, then Gravy [Graves] got one on the short side, so we were up 2–0 after one period. I felt really good then, because we were pretty good when we were playing with a two-goal lead.

"We led 3-2 [after Vancouver's Trevor Linden scored with 15:10 remaining in regulation], and it seemed like the time would never end. The only way to stay sane during that was to tell ourselves, 'It's going to be OK. It's going to be OK. We're going to win.' That's the only way to do it; otherwise, we'd have just gone nuts. I remember doing that. Of course, we were scared and nervous. Our whole lives, our whole world was in front of us. We tried to keep the faith as much as we could.

"It looked like we had won, but they called us for icing with a little over a second to go. I know Brian [Leetch] had already thrown his stick in the air, and then the whistle blew [when linesman Kevin Collins called icing]. People were in pandemonium; they were just sick to their stomachs that there was this one last face-off.

"I turned to my wife and told her, 'They never score in these situations. No one ever scores in these situations. We're fine. We're fine.' I think it was just me giving myself therapy. I was pretending it was for her because she was crying, but it was more for me, to medicate myself. Everyone was really worried.

"I was down behind the bench with my family [when the horn finally went off]. I was with my wife and my mother and my friend from Toronto and some other friends, and it's funny, I didn't know how to act. I wondered, 'Do I go down on the bench? Do I go out on the ice? What do I do?' I was the one who orchestrated where all the police would go and how we would take care of all the other issues—all those meetings. But me, myself, I didn't know how to act. The whole thing was surreal at that point.

"We had a lot of alumni there too. One thing we had always tried to make them feel a part of it. We said, 'This is for all the Rangers, for everyone who's worn the uniform, and for all the fans. We tried to deflect a lot of the stuff away from that exact team and give credit to all these other people. The Ranger alumni hadn't been cherished up until that time, and that was one way of paying tribute to them. We had a lot of them there.

"It was really so surreal. It flashed by so quickly, like the birth of a child. It happens so quickly, and you'd like to relive it, but of course, you can't."

Afterword

The Rangers were the toast of the town in the summer of 1994. There were parades and celebrations the likes of which New York hockey fans had never seen. Unfortunately for the Rangers, the Smith-Keenan marriage that produced New York's first Stanley Cup in 54 years didn't last.

"We had our Cup. We had the result we wanted," Smith says more than a decade after Keenan departed to run the St. Louis Blues only weeks after winning the only Stanley Cup of his career. "He didn't want to stay. He wanted whatever he wanted. It wasn't strictly a power issue. It was money, power, everything.

"So Mike left, and then we had the lockout, and that was a shame. We didn't get a chance to go through the league as Stanley Cup champs. [There were no East-West games in 1994-95 due to the reduced postlockout schedule.] We didn't get to celebrate the Cup as true, normal champions. And then we got knocked out [by Philadelphia] in the second round.

"We weren't built to be a dynasty. It was a team that wasn't winning the Cup in their prime. Most of them were later on in their careers. A dynasty is built from a team that's just peaking and happens to win, and throughout their peak, they keep winning or coming close to winning. The Islanders and Edmonton were like that. We were built to win the Cup and try to adjust from there and see if we could ever do it again."

Unfortunately for Smith and the Rangers, they couldn't. The Rangers made the second round again in 1995-96, then, after the addition of Wayne Gretzky in the summer of 1996, the team beat Florida and New Jersey before falling to the Flyers in five games.

Then everything came apart. Messier left as a free agent and signed with Vancouver. The team missed the playoffs in 1997-98. With the team on the way to a second straight playoff miss, Gretzky stunned everyone by announcing in the final week of the 1998-99 season that he was retiring. And with the team on the way to a third straight non–playoff season, Smith was let go on March 28, 2000.

Smith has stayed around hockey as a scout, television analyst, and part-owner of a minor-league team. He's rightly still proud of what the Rangers accomplished under his watch—even if the price was an unhappy ending.

"When I came to New York, in that time, everyone was saying, 'If you ever won the Cup, they'd make you the mayor. They'd make you the governor. They'd put a statue of you in front of the Garden. They'd be insane,'" he says. "So you come to New York and actually do it—even today, it seems like a fairy tale, doing something that everyone said was impossible to do. Everyone gets their joy and happiness and gets what they always wanted for their favorite team.

"I knew that that team had to go down. I had to use up every single bit of currency to get that team positioned the way it was. It was go-for-broke, do it. I'm sure that if you told Ranger fans in the summer of 1992 or 1993, 'We're going to have to make some hard decisions and trade some of the future, and you may not like what you'll see in the late '90s, but you'll be

Stanley Cup winners, you'll experience that—Rangers fans would have traded 20 years of no playoffs for that."

Smith's tenure in New York might not have ended the way he or the team would have wanted, but no one can take the memories of June 14, 1994, away from Ranger fans or from the man who built the team that finally won the Stanley Cup again.

CHAPTER 23

WAYNE GRETZKY

The Skinny

Wayne Gretzky's nickname was "The Great One." Seldom has a nickname fit its owner so perfectly.

If Mozart played hockey, he'd have been Wayne Gretzky. Like the musical prodigy of two centuries earlier, Gretzky saw things that no one else did—and he did amazing things at a young age. He could skate at age two. When young Wayne was six, his father, Walter, built a rink in the family's backyard in Brantford, Ontario. "It was for self-preservation," Walter said years later when asked why he built the rink. "I got sick of taking him to the park and sitting there for hours, freezing to death."

Wayne practiced for hours, honing his skills and absorbing the game of hockey from his dad. Walter's most important lesson for his son was "Skate to where the puck is going, not to where it has been."

Wayne was a fast learner. From the time he was in grammar school, he played in leagues that were for children well above his age. When he was six, he was playing with 10-year-olds. In his last season as a peewee, he scored a mind-boggling 378 goals. Every year he moved ahead, starring in (if not dominating) leagues in which he was easily the youngest player.

At the age of 14, Gretzky left Brantford after deciding that the pressure of playing in his hometown was too great and the carping by jealous players and parents was making him unhappy. He played a year in Toronto, where his skills and hockey genius more than made up for his lack of brawn. The next season, 1977-78, he played his only campaign in major junior hockey, scoring six goals in his first game and finishing second in scoring to future NHL star Bobby Smith while playing with Sault Ste. Marie of the Ontario Hockey Association. That's where he also began wearing the number that became associated with him: 99, because his favorite number, 9 (the number worn by Gordie Howe, Gretzky's favorite player), had been taken by teammate Brian Gualazzi.

Gretzky would have loved to go to the NHL, but the draft age at that time was 20—meaning he'd have had to spend three more seasons in juniors. However, the rival World Hockey Association had no such rule, and Gretzky signed a personal services deal with Nelson Skalbania, owner of the Indianapolis Racers.

His time in Indy lasted all of eight games. The Racers crashed into bankruptcy, and Skalbania sold Gretzky's contract to the WHA's Edmonton Oilers. Though at 5-foot-11 and about 160 pounds he often looked more like a stickboy than a hockey star, no one laughed when Gretzky took the ice. He won the rookie of the year award with 46 goals and 110 points while leading the Oilers to the league finals.

The NHL absorbed four WHA teams in the summer of 1979. Luckily for the Oilers, no NHL team controlled Gretzky's rights because he had never been drafted. So Gretzky remained an Oiler.

A lot of "experts" pooh-poohed Gretzky's WHA accomplishments, saying that he wouldn't be able to match his scoring numbers in the "tougher" NHL. They were right. Gretzky didn't match them—he improved on them, finishing with 51 goals and tying the Kings' Marcel Dionne for the scoring lead with 137 points. Dionne got the Art Ross Trophy because he scored more goals, but Gretzky took home the first of his eight consecutive Hart Trophies as league MVP.

Glen Sather, who had brought Gretzky to Edmonton and even housed him for a while, now began to surround him with talent, building the greatest offensive machine in NHL history. Gretzky won the Art Ross and Hart Trophies in 1980-81 while leading the Oilers to the playoffs, then sparked the second-year team to a first-round sweep of the Montreal Canadiens before a second-round loss to the defending-champion New York Islanders.

Notes on Wayne Gretzky

Name:	Wayne Gretzky
Born:	January 26, 1961 (Brantford, Ontario)
Position:	Center
Height:	5-foot-11
Playing Weight:	175 lbs
How Acquired:	Signed as a free agent on July 21, 1996
Years with Rangers:	1996-97 to 1998-99
Stats as Ranger:	234 games, 57 goals, 192 assists, 249 points, 70 PIM
Accomplishments:	Hockey Hall of Fame 1999
	Lady Byng Trophy 1998-99
	All-Star Game 1997, 1998, 1999
	Led NHL in assists 1996-97, 1997-98
	Retired as all-time NHL leader in regular-season goals (894), assists (1,963), and points (2,857); playoff goals (122), assists (260), and points (382)

But even in defeat, he impressed his rivals. "With a player of Gretzky's skills," Islanders coach Al Arbour told reporters after Game 3, a 5–2 win by the Oilers in Edmonton, "you just hope to contain him. But a player that great can't be contained forever."

By 1981-82, all the pieces were in place. With other stars like Paul Coffey and Kevin Lowe on defense, Jari Kurri, Mark Messier, and Glenn Anderson up front, and Grant Fuhr and Andy Moog in goal, the Oilers decimated opposing defenses. But it was Gretzky who put up numbers that no one had ever seen before. Rocket Richard and Mike Bossy were the only players in NHL history to score 50 goals in 50 games; Gretzky, then all of 20 years old, did it in 39 by scoring five times on December 30 against Philadelphia. He finished with 92 goals—and thought he should have had more.

"I was disappointed I didn't get 100," he said in an article commemorating the 20th anniversary of his historic season. "I had more than half a season to get the second 50. I thought I should have been able to do it."

Gretzky finished the season with 92 goals and 212 points, both NHL records. The Oilers cruised to the Smythe Division title and were big favorites against Los Angeles in the opening round of the playoffs. But they were stunned by the fourth-place Los Angeles Kings, who overcame a 5–0 deficit to win Game 3 of the best-of-five series, then shocked the Oilers and their fans by winning Game 5 in Edmonton, 7–4. Despite scoring 12 points in the five-game series, Gretzky was crestfallen.

"That loss was painful," he remembered nearly two decades later. "But it helped us grow."

The Oilers showed no ill effects from the playoff loss in 1982-83, again rolling to the division title. Gretzky led the league with 71 goals and 196 points. This time, the Oilers made it all the way to the Stanley Cup Finals against the Islanders. The series opened in Edmonton, where the three-time champions, playing without superstar Mike Bossy, shocked the Oilers with a 2–0 victory. The Oilers never recovered, going down in four straight games, including a 4–2 loss in Game 4 at the Nassau Coliseum, where the Oilers had yet to win a regular-season contest.

But Gretzky said the loss to the Isles taught him and his teammates a valuable lesson.

"Kevin [Lowe] and I walked by the Islanders' locker room on the way to the bus," Gretzky remembered many years later. "We were expecting to see the Islanders celebrating. There was a celebration going on—the friends and coaches and staff were celebrating. But the players weren't. They had ice bags and bruises, black eyes and bloody mouths. We were fine and healthy. They had sacrificed everything they had. That's when we knew what we had to do to win a championship."

The goals and points kept coming in 1983-84. Gretzky had 87 goals and 202 points, again cruising to the scoring title and Hart Trophy. Once again, the Oilers cruised to the division title and rolled through the Western Conference playoffs, earning a rematch with the Islanders. This time, though, the results were different.

Wayne Gretzky. *Courtesy of the John Halligan Collection*

The Oilers won the opener on Long Island, 1–0, on a goal by fourth-line forward Kevin McClelland. After a 6–1 loss, the Oilers came home and finally got their offense rolling, winning back-to-back 7–2 games before a 5–2 victory finally made the Oilers champions.

"There isn't a word I know that describes this," a celebrating Gretzky said in the boisterous Oilers locker room.

With their names on the Stanley Cup once, the Oilers wasted little time making it twice. With Gretzky piling up 72 goals and 208 points, they raced through the division, walloped the West, and beat Philadelphia in five games to repeat as champions.

It looked like the Oilers would make it three in a row in 1985-86. Gretzky had "only" 52 goals, but piled up 163 assists for 215 points, an NHL record that still stands. The Oilers blew out the Vancouver Canucks in the first round and were expected to douse their Alberta rivals, the Calgary Flames, in the second. But the Flames, one of the few teams in the NHL not intimidated by the Oilers' speed and skill, had other ideas. The teams split the first six games and were tied 2–2 in the third period of Game 7 when rookie defenseman Steve Smith accidentally put the puck into his own net. The Oilers couldn't get another goal and were beaten 3–2.

"Anytime you lose, it's difficult," Gretzky said afterward, "but this is awfully disappointing. We never even considered that we wouldn't get through this and advance to defend our title. But as hard as it is to win one Stanley Cup, it's even harder to hang on to it. For us it's going to be a long summer. It was just one of those things, but unfortunately it came in the seventh game, and a thing like that hurts everybody."

As they had three years earlier, the Oilers quickly got over their hurt. They finished with the best record in the NHL as Gretzky piled up 62 goals and 183 points. One of those was an assist on a goal in Chicago on February 1 that moved Gretzky past Hawks' great Stan Mikita into fourth place on the all-time scoring list—at age 26. The Oilers cruised through the Western Conference playoffs and outlasted Philadelphia in seven games to regain the Stanley Cup.

The Oilers and Gretzky both struggled in 1987-88. Calgary passed the Oilers to finish first in the Smythe Division, and Gretzky had his first major injury, a sprained knee that sidelined him for 13 games. That helped cost him the scoring title—he finished second to Mario Lemieux with 149 points, including a league-leading 109 assists. One of them came on March 1 and was the 1,050th of his career, moving him past Howe's record—in 1,086 fewer games than his boyhood idol needed to get 1,049.

In the playoffs, the Oilers avenged their shocking loss to Calgary two years earlier on the way to the Stanley Cup Finals, where they "swept" Boston in five games (Game 4 at the Boston Garden was tied 3–3 late in the second period when a power failure ended the game; the Oilers won the Cup at home by taking Game 5.)

After the win, the Oilers initiated a practice that has since become common—getting the whole team together on the ice for a photo with the Cup. "We got everyone in it," he remembered years later. "Anyone who had a hand in the Cup was in that picture. That was the most talented team we'd ever had." Little did he know it would also be his last in Edmonton.

On July 16, 1988, Gretzky married Janet Jones, an actress-dancer he had first met seven years earlier. Just 25 days later, the ex-bachelor found himself an ex-Oiler. In the biggest trade in NHL history, Gretzky was sent to the Kings in a five-player deal that also saw the Kings send the Oilers $15 million.

"After spending some time with [Kings owner] Bruce McNall," he told heartbroken Edmonton fans, I decided for the benefit of myself, my new wife, and our expected child in the new year that it would be better for everyone involved to let me play for the Los Angeles Kings."

Gretzky quickly made himself right at home in L.A. He scored a goal on his first shot in a Kings uniform, then added three assists as the Kings routed Detroit 8–2 in their opener. The Kings finished second in the Smythe Division behind Calgary—but ahead of Edmonton, setting up a first-round meeting with his former team. With Gretzky leading the way, the Kings stunned the defending champions, rallying to win the series in seven games, with No. 99 himself scoring two goals in Game 7, including an empty-netter that iced the win.

"Not to get too emotionally excited, because we still haven't won anything, but this was a gigantic step for this organization," Gretzky said after the win. His concerns about the next round were prescient: the Calgary Flames swept the Kings in four games.

By now, Gretzky was nearing the most famous record in NHL history: Howe's career mark of 1,850 points. Appropriately, points No. 1,850 and

1,851 came in Edmonton. On October 15, 1989, he set up a goal by Bernie Nicholls in the first period to tie Howe's mark, then scored on a backhander with 44 seconds left in regulation to break it. After the game was stopped to honor Gretzky, he capped off one of the most memorable nights of his career by scoring the game-winner in overtime for a 5–4 victory.

"It was only fitting that I did it here," he said. "I played a lot of years here. We won four championships here. And the two most important things are that the fans, who were great to me, were part of it and got to see it. And both teams who were so important in the record were there. I think they both deserved to be on the ice at that time."

By now, Kings tickets were a hot item in L.A., where Gretzky had become a megastar. The only thing he couldn't do was get his team past the second round of the playoffs—until 1992-93. Though he missed nearly half the season with back problems, Gretzky still put up 65 points in 45 games. He led the Kings past Calgary and Vancouver to their first division title, then lifted L.A. to its first Stanley Cup Final in a seven-game victory over Toronto. With the Leafs leading the series 3–2, Gretzky scored the overtime winner in Game 6. Then he fulfilled his promise to get the Kings into the Finals, scoring his record eighth postseason hat trick to lead Los Angeles to a 6–3 win in Toronto in Game 7.

Gretzky said he was motivated partly by public speculation that his best days were behind him. "When you are Wayne Gretzky, you take the roses when they are thrown at you and you have to take the heat," he said. "I took the heat. I stood up, and I answered the bell."

The Kings won the first game of the Finals in Montreal and appeared to have the second game won before Marty McSorley's illegal-stick penalty gave the Canadiens a late power play. They scored the tying goal, won in overtime, and went on to end the Kings' dreams of winning their first Stanley Cup.

Gretzky led all playoff scorers with 15 goals and 40 points. He also led the NHL in scoring in 1993-94, winning his 10th Art Ross Trophy with 130 points. But the Kings missed the playoffs in 1994 and the lockout season of 1995. With the Kings heading for a third consecutive nonplayoff season, they traded Gretzky to St. Louis on February 27, 1996, for two young players and some draft picks—frustrating Rangers' general manager Neil Smith, who very much wanted Gretzky in New York.

"The Kings asked me if I'd like to play in St. Louis," Gretzky said after the deal was made. "I told them I'd love to play in St. Louis. They wanted me. They're excited to get me. I'm thrilled to be there."

Gretzky and Brett Hull helped the Blues get to Game 7 of the Western Conference finals, but they were eliminated in a heartbreaking 1–0, double-overtime loss in Detroit.

With his contract expired, Gretzky was now a free agent for the first time in his career. Smith launched a full-court press to bring The Great One to the Garden.

The Setting

The presence of Messier, his old friend and longtime teammate in Edmonton, was a major factor in bringing The Great One to the Big Apple.

"I guess probably what tipped the scale was the chance to play with Mark and the opportunity to get a chance to play with a team that is really focused on trying to win a championship," Gretzky said after signing with the Rangers in July 1996. "I'm probably one of the first free agents to ever come to New York that came for a less-money situation," he added with a smile after signing a two-year, $10 million contract. "This will be my last stop. I'll make that clear."

After playing the previous couple of seasons on teams without a lot of talent, Gretzky was happy to come to a team that was only two years removed from winning the Stanley Cup and boasted a roster of stars such as Messier, Brian Leetch, and Mike Richter, among others. But renewing ties with Messier was the key: "Mark is the most unselfish player that I've ever had the opportunity to play with," he told reporters. "It was a huge factor in my decision. When I go to the rink, I know all the pressure will not be on my shoulders."

At age 35, there were some who thought Gretzky was slowing down. But putting on the Rangers colors and reuniting with Messier put some spring back in his step. Unlike his time in Los Angeles, he wasn't being asked to carry a franchise. "I can go to the rink and enjoy playing the game," he said.

With Gretzky and Messier leading the way, the Rangers again made the playoffs, earning a first-round berth against the Florida Panthers. Gretzky, who had led the NHL in assists during the regular season and tied for fourth in the league scoring race—though with a career-low 97 points—showed that he still had his scoring touch by beating ex-Ranger goaltender John Vanbiesbrouck three times in a 6:23 span during the second period of Game 4, giving the Rangers a 3–2 win and a 3–1 lead in the series.

The first two goals were short slap shots from the left of Vanbiesbrouck, both off great setups, one by Leetch, the other by former Kings teammate Luc Robitaille. On the third goal, he brought back memories of the glory days in Edmonton, Gretzky raced down the right side, stopped on a dime, spun, and then ripped another slap shot past Vanbiesbrouck.

"Those things happen," Gretzky said afterward. "I guess they happened a little bit more when I was younger."

The Rangers closed out the Panthers, then upset the New Jersey Devils to make the Eastern Conference semifinals. Gretzky set up Leetch for the winning goal in Game 2, a 2–0 victory, added a goal and an assist in Game 3, and scored again in Game 4. He set up the first goal in Game 5, a 2–1 overtime victory that put the Rangers into the Eastern Conference finals against Philadelphia.

The Rangers struggled in the opener, with Gretzky setting up their only goal in a 3–1 loss. But in Game 2, the Great One once again lived up to his name, scoring three goals in a 5–4 victory that brought back echoes of Edmonton. Gretzky scored twice on the power play and once at even strength while playing on a line with Messier—a rarity for most of their time together.

"Obviously, it's different," Gretzky told reporters. "The only thing Mark and I talked about was regrouping and getting some speed, so I wouldn't get the puck standing still and I wouldn't get run into the boards. Even though we didn't play a lot together, we're pretty comfortable together."

Gretzky also said after the game that he'd been "a little bit lucky." Messier, who scored what proved to be the winning goal, said his friend's luck "had been pretty good for 20 years."

Though Gretzky had a goal and four assists in the next three games, the Rangers lost all three to the Flyers, ending their dreams of another Stanley Cup. And they suffered a bigger loss that summer: Messier, a free agent, signed with the Vancouver Canucks.

The Rangers added another future Hall of Famer, Pat LaFontaine, during the off-season, but things didn't go well. Though Gretzky finished the season with 90 points and again led the NHL in assists, the team missed the playoffs.

Still, the personal milestones continued to come. On October 26, 1997, he had a pair of assists. The second, a pass that set up a goal by Ulf Samuelsson in a 3–3 tie with Anaheim, was the 1,851st of his career, giving him more assists than Hall of Famer Gordie Howe (second on the all-time scoring list) had points.

"It was a pretty exciting time," said Gretzky, who had been frustrated in previous games when teammates failed to finish his setups. "I was kind of speechless when it happened."

Garden fans saluted Gretzky after each of his assists with a standing ovation that lasted several minutes and chanted his name. "I was fortunate to play with some of the greatest players to ever play the game," he said afterward. "And, fortunately, they were unselfish, so it was luck."

Though Smith retooled the roster that summer after the team missed the playoffs, little went right for the Rangers in 1998-99 either. Gretzky's passes were still sharp, but his teammates were increasingly unable to turn them into goals. With the focus of the game steadily turning to defense, Gretzky was taking a battering on most nights.

The Rangers were eliminated from the playoff race in early April. With the team in need of rebuilding, Gretzky began to ponder retirement after 21 years as a pro, 20 in the NHL, and three as a Ranger.

"I'm done," he said on April 16, 1999, one day after being saluted by Canadian fans in Ottawa after the Rangers played a 2–2 tie. "It's just time. Of course I'm sad. I've played hockey for 35 years—since I was three years old. I'm going to miss it. In my heart, I know I've made the right decision. This is the right time. I've got peace of mind."

Hockey fans had one final chance to say good-bye to No. 99. His last game was to be the Rangers' season finale, a Sunday afternoon game against the Pittsburgh Penguins on April 18.

The Game of My Life

RANGERS VS. PITTSBURGH PENGUINS—APRIL 18, 1999

"I had made the decision earlier in the week that it was time to retire. I played my last road game on a Thursday night in Ottawa, and they gave me the first, second, and third stars, even though I didn't have any points and we tied the Senators 2–2.

"Coming to the Garden that Sunday was odd. On one hand, I was just going to play a game, the last game of a long season. On the other, I knew I would never be taking the ice again as a player.

"The pregame ceremonies were terrific. John Davidson, the Rangers TV analyst and an old friend, was the MC. He started with a nice introduction, saying that this was one of the great moments in Madison Square Garden history. I skated out onto the ice, and the crowd cheered so long that I got tired of waving and went over to the Penguins' bench to shake hands with some of their players.

"They introduced Mom, Janet, and the kids. Adam Graves, Jeff Beukeboom, and Brian Leetch represented the Rangers. Then came some old friends.

"First, they introduced Glen Sather, my first coach in Edmonton. I gave him a big hug—then Mario, the best player I ever played against. And Mess, the best one I ever played with. He was back for the day after his second season in Vancouver, where he had signed after we went to the semifinals in 1997.

"They gave me the official score sheets from 30 of the games I broke records in. And they gave me another car—I'm not sure how many that made for my career, probably 17 or 18. The best part was when they drove the car onto the ice and I saw that my dad was a passenger. I couldn't believe it. That was really classy. When they brought the car out, I almost fell over when I saw my dad.

"Someone asked me later if I was going to keep it. 'Oh yeah,' I laughed. 'What was that line that [Jack] Nicholson said? 'I think I earned it.''

"They also had my number painted on the ice behind the nets—in my 'office.' And the commissioner, Gary Bettman, officially announced that after my retirement, no one in the NHL would ever wear No. 99 again. I was really moved. When I first put that number on in 1977, I didn't expect that one day they wouldn't let anybody else wear it again.

"They even changed the Canadian national anthem for me. Brian Adams sang it, and at the end he sang, 'O Canada, we stand on guard for thee. We're going to miss you, Wayne Gretzky.' The new words at the end—wow. I didn't think those words were going to stick. But it was flattering.

"After all that, it was tough to play the game. I had an assist when Brian Leetch scored late in the second period to tie the game at 1–1; Brian will go down as the player who scored the last goal I ever set up. I even had a chance to get one last goal, but Tom Barrasso beat me to the puck late in the third period.

"I managed to keep everything together until [coach] John Muckler called a time-out in the final minute. He came over and told me that he'd just had a grandson—his daughter lives in Edmonton—and that I had to get the game-winner. Maybe when I was younger, I might have gotten it. But not this time. That's why I knew it was time to retire. I knew it would kill me not to play, but time does something to you, and it was time for me to retire. I felt confident about my decision. I didn't waver once in the seven days between the time I made it and my final game.

"The decision really hit me during that time-out—there were about 30 seconds left and I said to myself, 'My goodness, I've got 30 seconds to go.' That's when it really got me.

"As it turned out, I had a little extra time. We were tied 1–1 after regulation, so we went into overtime. It would have been nice to win, but Jaromir Jagr scored early in OT to win it. Maybe it was fitting—he was the best young player in the game then. The torch was passed, and he caught it. Jagr told me after the game that he 'didn't mean to do that.' I told him that's what I used to say.

"The fans booed when Jagr scored—something they don't do these days, not with him playing so well for the Rangers. Then they started chanting for me. The Penguins lined up and shook my hand like it was the end of a playoff series. I had my teammates come to center ice, and we took a team picture together. I think I was the first one to have a team do that; we did after we won the fourth Stanley Cup in Edmonton in 1988, and everyone does it now.

"I finally got off to the dressing room, and they played a video of some of the highlights from my career, from back in the Edmonton days all the way to that last road game in Ottawa.

"I went back on the ice and picked up a bouquet someone had thrown on the ice. Then some hats—I put on a Yankee hat that someone had tossed out there. I made a lot of curtain calls, but the fans wouldn't stop cheering. I wanted it to be a celebration. I didn't want everybody crying and all that stuff. I cried, though. I broke down a couple of times. They were tears of joy because I was kind of thinking of all the fun things, you know, the days of hard work together and … tears of joy. No question.

"After that, I went in for my final press conference. I still had my uniform on, and I told everyone that I hadn't had time to take it off, but then I admitted that, subconsciously, I didn't want to take it off. I knew I was never going to put it on ever again. After the writers had asked all their questions, everyone left and I just sat there. I wanted to savor everything for one last time.

"Maybe the nicest moment was when my dad came up me after the game and told me how proud he was of me. When you're a son, you want to hear things like that.

"I spent my last three seasons in New York and enjoyed them a lot. Considering the Rangers' history and tradition, it was probably appropriate that when I stepped off the ice for the final time, I did it in a Rangers uniform."

Afterword

Gretzky joked after his last game that he was "going bowling." But even in retirement, he stayed busy.

The start of the 1999-2000 season found The Great One back in Edmonton, where the Oilers retired his famous No. 99. The NHL followed suit at the midseason All-Star Game in Toronto, where the league officially mandated that no other player would ever wear that number again.

By the summer of 2000, Gretzky was officially back in the game. He became a minority owner of the Phoenix Coyotes, helping the NHL to build a successful franchise in the Southwest. He eventually became managing general partner in charge of all hockey operations. That November, he was named executive director of Canada's 2002 Men's Olympic Hockey team, again overseeing hockey operations and having the final say on personnel.

The magic touch that Gretzky always showed on the ice followed him into his Olympic efforts. Under Gretzky's aegis, Team Canada ended a 50-year gold medal drought, beating the United States 5–2 in the championship game.

Gretzky stayed in the Coyotes' front office until the summer of 2005, when he moved down behind the bench as coach while keeping his management role. He also served a second stint as the head of the Canadian Olympic Team. But neither worked out as well as he had hoped in 2005-06. Despite some flashes of inspired play, the Coyotes missed the playoffs. Team Canada, one of the favorites for the gold medal at the Turin Games, didn't make the Olympic medal round.

The Olympics came just weeks after Gretzky suffered the double heartbreak of losing both his mother and his grandmother.

His mom, Phyllis Gretzky, succumbed to lung cancer at age 64. She died less than a week before Christmas. "People in Canada knew her as a hockey mother, but we knew her as just a wonderful person," Gretzky said during the eulogy. "If we got in trouble and needed to get out of trouble, we went to our mother. She cherished the moments she had, not only with her kids, but with her grandchildren. Her eyes used to light up each and every day if she got a phone call from a grandchild, a note, a letter, or a gift."

Three weeks later, his grandmother, 84-year-old Betty Hockin, died of a heart attack. "It's been a sad time for the family," he said.

Canada's offensive struggles at Turin sent the 2002 gold medal winners home empty-handed. "I feel tremendously responsible that we didn't win," he said after Russia's 2–0 victory ended Canada's hopes.

Gretzky said he liked coaching even though the Coyotes missed the playoffs. "It's enjoyable, and yet it's also a difficult job in the sense that you're responsible for 23 players to be ready each and every night," he said after the regular season ended. He showed how much he liked coaching by signing a five-year deal to continue as the Coyotes' coach. The Great One may just enjoy phenomenal success behind the bench, too.

CHAPTER 24

JAROMIR JAGR

The Skinny

How happy were the Rangers to see Jaromir Jagr come to Broadway in January 2004? Consider that when GM Glen Sather brought him to New York, Jagr had more points against the Rangers (78 in 56 games) than against any other team with the exception of the New York Islanders. Most of that damage was done during Jagr's tenure with the Pittsburgh Penguins, who got the chance to draft him with the No. 5 overall pick in the 1990 Entry Draft as a consolation prize after a heartbreaking season-ending loss cost them a playoff berth.

It's easy to forget now, but the Penguins actually gambled a bit when they took Jagr. He grew up in Kladno, then part of Czechoslovakia, where he played for his hometown team. His size and skills quickly earned him a lot of attention from scouts. He starred for his country at the 1990 World Junior Championships, scoring 18 points in seven games and leading his team to the bronze medal.

Scouts may have loved Jagr, but many NHL teams were hesitant about using a high draft pick to select him. Jagr, unlike other top-rated Czechoslovak players such as Petr Nedved, was still in his homeland and had a year remaining on his contract with Kladno. After that, he probably would have to spend at least two years in military service.

But the Penguins, who already had stars like Mario Lemieux, took the risk and selected him fifth. They were rewarded when the Soviet Bloc dissolved that summer—and Jagr, suddenly free to move to the NHL after Kladno released him, arrived in North America as an 18-year-old rookie. As a symbol of his pride in his country, Jagr chose to wear No. 68, which symbolized the year of the Prague Spring, a short-lived surge of social reform in 1968 that was cut short when Soviet tanks rolled into Prague.

Jagr joined a team that was just getting ready to win. With stars like Lemieux, Paul Coffey, and Joe Mullen, the Penguins didn't need Jagr to be a superstar right away—just a solid contributor. And that's what he was. He scored his first NHL goal in his second game (against New Jersey's Chris Terreri) and notched his first hat trick against the Boston Bruins in February. The teenager finished with 27 goals and 30 assists for 57 points, making the NHL All-Rookie Team while giving the Pens another offensive option. He was even better in the playoffs, going 3-10-13 (leading all rookies in playoff points) as the Penguins won their first Stanley Cup, with Jagr becoming the youngest player ever to get a postseason hat trick.

In 1991-92, Jagr improved to 32 goals and 67 points while making the All-Star Game for the first time. In the playoffs, he was a force, scoring 24 points in 21 games to help the Penguins repeat as champions.

By then, his strength and skills had certainly impressed his teammates. "He can carry a couple guys and walk around the net and still have control of the puck," defenseman Ulf Samuelsson said. "He's going to be one of the top three players in the league in the next couple years." Added Paul Stanton, another defenseman, "He doesn't shy away from an uneasy situation when you need a goal. He likes the pressure. He's the kind of player people come to watch. Guys like him sell tickets."

Jagr took another step forward in 1992-93, improving to 34 goals and 94 points as the Penguins won the Presidents' Trophy with a team-record 56 wins and 119 points. The Pens ended their season with a 17-game winning streak, a league record. In January, he made his second All-Star Game appearance. In the playoffs, Jaromir scored nine points in 12 games, but the Penguins' bid for a third straight Cup was derailed by the Islanders in the Patrick Division finals.

Jagr led the Penguins with 67 assists and 99 points in 1993-94 as the Penguins won the Northeast Division with 44 wins and 101 points. But the Pens again were upset in the playoffs, losing to Washington in the first round, even though Jagr had six points in six games.

Notes on Jaromir Jagr

Name:	Jaromir Jagr
Born:	February 15, 1972 (Kladno, Czech Republic)
Position:	Right wing
Height:	6-foot-3
Playing Weight:	245 pounds
How Acquired:	From Washington for Anson Carter—January 23, 2004
Years with Rangers:	2003-04 through present
Stats as Ranger:	113 games, 69 goals, 83 assists, 152 points, 84 PIM
Accomplishments:	Set team records for goals (54) and points (123) 2005-06
	First-Team All-Star 2005-06
	Lester B. Pearson Award 2006

Jagr was understandably overshadowed by Lemieux for much of the early part of his career. The media quickly discovered that if you rearranged the letters in *Jaromir*, you could spell *Mario Jr*. That was the impression most people had of the skilled winger, who shared many physical attributes with his captain. Both were big, strong, offensively skilled—and had long, dark hair that flowed out from beneath their helmets. Even their jersey numbers, 66 and 68, were similar. Moreover, Jagr idolized his older teammate.

"He's the best. He's unbelievable," Jagr said of Lemieux. "I try to do some of the things he does in practice."

But with Lemieux on a one-year injury hiatus for the lockout-shortened 1994-95 season, Jagr stepped up and won the Art Ross Trophy with a league-best 70 points in the 48-game season. He was a First-Team All-Star and the runner-up (to Eric Lindros) for the Hart Trophy. He added 15 points in 12 playoff games.

That proved to be just a warm-up for 1995-96. Jagr was unstoppable, setting NHL records for assists (87) and points (149) by a right wing while finishing second to Lemieux with 62 goals, including 12 game winners. He played in his third All-Star Game and was a First-Team All-Star for the second straight season. In the playoffs, Jagr piled up 23 points as the team made the Eastern Conference finals. "He steps up to the plate when the game is on the line," coach Ed Johnston said of Jagr. "He wants the puck. We look to him for the big plays at the right time."

In 1996-97, Jagr finished with 47 goals and 95 points in just 63 games, missing 18 with a groin injury. He was a Second-Team All-Star.

With Lemieux's retirement that summer, Jagr stepped to the forefront in 1997-98, winning the Art Ross Trophy with 102 points, making the All-Star Game and being named a First-Team All-Star. He retained the Art Ross Trophy in 1998-99 by piling up 127 points, including 83 assists, and won the Hart Trophy as the NHL's MVP and the Lester Pearson Trophy (most outstanding player as voted by his peers). At the end of the season, the *Hockey News* ranked him as the best player in the game.

In 1999-2000, Jagr won his fourth Art Ross Trophy with 96 points and came up one vote short of the Hart Trophy, though he did win his second Pearson Award.

In 2000-2001, Jaromir won his fifth Art Ross Trophy with a league-best 121 points. On November 13, 2000, he registered his first four-goal game and scored his 400th goal. Six weeks later, on December 27, he piled up four points in a 5–0 victory against the Maple Leafs on Lemieux's comeback night. Three nights later, he scored his 1,000th point in a game against the Senators.

But by then the Penguins were struggling financially, and Jagr was one of the highest-paid players in the NHL. Though he was frequently rumored to be on his way to the Rangers, Jagr was traded to Washington on July 11, 2001, for three young players and draft picks.

"I didn't feel right in Pittsburgh," he said a few months after the trade. "It was time to move on. I had a great 11 years in Pittsburgh—I won five scoring titles and two Stanley Cups. I learned a lot, but I'm ready to start a new era."

The Caps gave him a big contract, but he lacked the supporting cast he'd had for most of his time in Pittsburgh, and the "new era" quickly fizzled. Jagr finished with 31 goals and 79 points, his lowest full-season total in a

Jaromir Jagr. *Courtesy of John Kreiser*

decade. In 2002-03, he improved to 36 goals and finished with 75 points as the Caps made the playoffs.

On January 11, 2003, he scored seven points in a 12–2 victory over the Panthers. On February 4, Jagr scored his 500th goal in a 5–1 victory against the Lightning. The Capitals lost their opening-round series against the Lightning, but Jagr led the team with seven points in six games.

The Caps slid backward, however, in 2003-04. With the team on its way to missing the playoffs, Jagr wanted out, and on January 23, 2004, the Caps obliged, sending him to the Rangers for Anson Carter. Between the two teams, Jaromir scored 31 goals and 74 points in 77 games. He was 15th in the scoring race—his 11th consecutive top-20 finish. But the Rangers missed the playoffs for the seventh consecutive season, and Jagr was out of the postseason for the second time in three years,

Still, Jagr looked forward to his first full season in New York—but then the lockout came. Instead of the Big Apple, Jagr started the season in the Czech Republic and then played with Omsk in the Russian League.

As it turned out, he said later, the season away from the NHL turned out to be a boost for his career.

"I think the year off helped me a lot," he said. "I was playing in the Czech Republic and then in Russia, and even though it's a good league, you can still play well even if you don't play 100 percent. You can kind of mentally rest, even physically rest during the year. It was a lot of fun for me—like exhibition games. Mentally, I was fresher for the next season."

The Setting

The lockout was settled in July 2005, but no one gave the Rangers much of a chance to do anything in 2005-06. *Sports Illustrated* predicted that the Rangers would finish last overall in the 30-team NHL, and most other "experts" were similarly disparaging. A playoff berth was thought to be impossible; competing for the Atlantic Division title wasn't even a consideration.

The season started out as if the supposed "experts" were right. The Rangers opened in Philadelphia and quickly fell behind, 3–1. But with Jagr leading the way, the Blueshirts rallied for a 5–3 victory.

By Christmas, Jagr was piling up points like no Ranger in years, and the team was doing the same. Rookie goaltender Henrik Lundqvist became a Garden hero with his superb play, and a rebuilt defense proved more solid than anyone could have imagined. But Jagr was the engine that made the Rangers run. With a number of fellow Czechs on the roster, he enjoyed a comfort zone he hadn't had in several years.

"I always wanted to play in New York, and finally when I had a chance last year, there was the lockout," he said early in the season. "I had a chance to play in my country and in Russia, and when I came here, you know, I think we've got a pretty exciting team. I don't think it's only me, I think every player, even the whole organization is having a lot of fun!"

The fun kept coming, as the Rangers stunned the NHL by grabbing the division lead and battling for first place in the Eastern Conference.

One key was that Jagr developed a rapport with coach Tom Renney, who said he learned in Vancouver that European stars need to be given a little more latitude. Jagr said that while he's followed Renney's instructions, "I know one thing: the more I'm going to score, the better chance the team has to win."

His teammates followed his example. The result was a work ethic unseen at Madison Square Garden in years.

"The most impressive thing about the Rangers is their work ethic and the way the whole team has bought into it, from Jagr down to the last guy on the bench," then-Islanders coach Steve Stirling said prior to a 6–2 midseason win by the Rangers at the Nassau Coliseum.

Jagr led the NHL in scoring when the Olympic break came, and showed no signs of slowing up after play resumed following the Turin Games. By the time the Rangers headed back to the Nassau Coliseum on March 29, Jagr had tied Jean Ratelle's 34-year-old team record for points in a season and Adam Graves' 1994 team mark of 52 goals. With the Islanders struggling, thousands of Ranger fans filled the Coliseum in hopes of seeing Jagr make history.

It didn't take long.

The Game of My Life
RANGERS AT NEW YORK ISLANDERS—MARCH 29, 2006

"I changed the blades on my skates [before the game]. They were a little bit higher. They were very good for passing, but the goals weren't there. I knew it right away in the warm-up. Every time I had a shot, I didn't look up. I had to look down. It wasn't there. I had to adjust them.

"I had a pretty good feeling that with 10 games to go, I should be able to get a point as long as nothing happened to me. But it wasn't something I was thinking about. I knew the line was going to play good and that I should be able to do it.

"I had a chance on the first shift; we had some great chances on that first shift. I wanted to do it on the first shift, but it took a little longer. But I'm glad I did it in the first period [a pass to Petr Prucha that set up the Rangers' first goal].

"I had a couple of chances to get the goals record. It looked like I scored in the second period, but I knew right away that it wasn't my goal. I felt like, 'I'm not going to score today.' I saw it right away. I thought the shot was going to miss the net if [linemate Martin Straka] wasn't there. Marty never goes to the net … until finally. First time he went to the net." [The goal was awarded to Straka.]

"I had a breakaway in the third period, but I was thinking that someone was behind me and was going to catch me. That's why I shot. I don't think it was a good shot [it went into goaltender Rick DiPietro's pads]. I wish I could take it back.

"At one point, DiPietro batted my stick. I couldn't find it. It was up in the air. I didn't know where the stick was. He didn't say anything to me. I just laughed. I don't know what he was doing. I wasn't holding my stick very tightly, and he flicked it away. For five seconds or so, I couldn't find it. I didn't say anything. I just laughed.

"It could have been a lot more [points]. We had a lot of chances; I had a lot of chances. Sometimes, like tonight, it looks so easy; other times you can't get anything, no matter how hard you try, you can't do anything. Some of the fans were chanting 'MVP.' Nobody ever chanted for me, not even in Pittsburgh. But there were a lot of Rangers fans here.

"It's a big honor [to set the scoring record] when you consider all the great players who've played for this organization. It was tough to [set scoring records] in Pittsburgh because Mario was there.

"I don't want to compare myself to Mario. He was always my idol, and he's always going to be my idol. No disrespect to Wayne Gretzky, but I always said that if Mario didn't have the health problems, I think he would break the records. Maybe not all of them, but I think the scoring and the goals for sure.

"Every season is different. This is a new era. During the early '90s, it was a lot easier to score. There weren't that many good players. Every team had probably two good lines, but the other two lines weren't that good. If you had good coaching, you could take advantage of that. During the late 1990s and the early 2000s, the league got better—it was a lot tougher to score. The goaltenders got a lot better. It was kind of impossible to score.

"I always thought that to be great, you have to help the team win the Stanley Cup—and that it really doesn't matter what you do in the regular season. Of course, it matters—with the Rangers, we haven't made the playoffs for such a long time. But let's wait and see what we can do in the playoffs. I always felt like I was on a team to win the Cup. Mario did it for us. I wish that one day I can do it for the young guys like Mario did it for me."

Afterword

Jagr did get the team record for goals scored, but not without another near miss. Against the Islanders at the Garden on April 6, it again appeared he had broken Graves' record when Straka's pass seemed to hit him and deflect pass DiPietro. The goal was announced as Jagr's, the sellout crowd at the Garden saluted him, and chants of "MVP" rocked the building. But after the second period, Jagr went over to the officials and told them the puck hadn't hit him (it went into the net off Islanders center Wyatt Smith). For the second time, Straka was credited with what first appeared to be a record-setting goal for Jagr. "I said I didn't touch it and it wasn't my goal," Jagr said afterward. "Can you imagine if they had given it to me, and after the game you guys would ask me the stupid questions over and over and over forever?"

Said Straka: "I tried to pass to him, and then they booed me when I scored a goal. I told him, 'Keep the goal. I don't want to hear the booing.'"

Jagr finally broke the record in the Rangers' next game, scoring the team's first goal in a 4–3 overtime victory in Boston. "It's a little bit of a relief. I don't think it's just for me; it's for my linemates," he said after getting the record-setting tally, a blistering wrist shot from between the circles that beat goaltender Tim Thomas between the pads. "I think they feel the pressure too, and sometimes they're giving me the puck too much. Maybe they should shoot it and let me go for the rebound, but now we can just play hockey."

No one was more impressed with Jagr than the man whose goal-scoring record he broke.

"He's playing in a league by himself right now," Graves said. "He gets the puck, and you can't get it off of him, which is why the game is so great now. He is far and away the best player in the world right now, and there isn't anybody remotely close to him."

Jagr finished the season with 54 goals and 123 points, both team records. But the Rangers struggled down the stretch, losing their last five regular-season games and falling from first place to third in the Atlantic Division. That set up a first-round meeting with the red-hot New Jersey Devils—a series in which nothing went right for Jagr or the Rangers.

New Jersey rode five power-play goals to a 6–1 win in the opener. But far more damaging to the Rangers was a shoulder injury to Jagr. He was hurt late in the third period while he took a swipe at New Jersey center Scott Gomez and left the ice immediately.

Jagr didn't play in Game 2, a 4–1 loss, and though he tried to play in Game 3, it was obvious during the 3–0 loss that the shoulder was still hurting. Jagr started Game 4, but left in the first minute of the 4–2 loss after being checked by Devils defenseman Brad Lukowich. "I knew as soon as I got hit that it wasn't going to be good," Jagr said.

The sweep was disappointing after the elation of a vastly better-than-expected regular season. "It's kind of sad for our fans and for the guys here," Jagr said after the Rangers' season had ended. "The way we played in the middle of the season and other parts of the season, we thought we had a pretty good chance if we played the same way. We proved ourselves. Nobody gave us much chance before the season. We proved if you work hard in the league, you're gonna be rewarded, and that's what happened to us. A lot of guys got a chance to play in the NHL who hadn't had a chance before, and they took advantage. It's tough to go from a team that didn't make the playoffs for seven or eight years to be a Stanley Cup champion. That would be a miracle. It's slow progress, but I think we made a good step."

On May 4, the same day he was named as a finalist for the Hart Trophy, Jagr agreed to have surgery on his left shoulder. Had he not opted for the surgery and been injured again, he could have been idled for three to four months. This way, he's expected to be back in time for the start of the 2006-07 season.